MANAGING EDUCATION FOR RESULTS

MANAGING EDUCATION

FOR RESULTS

Richard W. Hostrop

An ETC Publication
1973

Library of Congress Cataloging in Publication Data

Hostrop, Richard W.
　Managing education for results.

　Bibliography: p.
　　1.　School management and organization.　I.　Title.
LB2805.H68　　　　371.2　　　　72-8120
ISBN 0-88280-000-0　　　　　　　　　　　　　　　　$7.95

Copyright (c) 1973 by ETC PUBLICATIONS
　　　　　　　　　　　　18512 Pierce Terrace
　　　　　　　　　　　　Homewood, Illinois 60430

Printed in the United States of America

CONTENTS

ABOUT THE BOOK

MANAGING EDUCATION FOR RESULTS is among the very first comprehensive books concerned with modern management principles and practices in education.

The author builds a strong case that every knowledge worker is, or potentially is, a manager. He persuasively argues that counselors, educational technologists, librarians, and teachers as well as principals and deans, superintendents and presidents must *administer, plan,* and *lead* if education is to produce effective results.

Though MANAGING EDUCATION FOR RESULTS rests on clearly explained solid modern management principles and theories, it also describes in clear language and with numerous concise examples, in every knowledge worker area, "how to" immediately begin the management implementation process. In short, the practicing knowledge worker can begin the practice of managing education for results with the management techniques and tools explained in this most helpful work. Finally, the book can serve as a valued textbook in schools of education, schools of library science, and schools of media technology for would-be managers of knowledge and learning.

ABOUT THE AUTHOR

Richard W. Hostrop received 3 degrees from the University of California at Los Angeles, including a doctorate. There he concentrated in the areas of psychology, educational technology, and academic and library administration.

Dr. Hostrop has been both a teacher and a principal of elementary and secondary schools. He has served as a superintendent of schools in a large unified school district. Moreover, Dr. Hostrop has served as both an instructor and a community college president. Currently, Dr. Hostrop serves as Professor of Management at Federal City College in Washington, D.C.

Dr. Hostrop is the author of a dozen noted books and serves as a consultant to business and government as well as to academic organizations.

FOREWORD

Modern management principles are rooted in various social science disciplines. It would, therefore, be thought that since these principles were developed in the university that the educational establishment would have been the first to synthesize them into their operating structure. But this did not happen. Instead, the business and industrial establishments were first to synthesize these principles from the social sciences. They began about 1950 to develop and utilize many of the techniques and tools discussed in this book. Twenty years later, management refined and proven, was rediscovered by the educational establishment. The educational establishment found that the simple "two-wheel cart" of administration simply would not continue to do in the complex space age.

Many leading educational systems are seriously studying what can be learned from the economic sector of society with respect to how to get things done more efficiently and effectively. Some have adopted those management techniques and tools which do not come to grips with individual or group accountability but which, nevertheless, are valuable in improving decision making. A few have accepted the concept of accountability for results through the system of management-by-objectives; others are in the process of studying or adopting the concept.

Though such terms as "Delphi Technique," "PERT," "PPBS," "MIS," "MBO," and others are beginning to appear in a scattered way throughout the educational literature, it still remains essentially true that primary management information must be obtained from reading the *Harvard Business Review* and books written by professors of business administration and management. As a consequence, literally tens-of-thousands of educators have never heard of any of the aforementioned terms. The purpose of this book is not only to bring to the attention of educators effective and efficient business and industrial management practices which are applicable to education, but to "translate" these practices through *educational* examples rather than economic ones.

Because of the widely proven value of management principles in the economic sector of society, and because of a growing number of successful examples in the educational sector as well, it is the thesis of this book that 1) school administration courses need to become school management courses; 2) that school administrators need to become school managers; 3) that classroom teachers need to become classroom managers. The principles discussed in

MANAGING EDUCATION FOR RESULTS are equally applicable to other knowledge workers as well: counselors, educational technologists, librarians. It is the aim of this book to aid in making these imperative transitions in order for formal education to remain a viable alternative to other pressing nonformal educational alternatives.

Washington, DC   Richard W. Hostrop

Dedicated to education managers: trustees, administrators, teachers, counselors, educational technologists and librarians, in whose hands lie the nation's greatest resource, its students.

PART I

ACCOUNTABILITY THROUGH GOALS AND OBJECTIVES

Chapter 1

THE CALL FOR ACCOUNTABILITY IN EDUCATION

School administrators and school teachers alike are responsible for their performance, and it is in their interest as well as in the interests of their pupils that they be held accountable. Success should be measured not by some fixed national norm, but rather by the results achieved in relation to the actual situation of the particular school and the particular set of pupils – Richard M. Nixon.

On February 14, 1970, James E. Allen, in his then capacity as U.S. Commissioner of Education, asserted before the American Association of School Administrators that the public's disillusionment and lack of confidence in their schools was "in large measure our inability to substantiate results." He stressed that "the strengthening of the concept of accountability is imperative."

Less than a month later, on March 3, 1970, President Nixon echoed the call for accountability in education by his Commissioner of Education when he sent to Congress a special message on educational reform accompanied by the above headnote.

It is to be noted that stress was placed by both the highest educational official and the highest elected official in the land on "accountability" through "measurement" and "results." These three words are at the very core of modern management principles. *Management is the acceptance of personal accountability determined by measurable results.*

President Nixon also noted another important concept of modern management when he declared that school administrators and school teachers ("managers") should only be held accountable for the results inherent in a particular situation ("school") with a given set of raw materials ("pupils"). In short, an educational manager can only be expected to be held accountable for measurable results ("performance") within those areas in which he has primary authority.

Why Management?

That academic administration no longer works is plainly evident. Educational costs have been allowed to soar at a rate far outstripping national productivity, yet with no clear measurement of results obtained. Consequently, the homeowner has demonstrated his displeasure by rebelling at the ballot box when school officials call for tax rate increases and more bonding power.

The public is not only disenchanted with what it perceives to be an insatiable appetite for tax monies by the educational bureaucracy. It cannot understand why faculties have found it necessary not only to unionize, but to strike; often the public concludes this is the fault of oppressive and insensitive administrators. The public cannot understand why administrators cannot control student protests and sit-ins; why students are not more severely punished for property damage. The public cannot understand how a young person can graduate from high school barely able to read, write, or compute. In short, the public no longer accepts administrative public relations bulletins. The public is demanding that trustees and administrators, teachers and students, *prove* that society is getting value for dollars received.

What the public is rightfully calling for is accountability. It wants its educators to stop being firemen of crises and to instead become managers of crises prevention.

What is needed to improve the existing condition in education is a shift away from school and classroom administration, which focuses on present events, to management which focuses on future outcomes. Administration tends to be reflexive reaction to unforeseen events whereas management tries to foresee events by planned action.

Though administration worked well enough in the pre TV age, it no longer can. Through the wonder of hovering space satellites, the earth has become a global village. What happens at Berkeley today may happen at Columbia tomorrow. This time compression of information availability requires an equally sophisticated receiving and processing system. For education to respond effectively to the new reality of near instantaneous information dissemination requires new techniques and new tools. Management is part of the new reality. Management can effectively respond to the public call for accountability in education.

Management as an Accountability System

Unless an organizational structure has built into it a system which concisely accounts for who is accountable for what, in measurable or succinct terms, its structure is an administrative rather than a management one. Indeed, by definition, most educational organizations are misnamed as "systems." *Webster* tells us that a "system" consists of "a coordinated body of methods or a complex scheme or plan of procedure." Not many school, college, or university "systems" can lucidly demonstrate that they employ a coordinated body of methods, utilize complex schemes, or have a plan of procedure. The few but growing number of true systems *can* demonstrate that they do coordinate a body of methods, utilize complex schemes, or plans of procedure so as to achieve measurable or succinct objectives towards predetermined goals. The former are administrative organizations, the latter are management systems. Administrative organizations are *input* oriented organizations. Management systems are *output* oriented systems. Input organizations cannot demonstrate accountability because the structure militates against measurement of results. Output systems can demonstrate accountability because the structure cannot function without precise ranges of measures or concise descriptive results.

The systems approach to the management of education is a humane system — much more so than our present Procustean system of egg-crate classrooms using the *same* textbook for 30 or more *different* learners. The systems approach, as a measurable results oriented system, by definition, is an individualized system. Instead of 30 or more different learners using the same textbook at the same time it demands that few, if any, students use the same book, or any other material, at the same time. The implications of non-Procustean education have radical implications for management. The implications have to do with such far-reaching effects as to where learning is to take place, what the learning place is like, the materials to be purchased, and particularly the kinds and types of learning managers the system employs.

The foregoing should make it plainly evident that management must begin, with the aid of the community it serves, to define for itself education's output, "an Educated Person." Management's 2nd step is to reexamine its curriculum in view of its judgment as to what the 1st half of the 21st century is likely to be like so as to prepare today's students for *that* world. Management must then design the requisite future-oriented curriculum, with its measurable learning tasks, so as to achieve the system's goal: An Educated Person for the 21st Century. To accomplish these ends only a systems (systematic) approach will do.

What the systems approach (management) demands of education can only be described as radical. It requires that *society,* represented by school trustees and/or representative local citizen groups, define rigorously and in detail precisely what are its goals and how goal attainment is to be *proven*. But the *means* for attaining society's goals is the job of educational management.

The systems approach, as used in education, is not confined only to educational decisions made at the local system level. In fact, there actually are 4 distinct levels in which the systems approach is being used: 1) between 2 or more nations to between all nations of the world; 2) between school systems of entire states, regions, or nation; 3) application designed to understand the workings within individual school districts or institutions; 4) application to individual courses and teaching methods.

On the international level a number of interchanges employing the systems approach have occured, especially under the auspices of UNESCO.

At the national level the *National Assessment of Educational Progress* program is undoubtedly the most ambitious educational example of the use of the systems approach. The program not only provides a kind of continuing national census of what people have learned but suggests from juxtapositions of various factors corrective means for overcoming educational deficiencies. Beginning with the first report in the early 1970s, an important means for assessing the product of education – learning – has resulted. Even more important outcomes have been well-founded decisions by trustees who have acted on the findings by reordering priorities and by educational managers who have carried out the trustees' mandates.

At the state level, California and New York are particularly well along in the use of the systems approach. By the use of cost-effectiveness and analysis and program budgeting they have been able to reduce to some extent the guesswork in allocating resources and deploying educational personnel so as to maximize the effectiveness of the system.

Another level where the systems approach is used is within individual courses and the accompanying teaching methods. It, of course, is not enough to relabel courses or subjects to simply give them a 21st century look and sound. If only the "packaging" is new nothing new has happened. The subject content must coincide with its label so as to be directed toward what society has defined as an Educated Person. This done, the role of the teacher as implementer becomes crucial.

The enormity of the challenge to properly manage education can be seen when we view the world as a backdrop to its number one problem, reading. Throughout the world, according to UNESCO, there are more than 500 million illiterate adults – about 60 percent of the world's adult population! Though not so accute in industrialized nations, reading, nevertheless, remains a serious problem. In the United States reading continues to be the number one educational problem with an estimated 25 percent of the population *functionally* illiterate (reading below 5th grade level). (5.22).* So serious is the problem in the United States that the federal government in 1970 embarked upon the Right to Read (RIR) program with its goal being to "assure that 99 percent of all people in the United States who are 16 years old and 90 percent of all over 16 will be functionally literate by 1980." (20:340).

To overcome illiteracy, and to solve other educational problems, management is confronted with four major realities: 1) the sharp increase in popular aspirations for education; 2) the acute scarcity of economic resources; 3) the inherent inertia of educational systems; 4) the inertia of society itself. The challenge to educational management on the grand scale requires procedures which will result in substantial mutual adjustment and adaptation by *both* education and the larger society. But the greater adjustment is required by education because it is education that is part of society, not society part of education. This requires that educational management be aggressive in its advocacies while at the same time remaining flexible to alternatives.

Education as a System

An educational system, as a system, share in common with other systems (the human body, the military, the church, business, etc.) a set of *inputs,* which are subject to a *process,* designed to attain certain *outputs,* which are intended to satisfy the system's objectives and goals. Together, these form a dynamic, organic whole. And if one is to assess the health of an educational system in order to improve its performance, and to plan its future intelligently, the relationship between its critical components must be examined in a unified vision. Figure 1-1 presents a simplified diagram showing some of the more important internal components of an educational system.

An example of how the interaction of the component parts interact on each other might be a decision to diversifiy secondary vocational education where none had existed before. To implement this decision would likely require far-reaching changes in the system's academic structure, in the curriculum and teaching methods, in facilities and equipment, and in the distribution of teachers and the flow of students within the structure. In short, virtually every component is substantially affected by such a change.

Citations refer to the bibliography to be found on page 235. The number preceding the colon refers to the bibliographical source; the number following the colon refers to the page number(s) of the citation

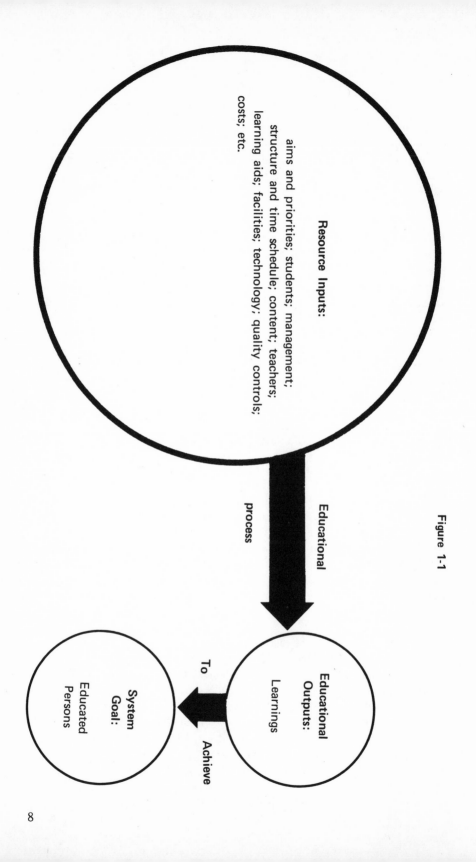

Resource Inputs:

aims and priorities; students; management;
structure and time schedule; content; teachers;
learning aids; facilities; technology; quality controls;
costs; etc.

Educational

process

Educational
Outputs:

Learnings

To

Achieve

System
Goal:

Educated
Persons

Figure 1-1

8

Figure 1-1, however, does not show the whole of what must be looked at in a systems analysis. It is confined to the internal components of the system, detached from the environment. Yet it is society which supplies the educational system with the means of functioning — just as the educational system, in turn, is expected to make vital contributions to society. This requires that education's inputs and outputs must be examined with respect to their external relationships to society, for these reveal both the resource constraints that limit the system and the factors that ultimately determine its productivity to society. Figure 1-2 shows the multiple components of the inputs from society into the educational system, followed by the multiple learning outputs from that system which flow back into society, upon which they ultimately have many diverse impacts.

Figures 1-1 and 1-2 raise many questions which will be dealt with throughout the remainder of this book. They include such matters as further explication of "management", the nature of educational "instructional systems" and "technology", the meaning of "efficiency" and "quality", and skepticism about the reliability of source inputs as indicators of the quality of educational outputs. They include the need to define the difference between the internal and external ways of judging the quality and productivity of an educational system's performance, and to suggest how these different angles of vision can lead to different judgments. They include the need to identify key and reliable indicators as to the probable efficacy of an educational system's input as determiners of the quality of a system's output.

Inputs of Educational Systems

Students, obviously, are the primary input of any educational system. Their development is the educational systems prime object, their attitudes greatly affect its process, and in the end they are its prime outputs.

Society rightly expects to find that the school experience will have made a desirable difference in the lives of their children. Children, of course, are shaped not only by the school but by their families, friends, church, mosque, synagogue, or temple — and other environmental forces as radio, television and travel — each in its own distinctive way, yet interdependent in forming the whole person. But society has a right to expect that the school will provide children with attitudes and skills that he cannot get any place else. In short, *schools are expected to make a difference.*

Though there is a temporary leveling off of students entering first grade, the percentage of students in school is rapidly accelerating — post secondary

Inputs from Society

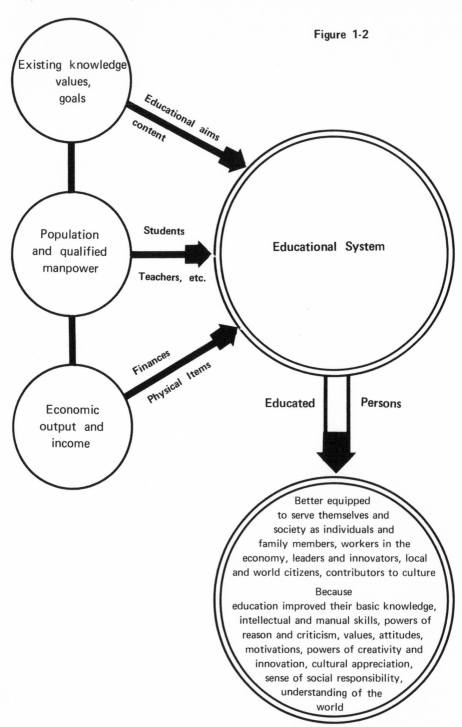

Figure 1-2

10

schooling on the one hand and pre first-grade enrollments on the other. The pattern of phenomenal educational growth may be seen in the fact that though the population of the United States has increased 2.5 times from 1900 to date, the proportion of the age group attending secondary schools jumped from 12 percent in 1900 to well over 90 percent in 1973. Likewise, for the same period, higher education enrollments soared from 4 to over 50 percent for the corresponding age group. Other technologically advanced nations have had a similarly dramatic rise in the rate of school enrollments.

Teachers, next to students, are the largest, most crucial inputs of an educational system. They are also, by all odds, the most expensive inputs of an educational system. Their cost, typically consuming between 75 - 85 percent of the educational budget, is at the heart of the financial crisis facing the schools. Too, they play the central role in output results. Thus their unit cost in relation to students and the index of learning results, as measured by student achievement, demands close scrutiny. To hold down unit costs, while simultaneously maximizing learning results, is undoubtedly the number 1 challenge to educational management.

Money "fixes everything" is only a half truth, notwithstanding the old cliche that "nothing is wrong with education that more money won't fix:" It too easily diverts educators from digging deeper to the other sources of education's problems. There are, in fact, extremely important constraints besides money which can limit the rate at which an educational system can expand, change, and improve — and sometimes these prove even more unyielding than the money factor. The introduction of promising innovations is 1 major example with its often concomitant militating NIH (not invented here) syndrome.

Though nonmonetary factors are of critical concern in solving a number of educational problems it still remains true that money is an absolutely crucial input of any educational system. It provides the essential purchasing power with which education acquires its human and physical inputs. With too little money, education can be left helpless. With an adequate supply, its problems become more manageable even though they do not vanish.

One simplistic solution to the school money crisis often suggested by the public and teacher groups is to cut down on the number of administrators (and other "excesses" and "frills"). But how effective are these proposed solutions?

The 1971 *Gallup Survey of Public Attitudes Toward Public Schools* disclosed that if a school system were forced to reduce services the public most favored that its schools 1) reduce the number of administrative personnel, 2) operate schools on a 12-month basis, 3) reduce the number of counselors, and 4) charge rent for the use of textbooks rather than providing them free to students. The public least favored 1) reduction of special services such as hearing therapy, reading, and speech, 2) reduction of the number of teachers by increasing class sizes, 3) reduction of teachers' salaries by a fixed percentage, and 4) reduction of janitorial and maintenance services.

Using the *Cost-Ed Model* (2:246-47) applied to some of the public's *most* preferred choices, and using the data gathered for analyzing the typical secondary school, simulated costs were reduced as follows:

District administrative staff cut by 10 percent

Counseling staff cut by 10 percent

Rent amounting to one-third of the total cost of textbooks and library books charged to students

Cost-Ed analysis reveals that these changes would have the effect of reducing the average per-student cost of secondary education by $6.70 or less than 1 percent of total costs.

In order to compare the results of the public's preferences still further, Cost-Ed analysis was applied to some of the suggestions which the public was *least* favorably disposed towards as a means for reducing school costs:

Increasing the average class size by 10 percent

Reducing the average teacher salary by 10 percent

Reducing janitorial and maintenance services by 10 percent

Cost-Ed analysis reveals that these publicly opposed changes would decrease the cost of educating the average American secondary student from $912.59 to $832.55, a reduction of $80.04 per student of 8.8 percent of total costs.

In terms of "trade-offs" between what the public considers to be the most and least desirable means for achieving cost savings simulated results reveal the following:

Boards of trustees would have to increase the student/administrator ration from 406:1 to 564:1 to save the same amount of funds as by increasing the student/teacher ratio from 29:1 to 29.7:1.

Savings incurred by renting books rather than providing them free of charge could be equaled by increasing class size by less than one student or by reducing the average annual pay of teachers (eg, by hiring younger teachers or paraprofessionals)by less than 1 percent.

A decrease in annual pay of teachers by 5 percent would free enough resources to increase audio-visual materials and books by 170 percent.

A 30 percent decrease in classroom janitorial and maintenance costs could pay for a 100 percent increase in books and audio-visual materials.

A 12-month school year, creating greater utilization of school facilities and higher annual salaries for staff, would reduce education costs for the typical secondary student by 7.2 percent.

It seems evident from the sobering results revealed by Cost-Ed analysis that there is no simplistic solution to the financial problems facing education.

It is self-evident, too, that there is not a limitless amount of money for education. As important as funds seem to educators, and as important as education is to society, education must compete for funds along with other agencies of society: the military, highways, welfare, parks, police, firemen, ad infinitum. The competition for finite funds is not just limited to the aforementioned either. There is fierce rivalry for "education money" among and between the various segments of education itself: elementary versus secondary; secondary versus higher education; private education versus public education; formal versus nonformal education.

There is, moreover, consistent evidence that the per unit cost of education is rising faster than the rise attributed to inflation. What this, of course, means is that education has been receiving an increasingly larger share of the total GNP (gross national product). But it is also a well-known fact that since 1960 considerably more local tax and bond referenda have failed at the polls than have passed. In 1960, 60 percent of the tax issues presented to the public passed, by 1970 only 10 percent were passed. So bad has the situation become that some public schools have even had to shut down for a period of several days to several months simply because the schools ran out of funds. To ensure equal educational opportunity it seems certain that most, if not all, financial support for schools will shift away from local school districts to the state. And the states increasingly will call upon the federal government for educational aid. The 1971 *Serrano v. Priest* decision declaring the local property tax unconstitutional as the chief means of financing local public education assures this trend. But even so, education cannot expect to receive a much larger increase than its current 8 percent of the nation's total GNP, a higher percentage than any European nation.

Roger A. Freeman has particularly well summarized the degree of input effort the United States has put forth in the support of education during the past several decades. In an address he made in 1971 as a senior staff member of the Hoover Institution at Stanford he said:

> With only 6 percent of the world's population and between one-fourth and one-third of its developed resources, the American people now invest in educational institutions annually almost as much as all other nations combined.
>
> Nothing testifies more eloquently to the American faith in education than the priority which the people have granted it in financial terms.
>
> Over the past 20 years the support of schools and colleges from all sources has multiplied eight times while personal consumption expenditures for business or personal investment multiplied only slightly more than three times.
>
> Expressed in dollars of constant value, personal consumption doubled while educational spending expanded five-fold.
>
> Over the same period the number of employees in private industry increased 38 percent while it tripled (203 percent) in public education. In the rest of government manpower grew 87 percent.
>
> These are impressive facts which make charges of neglect or starvation of education look plain silly.

What all the preceding adds up to is one simple fact: productivity has not kept apace with educational costs — especially salary costs. In a pioneering study in the United Kingdom, which caused a great deal of controversy there, it was concluded that education's productivity has actually been *declining.* (4:47-8) Though its author makes no claim to infallibility or to the universal applicability of the findings there to other countries, there is good reason to believe that similar studies made elsewhere would reach similar conclusions.

In the United States for each teacher added to the roster of an educational institution the school budget must be expanded by an amount equal to the average income of 2.1 members of the population as a whole. Plainly put, teachers have become too successful at the bargaining table. So successful have teachers become in obtaining financial gains that for the first time since 1938 there are now more teachers than jobs available. Because of the wide differences in income ratios between current teacher salaries and the average per capita income, school systems have reached the point where they simply do not have the wherewithal to keep hiring more teachers at these rates, let alone upgrade present rates. The only realistic means left for most school systems is to employ inexperienced teachers, with no advanced work, so as to hold costs down and/ or increase student/teacher ratios and increase class size with or without the addition of paraprofessionals. There are, of course, other means, too, such as increasing the ratio of teachers to support staff and/or administrators, but compared to any savings to be gained vis-à-vis the instructional budget such savings are small indeed as has been soberly shown. Society simply cannot afford educational salary rates much more than the current 2 to 1 to the general population. The limit has been reached if not overreached already. Nor can academicians any longer expect to receive average salary gains much beyond the average of the work force in general. In sum, academicians, on average, are no longer underpaid as compared to the total society. Future gains can only be those consistent with the general GNP and/or productivity − larger student/staff ratios and/ or greater student learning results which ultimately are reflected in an accelerated GNP, and thus a higher standard of living for all.

Outputs of Educational Systems

It has not been possible in the past to measure the full output and eventual impact of an educational system on society. Likely this will never be totally possible. However, by the local use of a measuring scale, modeled after the *National Assessment of Educational Progress* inventory, we can at least identify some of education's output at the local as well as at the national levels − comparisons with the past, weaknesses to overcome in the present. There are, of course, other means of measuring at least certain aspects of education's output. The easiest measure of output is the number of students emerging from the system on both a gross basis and as a ratio of entering students on a year-to-year basis. Some make the exit prematurely − these are the dropouts and the pushouts. Others complete the elementary school cycle and go on to the secondary cycle. Others complete the secondary cycle and go on to the postsecondary cycle. Still others complete a cycle and then enter the world of work.

In terms of "products," it is important to distinguish between "finished" and "unfinished" ones. Though the nonfinishers are not a complete loss they likely carry away less for themselves and society than would otherwise be true had they completed each cycle they entered — and as many cycles as they were capable of completing. The important fact, no matter how capable the learner, is that society *itself* makes a sharp distinction between those who have completed lower cycles vis-à-vis higher ones, those who have stopped within a cycle vis-à-vis those who have completed it.

Because of the premium placed upon education in recent years, and because of the complexity of society itself, the individual has remained in school much longer. In 1920 only 30 percent of the students entering the fifth grade completed high school; today more than 70 percent do. American educators now are worried over the fact that more than half of the students who enter two-year colleges do not finish. (4:70)

Though figures on graduates or dropouts (and pushouts) are useful indicators of an educational system's output, they, in themselves, do not provide a sufficient basis for evaluating the system's performance. Indeed, no one type of indicator does; we must examine as wide a variety of them as we can identify, then base our judgment on the combination. Though the search continues, we still must determine how well does education's output fit the manpower needs of national development.

Research into the relationship between education's output and the nation's manpower needs is disquieting. Educational systems are falling far short of turning out the right numbers and combinations of manpower needed for optimum development. On the other hand, society's employment structures and incentives are poorly geared to make the best use of educational personnel, and hence to serve the real needs of development. Though admittedly our measuring tools are inexact we nonetheless can spot a number of practical indicators of the disparity between what the educational system is turning out, what the economy can use at the moment, and what it will need for future growth. Though it cannot be expected that the correspondence between these can ever be perfect, it can be much better than it is. To glut the economy with secondary school teachers and engineers when society instead needs more special education teachers and engineering technicians are but two recent examples of dissonance between education's output and society's needs. Individuals who have been "turned out" without proper vocational guidance, and thus cannot find a job, rightfully feel embittered after their investment of time, money, and delayed income. It is little wonder then that such individuals become hostile to the educational system and even society itself. It is understandable that dissonant students have become dissident, and why they have joined their parents in calling for accountability — relevant curricula which will prepare them for careers that exist.

For education to improve its cost-benefit ratios there is mounting evidence that instead of employing more teachers to students that more paraprofessionals be employed. Paraprofessionals have been widely used in practically every profession except education. Indeed, Guy Hunter suggests that the optimum ratio of technicians (paraprofessionals) to professionals is between 3:1 to 5:1, depending upon the profession. (4:77-9) Countless studies reveal that teachers spend countless hours each year in noninstructional activities: clerical work, drill, correcting objective tests, discipline, etc. Certainly, it seems that it is only a matter of time before the widespread use of paraprofessionals (usually trained graduates of 2-year college programs) will become standard in education. Notwithstanding the holding down of costs by the use of paraprofessionals, increased student learning can be expected when arranged within cybernetic system models which make use of community resources and which focus on individualizing learning. (4:127)

The Coleman Report of 1966 and the Carnegie Corporation financed Armor Report of 1971 perhaps most pragmatically and dramatically point up what outputs from the educational system American society actually is getting for its inputs and what outputs it should be getting. Both studies report that:

> Such simple prescriptions as increasing teachers' salaries, lowering class size, and giving school systems more money do not work – at least they do not increase student academic achievement.

> Not much does work in schools independent of a child's socio-economic status and home background; the influence of the latter is far greater than that of the schools.

> Achievement of black students placed in an integrated setting improves only slightly.

> Black and white children are provided nearly comparable resources within general geographic regions.

> David J. Armor, with other Harvard University researchers, based on their second look at the Coleman Report, came up with some controversial conclusions and recommendations:

> Neither school upgrading nor integration by busing or other means will close the black-white achievement gap if the socio-economic gap is ignored. [Which means that employment programs, such as Model Cities, may be as important as such strictly educational programs as Title I.]

The least promising approach to better learning is to
increase school expenditures.

Educators should abandon the whole child approach
[music, art, social studies, getting along with others, etc.]
and concentrate on specific areas such as reading or
altering the way poor parents deal with their children.
It would be better to teach poor children something
than to continue to fail at teaching anything.

If these conclusions are sound, it almost inevitably follows that the nation's
taxpayers are at the moment wasting money by the warehouse full on hun-
dreds of school programs rooted in exactly opposite assumptions. Thus, to
be truly accountable to society boards of trustees and educators must decide on what learning is to be acquired in what way and for what purposes.

Learning for What?

Learning is the major output (product) of education but not its system goal.
Its system goal is an Educated Person. And "an educated person is one who
interacts with his physical and social environment in a manner that produces
personal fulfillment and social optimum in terms of his potential." (23:16)

The question, Learning for What?, is thus answered: to become an Educated
Person. The educational manager then implements and manages a future-
oriented system designed to turn out Educated Persons as illustrated by
Figure 1-3.

Figure 1-3

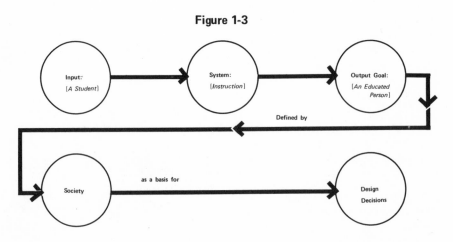

Managing education for results requires a systems approach. And *a systems approach is a method of designing, organizing, and managing the operation and interaction of personnel, media, and facilities so as to attain specific, measurable results, and in terms of specific constraints and priorities.*

The stated and defined system goal (an Educated Person) must become the fundamental basis for all decisions about the design and its management. Any significant design or operation decision which is not *demonstrably* effective and efficient in terms of objectives which are commensurate with the system goal can be successfully challenged by critics. It appears likely that many, if not most, of the management decisions currently being made as to design and operation of instructional programs are not made in accordance with a clear goal in mind. They are not made with regard to *if* the particular learning objective is important, *how* it is important, and if it is the *best* designed learning activity to achieve the system goal of producing Educated Persons.

Several diverse curricular examples, by way of illustration, are foreign languages, physical education, and handwriting.

It is generally agreed that most students in the United States who study a foreign language do not learn it. There are many reasons for this. For one, English has become the *lingua franca* of the world. Thus Americans have come to depend upon other peoples to have learned English. Secondly, most Americans have no strong motivating force to master another language because of the isolated geography of the United States from other non English speaking nations. In Europe, which is the approximate size of the United States, more than a dozen different languages besides English are spoken. There, thus, is both a felt commercial and travel need to master other languages. But perhaps an even more fundamental question than *if* foreign languages should be taught is *when* should such study begin? From all available evidence, waiting until high school to begin the study of a foreign language is pedagogically unsound. The best time to learn another language is when one is young. Certainly, the study should begin no later than age 8 or 9.

Should physical education be offered in school is another question. In much of Europe clubs of various kinds have provided for this organized physical outlet. In elementary schools "physical education" frequently consists of no more than "free play." In secondary schools the emphasis is on team sports, yet after one leaves school seldom does one engage in group sports. Instead, one largely participates in individual or duo sports: golf, bowling, horseback riding, tennis, swimming, and the like. Moreover, our high school and college physical education activities are seldom co-educational even though out-of-school this age group, more often than not, participate together in individual and duo sports just as do adults.

Elementary school teachers in 2nd and 3rd grade (why grades?) spend considerable time changing students initial manuscript writing over to cursive writing. Why? Is not manuscript writing more legible? Could not cursive writing be a self-taught skill for those who prefer cursive writing? Is there much resemblance of one person's handwriting to another's now even with cursive writing being taught? Would it not be better to invest this same amount of time, at say 8th grade, to teach everyone how to type instead?

There are, of course, many other subjects which we need to examine as viable for the 21st century as well. For instance, why is college freshmen English required? (Teachers in France do not find it necessary to teach "French" to their college students — nor do the Germans, Italians, Spanish or others find it necessary to teach their own language — instead, they improve their langugae skills as a natural and functional integrative part of other subjects.) Or why do English teachers assign themes when themes are never written in the "real world?" Should *textbook* reading, as a formal subject, be taught in our elementary schools? Why not read great children's literature instead, supplemented initially by programmed reading workbooks to provide needed basic skills? (No reading textbook every won a children's literature prize nor are any considered children's "classics" — great literature can never be produced by a textbook writing committee.) Why is there a lack of logically and systematically organized esthetic experiences program for most students? (Esthetic experiences are what give life zest — far richer is the man who knows *how* to live than one who accumulates funds so *as* to live.)

In short, as important as is knowledge acquisition, research, and community services in education, a fundamental question must first be posed — For what purpose? This requires a careful scrutiny of what we are now doing and what we are not doing; of turning more to research findings as in the Coleman and Armor Reports and relying less on "hunch;" eliminating that which makes little sense and adding those activities and practices which do. Truly, the public has loudly called for accountability in education. It is essential that we answer this call with affirmative action.

The call for accountability requires that goals and objectives are set and implemented, that there is a plan. The next 2 chapters will suggest some means whereby goals and objectives can be set and implemented so that the call for accountability is responsibly answered.

Chapter 2

SETTING GOALS AND OBJECTIVES

It simply never occurs to more than a handful (of teachers, principals, and superintendents) to ask why they are doing what they are doing – to think seriously or deeply about the purposes or consequences of education – **Charles E. Silberman**

The term "goal," as used throughout this book refers to a major end result, usually taking a year or longer to complete. The term "objective" on the other hand, refers to intermediate support tasks which must be success- fully completed in order to accomplish a given goal, usually taking less than a year to complete. Goals are to be differentiated from objectives, in that they express the broad general statements of an educational system's long-range pur- poses. Objectives, on the other hand, represent more specific and tangible statements.

But Why Set Goals and Objectives?

Perhaps Seneca put it best as to the result of having no goals and objec- tives when he wrote nearly 2 thousand years ago, "When a man does not know what harbor he is making for, no wind is the right wind" or as the Talmud says, "If you do not know where you are going, any road will get you there." Goals give purpose to ventures.

If an organization has no clearly spelled-out goals and objectives it has no future. Goals and objectives, by definition, imply "looking ahead." Also, by definition, goals and objectives subsume a concise result.

What should an elementary school try to do with limited resources? Educate the retarded or the gifted? Integrate children by busing or spend the saved busing money instead on schools where the lowest achievement occurs?

What should a secondary school try to do? Continue with physical education programs when students cannot read or diminish physical education programs and use the funds made available for special reading programs? Should emphasis be placed on teaching the "melting pot" theory of American society or the "vegetable soup bowl" theory – integration vis-a-vis pluralism?

What should the 2 year college try to do? Become more comprehensive so as to broaden educational opportunity or to contract so as to better assure the quality of what is offered? Should "standards" be kept high so as to screen out "unfit" university aspirants or should grades be eliminated altogether so that the es- poused "open doorness" is a reality rather than "revolving doorness"?

What should the 4-year college and universities try to do? Educate the able, or educate the masses? Teach the wisdom of the ages or prepare youths for the job market?

These examples serve to point out that educational organizations will increasingly be forced to choose among alternative emphases and priorities. This is done by establishing goals and objectives, setting priorities and establishing evaluative systems.

The concept of an "organizational goal" is just that — a concept, a verbal abstraction, and little more. But, as a conceptual tool it can be enormously useful in deliberating, determining, and evaluating policy and practice in education. A conception of organizational goals may serve as the basic element in a formulation of an organization's philosophy, ideology, and policies. Stated goals help tie together assumptions, values, and hopes for the organization into a coherent policy that then provides standards and guides for present and future decisions and actions. A policy formulation containing clearly enunciated goals also enables individuals and agencies outside the organization — parents and students, governmental units and funding agencies, etc. — to be clear about the organization's raison d'être and what can be expected of it.

In sum, there are at least 6 reasons why educational systems need to set goals:

1. As fundamentals of policy.

2. As general decision guides.

3. For planning purposes.

4. For management information systems.

5. For organizational evaluation.

6. For implementing accountability.

Education's Goals

For each organization there are 1 or more goals, though seldom as many as half-a-dozen. For example, most businesses have but 1 major goal — to make a financial profit. In education, there are 3 primary goals: (1) facilitating *learning* through education management; (2) creating *knowledge* through research and publication; (3) providing *community services* through consulting, forums, lectures, programs and performances, and the like. It is noteworthy that it is business, with its economic goal, that bridges the researcher's findings to the learners' need for knowledge by way of commercial publications. Organizations are interdependent, not independent.

In this book, the emphasis will be on facilitating *learning* because only "formal" learning is common to all segments and levels of education. Community services is not common to elementary school systems. Research is uncommon outside university systems.

Learning, as a product of education, implies change. Change is learning — no change, no learning; no learning, no change. Thus educators (administrators, teachers, counselors, educational technologists, librarians, et al) sole learning function is to facilitate positive behavioral change. If *measurable* learning results cannot be clearly demonstrated to others, we have not managed. We have only administered.

The *results* principle which holds true for education likewise holds true for the economic sector: no profit, no positive results. Business profit is money, education profit is learning. The success of these and other sectors of national life, in the final analysis, is based upon results, not good intentions. It is not surprising, then, that modern management theory is based upon what is known as "results management." Under this system of management the objective is to integrate the work of the individual with his own personal interests toward achieving the overall goals of the institution. Thus, the management objective for all organizations is to cause the individuals' work objectives to be consistent with the organization's goals. Indeed, individual and group program objectives have coherence only to the extent that they reflect organizational goals.

Setting Education's Goals

Before an organization can set its educational goals, it must first be determined *who* has primary responsibility for *what*. Broad society goals are set usually, in the final analysis, by boards of trustees — generally, however, only after they have received considerable input from staff, and increasingly students, and often others external to the organization by way of board advisory groups. But even the autonomy of boards of trustees is not entirely absolute when it comes to policy making. There still are the constraints of school codes and federal regulations, of state master plans and statewide coordinating councils. Then there still remains the internal dominance conflicts between faculty and administration over such items as scheduling and curriculum, over classroom organization and teaching strategies. Too, different levels of the educational ladder have different traditions — though educational unionism is tending to blur these distinctions. In short, conflict over who has ultimate authority in various areas must first be resolved before a group sets about to establish its goals and priorities.

Then there is the problem of how goal and priority determinations are to be made: by fiat? by committee? by survey? The premise taken in this book is that the committee approach (participatory democracy) is the best approach when it comes to goal setting though the committee may very well indeed wish to use survey methods such as the *Delphi Technique* (see Chpt. 4) to aid it in its deliberations.

A standing committee holding much promise for setting goals and objectives, priorities and evaluation, are *Councils for the Future.*

Councils for the Future

Public education in the common schools is at a crossroad of a crisis. If its practitioners can learn to manage, then the system will survive. But if its practitioners ignore this imperative the common schools will become nearly unrecognizable as business moves in with performance contracts and as the government moves in with educational vouchers. Nor will higher education be totally immune. It will only take the flood awhile longer to reach there. Alvin Toffler tells us why this is so: " . . . our schools face backward toward a dying system, rather than forward to the emerging new society . . . people tooled for survival in a system that will be dead before they are." (24:354)

The implications of Toffler's observation has profound implications for educational management. His suggestion for the need to establish "Councils of the Future" in every school and college is soundly based. Such councils are sorely needed in recognition of the fact that it now takes less than 15 years for knowledge to double. Because of this fact, instead of assuming that every subject taught today is taught for a reason, it should be assumed that little being taught can be justified as having relevant applicability 15 years hence. Only those subjects passing a stringent review as being future-relevant can be justified so as to be continued in today's curriculum. Management then is managing for the future which implies *planning* in stark contrast to administration which implies day-to-day *reaction* to present events.

As regards to today's curriculum one thing is certain. It is a mindless hold-over from the past. Instead of teaching being organized around such fixed disciplines as biology, economics, English, history, languages, mathematics, physical sciences why not around stages of the human life cycle: a curriculum based on birth, childhood, adolscence, marriage, career, retirement, death? Or around contemporary social problems? Or around significant technologies of the past but particularly of those of the future? Or around countless other imaginative alternatives?

One more thing is certain, before learning is managed it must first be decided what it *is* that is to be managed. Is management to manage the present factory system of education and its accompanying compartmentalized and departmentalized curriculum or is it to manage an individualized and relevant interdisciplinary curriculum? There is no question that educational managers must be held accountable for measurable learning results. But it first must be determined what the curriculum is to be. It can be correctly claimed, for example, that if we teach all of our high school students how to drive a car having a gear shift and a clutch we have achieved 100 percent measurable results. But have we managed? In this illustration we have 2 issues to ponder. The first is obvious, of what good is it to learn to drive a car with a gear shift and a clutch when practically no car no longer has either? But an even more relevant a question is should driver education be taught at all in our public schools vis-a-vis other pressing societal needs (especially in light of the fact that no proof exists that driver education training reduces accidents)? Thus educational management, of necessity, must begin not with managing learning but with the even more fundamental question of *what* the curriculum and its basic learning content is to be.

The establishment of a Council for the Future can aid in the process of curriculum revision and, of course, other goal setting activities as well, if desired. Membership on the Council should include not only administrators but teachers, students, and representative members of the community. Their charge may be to scrutinize, eliminate, add to the present curriculum, or begin anew. The past excuse of certain imposed required subjects by hierarchial educational levels now has little validity; college admission based upon ACT and CEEB scores, coupled with generous open admission policies, counter this past possible justification. The revitalized curriculum must, of necessity, be relevant to future needs — a society in which instead of changing *jobs*, on average, three times during one's working years, one will change *careers* three times. Learning is to become a life-long process in fact, not just in rhetoric.

Curriculum planning. Five-year, future-oriented curriculum planning becomes a necessary management technique. There must be a recognition, as the

5-year curriculum plan is *annually* updated to a new 5-year plan, that knowledge will grow increasingly perishable. Today's "fact" becomes tomorrow's "misinformation." This is no argument against learning facts or data — far from it. But a society, in which the individual frequently will be forced to change his job (and even career), his place of residence, his social ties and so forth, places an enormous premium on learning efficiency. Tomorrow's schools, colleges and universities must, therefore, teach not merely data, but ways to use it. Students must learn how to discard obsolete ideas, and how and when to replace them. They must, in short, learn how to learn. Indeed, *learning how to learn is now the chief learning goal of education.*

Psychologist Herbert Gerjuoy, of the Human Resources Research Organization, phrases the new imperative simply:

> The new education must teach the individual how to classify and reclassify information, how to evaluate its veracity, how to change categories when necessary, how to move from the concrete to the abstract and back, how to look at problems from a new direction — how to teach himself. Tomorrow's illiterate will not be a man who can't read; he will be the man who has not learned how to learn. (24:367)

Though Gerjuoy is undoubtedly correct that tomorrow's illiterate "will be the man who has not learned how to learn," today's challenge is not only preparing for tomorrow's learners but for the still more basic need for many who not only have not learned how to read for meaning but who have not learned how to read at all.

Besides revitalizing the curriculum, teaching students how to read, teaching them to read for meaning, and to learn how to learn students also need to be aided in achieving self-realization through learning how to relate to others, how to establish and integrate values, and how to choose and make decisions from a vast array of alternatives — ever mindful of the possible *future* consequences of each decision, not just mindful of the present consequences.

The curriculum of tomorrow must thus include not only an extremely wide range of data-oriented offerings, but a strong emphasis on future-relevant performance skills. Councils for the Future, in each educational organization, need to be established and to begin to shape an educational system via the setting of 1-year goals, 5-year goals, and 15-year goals which are relevant to what the world is likely to be like 3 decades hence. Figure 2-1 shows a form that has proved helpful in setting these short, intermediate, and long-range goals, a form which is *annually* updated.

Figure 2 - 1

"JONES" ELEMENTARY SCHOOL DISTRICT ORGANIZATIONAL GOALS

Date: **No.**

1975 - 1976	1976 - 1980	1981 - 1985	1986 - 1990

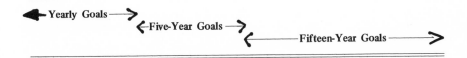

If the concept of educational Councils for the Future put forth by Toffler and others seems widely futuristic, it should be noted that Stanford University and Syracuse University already have such councils funded by the federal government as educational policy research centers. They are charged with the responsibility of forecasting the affective and cognitive skills that the people of tomorrow will need. In Paris, the OECD (Organization for Economic Cooperation and Development) in 1970 created a division with similar responsibilities. In 1971 the first meeting of the *International Society of Educational Planners* was held. These seeds of futurist studies in education are bound to multiply like dandelions on a warm summer day. Their time has come. To avoid future shock, educational institutions will have decreasing lead time to prepare students for the future. The accelerative thrust of information and change will transform academe itself — from today's somewhat placid waters to a raging maelstrom. The only relevant question is will the academy build the necessary information flood controls to channel information into a constructive rather than a destructive force. Management has a chance; administration not at all.

Councils for the Future not only support Cervantes' succinct insight into adaptational psychology: "Fore-warned fore-armed" but psychologists' research findings 400 years later. Studies of the reaction of astronauts, immigrants, new workers, and others facing new experiences for the first time almost uniformly point to the conclusion that those in similar groups who were never fore-warned do not do nearly as well as those who were. Whether the problem is that of getting off an interchange in an unfamiliar town, meeting someone new, teaching for the first time, playing the piano, solving a chess problem, or dealing with interpersonal difficulties, performance improves when the individual knows what to expect next.

Mentally processing advance data cuts down on the amount of processing and the associative adaption time. The mind is given the chance to mentally consider alternatives and to rehearse action before action is actually taken.

Even more important than the advance information itself is the process of *seeking out* such information. Seeking out information in anticipation of the need to adapt to changing conditions can be taught and should be taught. Indeed, not only are there Councils for the Future but there now are courses on the future in a growing number of institutions of higher education. The content of these courses is not only on what is to be, but on the *process* of becoming. It is a truism that those among us who are conditioned to consider future effects on immediate decisions include our most adaptable and successful citizens. Anticipating the future has become a habit with them. The administrator (manager) who begins an intensive and extensive soft sell of explaining educational needs to the electorate at least a year in advance of a planned referendum is more apt to be successful in putting over a rate increase than a hastily thrown together hard-sell campaign 3 months before the referendum. The teacher who studies the cumlative records of the students to be assigned to him in the fall before going on summer leave in the spring is more apt to do a better job in meeting his students' individual needs over those teachers failing to make such an effort. The student who upon taking a new subject first reads about the subject in an encyclopedia, studies the table of contents in his text or library book, thumbs through books and other materials before beginning to read, is more apt to be successful in that subject than those of like ability who have not acquired the habit of anticipation.

Of course, as the educational manager projects himself into the future he does so for varying lengths of time depending upon the purpose of the exercise. Projecting long range goals as far as 15 or more years into the future is not unrealistic for the educational planning of a new building, or for planning the curricular needs of society. Intermediate goals of 5 years in length are common for such tasks as forecasting future enrollments, analyzing the need and geographical placement of new buildings, projecting staffing and financial support requirements. Yearly goals become much more precise and of immediate practical benefit: study of a possible change in grading practices, recruitment of more staff from minority groups, introducing performance objectives into a social studies class, implementing student learning contracts into an English literature class, and the like.

Sociologist Benjamin D. Singer asserts that each individual carries in his mind not merely a picture of himself at present, a self-image, but a set of pictures as he wishes to be in the future. What this does Singer says is to provide a focus for the individual, "a magnet toward which he is drawn; the framework for the present, one might say, is created by the future." (24:373) And Robert Jungk, one of Europe's leading futurist-philosophers, has said, "Nowadays almost exclusive stress is laid on learning what has happened and has been done. Tomorrow . . . at least one third of all lectures and exercises ought to be concerned with scientific, technical, artistic and philosophical work in progress, anticipated crises and possible future answers to these challenges." (24:376)

Management is always more future-oriented than present-oriented. This applies equally to the practice of management by classroom managers (teachers) as to the practice of management by school managers (administrators). It has been suggested that each educational institution reexamine 1) its present course offerings as to its likelihood of being relevant to the needs of the 21st century and 2) to discuss if the current curriculum should continue to be organized by subjects rather than by concepts (eg, life cycles and/or major social issues as "peace," "human rights," the "good society," and the like). To aid in this process the establishment of Councils for the Future has been suggested inasmuch as psychological studies have revealed that man can make better adaptations and wiser decisions if he attempts to intelligently prognosticate the future rather than to simply analyze the past. This extremely important management vehicle needs to be set into early motion with the Council's first task to make recommended changes in the curriculum — projected on master charts into yearly changes, 5-year changes, and 15-year changes so as not to continue to turn out "people tooled for survival in a system that will be dead before they are." Only after this curriculum analysis has been made, and with it a systematic means of studied annual updating and implementation, can meaningful managing for learning results occur — except perhaps for the basic 3-R skills which need not and cannot wait.

Educational Goal Setting in Action

As education's goals are established, be it by fiat, committee, or survey they must be written in measurable terms or in concise descriptive terms when measurement is impossible or not fully adequate. Several curricular and affective and cognitive learning examples developed by the Louisville Public Schools (which have been modified for reader clarity) will serve to illustrate:

LOUISVILLE PUBLIC SCHOOLS

Criterion-Referenced Assessment for Inner-City Children

Federal Fund Request

In order for change in any system to be effective and based on reality, there must be a feedback system that is independent of, yet closely related to, the changing system. What is proposed herein is a feedback system based upon the double concepts of behavioral objectives and accountability. The development of that system will be as follows:

1. Teachers, counselors, principals and administrators will develop individual, teaching team and school objectives that are stated in measurable performance terms.

2. These objectives will then be used to develop appropriate measurement instruments that teachers, counselors and principals can use to make educational decisions about their students that are based upon fact rather than upon intuition.

3. The summation of this system will then be used as the reporting system to the public and other educational institutions as evidence of the relative success of the project

4. The level of involvement of this project will be elementary, junior high and senior high schools.

Board of Trustees' Goals

1. At least 50% of the students in the Louisville target schools will gain at least one full year in achievement in reading and at least 75% will gain beyond expectation based upon the past two years' performance as measured by standardized tests — pre and post.

2. At least 75% of the students in the target schools will be present in school more often during the project school year than they were in the previous school year and the 10% with the worst attendance records during the previous school year will show significant improvement in the project school year.

3. The self concepts of at least 50% of the students in the target schools will improve significantly as measured by pre and post data.

4. Students enrolled in the target schools will experience success in self-directed learning as measured by the increasing number of optimal assignments and projects completed during specified periods of the project.

5. Students at the target schools will develop more positive attitudes of citizenship as measured by a 50% reduction in the cost of vandalism at target schools as compared to the costs the previous years.

6. Students at the target schools will learn to deal more constructively with authority as measured by pre and post gain scores.

7. Students at the target schools will learn to settle personal disputes without overt hostile behavior as measured by a 25% decrease in the number of conflicts with peers and staff throughout the project.

Superintendent's Goals [Examples]

1. At least 50% of the students in the Louisville target schools will gain at least 1 full year in achievement in reading, and at least 75% will gain beyond expectation, based upon the past 2 years' performance, as measured by standardized achievement tests — pre and post.

2. At least 50% of the students in the target schools will gain at least 1 full year in achievement in mathematics, and at least 75% will gain beyond expectation, based upon the past 2 years' performance, as measured by standardized tests — pre and post.

3. At least 25% of the students in the target schools will gain at least 1 full year in achievement in social studies, and at least 50% will gain beyond expectation, based upon the past 2 years' performance, as measured by standardized tests — pre and post.

4. At least 25% of the students in the target schools will gain at least 1 full year in achievement in science, and at least 50% will gain beyond expectation, based upon the past 2 years' performance, as measured by standardized tests — pre and post.

5. At least 75% of the students in the target schools will be present in school more often during the project year than they

were the previous year, and the 10% with the worst attendance records the previous year will show significant improvement in the project year.

6. The self concepts of at least 50% of the students in the target schools will improve significantly, as measured by pre and post data.

7. Students enrolled in the target schools will experience success in self-directed learning, as measured by the increasing number of optimal assignments and projects completed during specified periods of the project.

8. Students at the target schools will develop more positive attitudes of citizenship, as measured by a 50% reduction in the cost of vandalism at target schools as compared to the costs the previous years.

9. Students at the target schools will learn to deal more constructively with authority, as measured by pre and post gain scores.

10. Students at the target schools will learn to settle personal disputes without overt hostile behavior, as measured by a 25% decrease in the number of conflicts with peers and staff throughout the project.

11. At least 75% of the parents in target schools will show a positive attitude toward school, as measured by a parent inventory questionnaire based on the Likert questionnaire.

12. At least 75% of the students in target schools will show a positive attitude toward school, as measured by a student inventory questionnaire based on the Likert questionnaire.

Principal's Goals [Example]

Date: December 4, 19 __

School: "Alpha"   **Principal: "John Doe"**

1. The average daily attendance of all students for the project school year will be at least 90%

2. The self-concepts of at least 50% of the students will improve significantly, as measured by pre and post data.

3. Students will experience success in self-directed learning, as measured by the increasing number of optional assignments and projects completed during specified periods of the project.

4. Students will develop more positive attitudes of citizenship, as measured by a 50% reduction in the misuse of school equipment and materials.

5. Students will learn to deal more constructively with authority, as measured by pre and post gain scores.

6. Students will learn to settle personal disputes without overt hostile behavior, as measured by a 25% decrease in the number of conflicts with peers and staff.

7. At least 75% of the parents will show a positive attitude toward school, as measured by a parent inventory questionnaire based on the Likert questionnaire.

8. At least 75% of the students will show a positive attitude toward school, as measured by a teacher-made student questionnaire.

9. At least 50% of the students will gain at least 1 full year in achievement in reading, and at least 75% will gain beyond expectation, based upon the past 2 years performance, as measured by standardized tests — pre and post.

10. At least 50% of the students will gain at least 1 full year in achievement in mathematics, and at least 75% will gain beyond expectation, based upon the past 2 years' performance, as measured by standardized tests — pre and post.

11. At least 50% of the students will gain at least 1 full year in achievement in social studies, and at least 75% will gain beyond expectation, based upon the past 2 years' performance, as measured by standardized tests — pre and post.

12. At least 50% of the students will gain at least 1 full year in achievement in science, and at least 75% will gain beyond expectation, based upon the past 2 years' performance, as measured by standardized tests — pre and post.

13. Each team will produce a log of the strategies, techniques and activities utilized in carrying out their objectives, including the resources, or lack of resources, that contributed to or hindered their success.

14. Each team will produce interim objectives for each of the above long-term objectives.

15. To make contact with the community through parent visitation, Neighborhood House, et cetera, at least 6 times a month to explain programs and listen to parent concerns about goals for children's education.

16. To have 75% of the school staff make contact with the community through parent visitation, Neighborhood House, et cetera, at least twice a month to explain programs, offer resources to community and to listen to parent's concerns about goals for children's education.

17. To have a minimum of 3 one-hour conferences with each staff member at "Alpha" during the school year, at which time criteria for evaluation, evaluation, mutual areas of concern and achievement of team and individual objectives will be discussed.

18. To spend at least 1 hour a week in each team's class and to critique at least 1 hour with that team each month.

19. To have 100% of the individuals and teams in "Alpha" write objectives in the areas of students' cognitive, affective, and social development and in the area of their own professional development by December 11.

20. To produce and publish a list of priorities for the use of the PLF's time and energy in administrating "Alpha" School by January 4.

21. To have at least 1 full staff meeting at which at least 90% of the staff will be present per month at which information may be exchanged, mutual areas of concern discussed, et cetera, beginning in December.

22. During the monthly staff meetings, the 3 teams will meet to discuss problems and problem-solving strategies for areas of conflict among teams.

23. To keep a daily log of critical incidents and a record of my interventions and contacts with teams and individuals.

24. To report to "Joe Smith" and "Bill Brown" at the end of each month what progress I am making in meeting these objectives.

Teaching Team Objectives [Example]

Date: December 11, 19 __

School: "Alpha"   **Principal: "John Doe"**

Team: 2   Grade: 3-4   Coordinating Teacher: "Jack Jones"

"Jan Bern", Teacher Corps Intern   "Laura Farrell", Librarian
"Kathy Bart", Staff Teacher   "Nora Smith", EMH Teacher
"Clint Calb", Teacher Corps Intern   "Sue Grey", EMH Teacher
"Earl Hitch", Paraprofessional   "Jane Green", Reading Improve-
"Glen Priz", Teacher Corps Intern   ment Teacher
"Mary Sams", Paraprofessional   "Mary Mason", Counselor
"Ann Spring", Paraprofessional

1. Terminal — By June, at least 75% of the 3rd graders will be able to divide 2-place numbers, as measured by a score of 70% on a teacher-made test.

   Interim — By February 28, at least 30% of the 3rd graders will be able to divide 2-place numbers, as measured by a score of 70% on a teacher-made test.

2. Terminal — By June, at least 50% of the 4th graders will have mastered long division skills, as measured by a score of 70% on a teacher-made test.

   Interim — By February 28, 75% of all students will be able to demonstrate mastery of borrowing and carrying 2- and 3-place numbers in addition, subtraction and multiplication, as measured by a teacher-made test.

3. By June, 50% of the students should be able to read and carry out directions written on their instructional level with 70% accuracy, as determined by the teacher.

4. Terminal — By June, 80% of the children currently reading in books 1-5 of the Project READ series should be able to identify words containing consonants and vowels with 80% accuracy, as measured by a teacher-made test.

Interim — By February 28, 60% of the children reading in books 1-5 and above should be able to identify independently words containing consonant blends and long and short vowels with 60% accuracy, as measured by a teacher-made test.

Also, by February 28, 80% of the children reading in books 7-12 will be able to master content clues with 70% accuracy, as measured by teacher-made tests.

5. Terminal — By June, 50% of the 4th grade children will score at least 70% on a vocabularly test taken from the **Magic Word,** a 4th grade level reader.

    Interim — By February 28, 25% of the 4th grade children will score at least 70% on a vocabulary test taken from 8 selected stories.

6. Terminal — By June, 75% of the 3rd graders will be able to identify at least 15 community workers and their roles, categorize 3 classes of foods and their geographic sources, 3 types of clothing materials and their sources, 2 concepts of cultural geography, and 3 concepts of transportation, as measured by a score of 70% on a teacher-made test.

    Interim — By February 28, the 4th graders will have reviewed and mastered the following concepts with 75% accuracy on a teacher-made test: 15 community workers and their roles, 3 basic foods categories and their sources, 3 sources of clothing materials, 2 concepts of cultural geography and 3 sources of transportation.

7. By June 75% of the 4th graders will be able to relate to teacher satisfaction 3 concepts of the earth in the solar system and demonstrate their ability to use 10 map skills, as measured by a teacher-made test.

8. By June, 75% of the 4th graders will be able to demonstrate knowledge of all of the capital letters, 10 types of punctuation, 3 types of sentence structures, 4 types of dictionary skills and 4 parts of speech, as measured by achieving a score of 70% on a teacher-made test.

9. By June, 90% of all students will have demonstrated their knowledge of 5 physical fitness skills by achieving a passing score on the May Physical Fitness Test.

10. By June, all 3rd and 4th graders will improve in good sportsmanship, as measured by a decrease in the number of fights, an increase in

teamwork and a decrease in observed incidents of unsportsmanlike conduct during sporting events, as measured by a teacher checklist.

11. By June, 75% of all 3rd and 4th graders will demonstrate an increase in positive self concept, as evidenced by an increase in the number of tasks completed, an increase in the number of positive verbalizations when given assignments and increased academic success, according to teacher records.

12. At least 75% of all students will have completed at least 1 art project (painting, papier mache; etc.) by February 28.

Individual Objectives [Examples]

"Jack Jones", Coordinating Teacher

1. By January 8, we will have rescheduled our Project READ Program so as to meet some of our objectives in the area of language arts with special emphasis on correlating the English skills. This will involve at least 95% of the students.

2. By February 28, at least 80% of our children will be participating in a program of scheduled music and art. At present I feel that only 25% of the family is participating.

3. By February 28, all student groups will be working with each team member, participating in some form of group discussion at least 2 times each week. The discussions should be an outgrowth of child-centered experiences.

"Laura Farell", Librarian

1. By May 15, I will have contacted at least 75% of the teaching staff in order to assist them in planning research activities for their students and/or specific units of work and to make available to them as many aids as possible (books, audio-visual, et cetera). I will maintain a log of these activities and materials suggested.

2. Given at least 1 hour per week of instruction time by the librarian, at least 75% of the children in such programs will, to the librarian's satisfaction:

    a. demonstrate use of the Card Catalog,

       b.   locate at least 4 divisions of books, ie, fiction, non-fiction and reference,

       c.   identify at least 8 kinds of reference materials, and

       d.   demonstrate the use of at least 5 types of reference books.

All will be recorded by a checklist for each child.

3. From December 14, until February 23, I will be available from 2:00 until 4:00 p.m. on Tuesday and Thursday to any staff member who wishes help in acquiring more skill in the use of the library and of audio-visual materials. I will maintain a log of the number of staff members who use this service and a record of materials requiring repair.

4. I will endeavor, by personal contact and individual suggestion, to bring about an increase in library skills, knowledge of materials and a desirable love for books by the students. This will be evaluated by an increase in the use of both books and materials as shown by library records.

5. I will critique at least once a month with each team to assure the future role of the library in the Focus Project, as recorded in my personal log.

6. To provide materials on opposing sides of controversial issues, I shall acquire books with opposing points of view (such as in the social science area — democracy versus communism).

7. I will endeavor to provide library materials that will enrich and support the curriculum, as evaluated by the increased use of these materials. Additionally, I will increase by at least 25% the books relating to the skills and achievements of Blacks.

8. I will publish supplements of the already issued brochure of any important materials or visual aids as they come to the library.

"Nora Smith", E.M.H. Teacher

1. Terminal — By the end of the school year, 50% of the class will be reading at 3.0 grade level and the remaining 50% at least at 1.0 grade level as measured by a standardized reading test.

Interim — By February 26, 50% will be reading at 2.4 level, as measured by a teacher-made test.

2. By the end of the school year, 50% of the class will be able to perform 2-place additions with regrouping, 2-place subtraction without regrouping and multiplication through the 6 table with 80% accuracy, as measured by a teacher-made test.

3. Terminal — By the end of the school year, 75% of the class will be able to tell time as demonstrated in a teacher-made test.

   Interim — By February 26, 40% of the children will be able to tell time.

4. By the end of the school year, at least 25% of the children will be able to:

   a. identify at least 12 seeds

   b. name at least 4 parts of plants, and

   c. name at least 4 plant classifications, as measured by a teacher-made test.

5. By the end of the school year, at least 25% of the children will be able to:

   a. name the 4 seasons and give verbally at least 2 related facts, and

   b. read a thermometer to the teacher's satisfaction.

6. Emphasis will be placed on the child and his relation to the community. To achieve this:

   a. there will be at least 15 minutes each day devoted to a review of the news related to the community and the child,

   b. we will visit the library for film strips and/or stories relevant to citizenship at least twice weekly, and

   c. we will make at least 1 field trip and/or invite 1 community resource person each week. A log will be kept of these activities.

7. A rating scale of behavior pertinent to self concept will be devised with the assistance of the counselor and administered by January 15, and again by February 26, and June 1. There will be significant positive changes in at least 75% of the children.

8. Each child will have a personal chart made visible to him as to his progress and achievement.

9. During the school year, each child will have at least 1 success experience on at least 80% of the school days, as recorded on checklist 1.

"Jane Green", Reading Improvement Teacher

1. All children in the Reading Center will be evaluated by comparison of form A of the Gates-McGinitie Revised Reading Test administered in October. Form B of the same test is to be administered in April. In this interval the achievement gained will be as follows:

    a. 60% of the 2nd grade students will gain at least 6 months, as measured by Level A tests;

    b. 95% of the 3rd grade students will gain at least 6 months, as measured by Level B tests;

    c. 50% of the 4th grades will gain at least 6 months, as measured by Level C tests;

    d. Of the 3 5th grade students, one will gain at least 8 months, the second, at least 6 months, and the 3rd, at least 4 months.

2. In order to provide success experiences for these children, each child will have his own bar chart to make visible to him his progress. The material chosen will be gauged so that each child will score at least 45 correct out of a possible 48 times.

"Mary Mason", Counselor

1. The average daily attendance of all students at "Alpha" School for the school year will be at least 90%. To help achieve this I will:

    a. greet at least 90% of the student body by name each time one is met,

b. telephone every child who is absent from school for more than 2 consecutive days,

c. chat casually with every child after he returns to school from any absence,

d. telephone every child who has had a record of heavy absence or truancy if he is absent,

e. visit every child who is absent for more than 4 consecutive days,

f. visit every child who is hospitalized for more than 2 days,

g. have a conference with parent and child who is known to be truant or who has shown a weekly absence pattern, and

h. have children with attendance problems drop by daily for a chat.

2. The average daily attendance of the lowest 10% of the attendance problems for "Alpha" School during the previous school year will show at least a 30% improvement during this school year. To accomplish this I will:

a. employ strategies a-h given for Objective 1, and

b. have individual counseling sessions of at least 20 minutes per week with children who are considered attendance cases by the team, school social worker and counselor.

Records will be maintained in my personal log.

3. The average daily tardiness at "Alpha" School will show a 50% improvement during this school year as compared to the previous school year. To achieve this I will:

a. greet children as they come to school each morning,

b. spend at least 3 mornings per week on the street and playground greeting those who arrive after 8:30 a.m.,

c. telephone parents or children who have been tardy at least once a week,

    d.   have conferences with parents of children who have already been tardy more than 5 times,

    e.   have individual or group counseling sessions of at least 20 minutes every 3 weeks with tardiness cases, and

    f.   have children who have had a record of tardiness drop by to see me before school each morning.

Records will be maintained in my personal log.

4.   The self-concepts of at least 50% of the students in "Alpha" School will show improvement, as measured by pre and post data of the C.P.Q. and E.S.P.Q. To achieve this I will:

    a.   know at least 90% of the student body by name and be able to discuss with each child something about his interests, concerns, achievements, family, et cetra, whenever the child is seen,

    b.   give praise and support for accomplishments within the team during daily visits of at least 15 minutes to the classroom area,

    c.   display pictures and writing articles to publicize children who are making some type of contribution to the community or school, and

    d.   have individual or group counseling sessions of at least 30 minutes every 2 weeks for children who are having peer-group problems.

5.   Students at "Alpha" School will learn to settle personal disputes without overt behavior, as measured by a 25% decrease in the number of conflicts with peers and staff reported to the office. Strategies used for the development of self concepts will be used.

6.   At least 70% of the students at "Alpha" School who have known physical or psychological problems, as diagnosed by health aide, school nurse or psychologist, will receive treatment by the proper agency during the Project Focus school year as shown by record.

The following strategies will be utilized:

a. diagnosing of defects will be done by routine health screening procedures by teacher or by self-referral to school nurse or psychologist;

b. parents of children who need care will be contacted to have a conference about the problem;

c. a referral will be made to the proper agency if the parent does not want to consult a private physician; and

d. follow-up of all referrals will be made to make sure necessary treatment has been received and recording pertinent data on school records has been done.

Records of these activities will be maintained.

7. Students at "Alpha" School who have been self-referrals to the counselor or school nurse at least weekly for reasons of dizziness, stomach aches, headaches, et cetra will show a 50% reduction of such referrals by the end of the school year.

To achieve this I will:

a. have conferences with parents to inform them of the self-referrals and to request that immediate medical attention be secured;

b. make referral to the proper agency if the parent does not want to consult a private physician;

c. make follow-up to be sure if there is need for medical attention record data on proper school records, and see that treatment is received; and

d. have individual or group counseling sessions of at least 30 minutes every 2 weeks for children who have been seen by a physician and do not have a medical problem.

A record will be maintained in the log.

8. Students at "Alpha" School will develop more positive attitudes of citizenship as measured by a 50% reduction in the misuse of the school building, school equipment and materials.

To achieve this, I will:

    a.   take photographs of destroyed equipment, destroyed property, defaced walls, littered floors, et cetra, and take photographs of properly cared for things to display and to use as the basis for group guidance classes, and,

    b.   have individual and group counseling sessions of at least 30 minutes every 2 weeks with students who have been referred to the counselor about vandalism.

A record will be maintained.

9.   At least 1 hour per week will be spent in each team's class to observe children or to work with individual children. Records of these visits will be kept in a log.

10.   At least 3 afternoons per week will be spent critiquing with teams who request it. Log record will be kept.

11.   At least 1 afternoon per month will be spent meeting with leaders of community agencies to discuss community resources, problems, or ways the school and agency can work for the support of a particular family. Log records will be kept.

12.   At least ½ hour per week will be spent in conference with the community coordinator discussing ways the counselor can work with particular families. Log records will be kept.

13.   At least ½ hour every week will be spent with the principal discussing ways the counselor can work with particular problems. Log records will be kept.

14.   At least 5 minutes per week will be spent with the Public Health nurse discussing children with health problems. Log records will be kept.

15.   At least 5 professional books on counseling techniques, group dynamics, child development, et cetra, will be read during the school year. An annotated bibliography will be kept.

As can be seen from the foregoing, the goal setting activities of the Louisville Public Schools were based upon performance goals which were capable of measurement, and which were specifically programmed for implementation. It is further to be noted that good goal programming requires that specific answers be written down as to 1) *what* should be accomplished (task), 2) *how* the task is to be performed (conditions), 3) *measures* to determine success (criteria), and 4) *who* will be responsible for achieving each goal (accountability).

Evaluation

Built into the system of setting goals, objectives, and priorities must be a provision for reviews of performance to take place during the process of working toward a given goal (see MBO Chpt. 13) — not at the end of the period when corrective action is not possible.

Assessment of an organization's effectiveness can be determined to the extent to which acknowledged goals and objectives are being achieved. Few, if any, decisions within a system or institution make sense unless they are taken with reference to accepted goals. Such goals provide the fundamental elements of an organization's policies, its ideologies, its values that provide a focus for loyalty, professional commitment, and genuine community.

We must always keep in mind, as goals, objectives, and priorities are set, that educational systems exist primarily to teach students. Thus, as the content and quality of the system is evaluated, it must be based on 1) what have students actually been learning, 2) how much have they learned, 3) how well and how fast did they learn, and 4) how much and how well are students learning today vis-à-vis previous years. Too often the focus is not on the output of the educational system but on its inputs — increase in enrollments, increase in budgets, increase in size of staff, increase in number of library books purchased, and the like. Insofar as output is concerned, it is a sad commentary that the public is more likely to know the win-loss record of the basketball team than the scholastic attainments of the institution's students. Yet, there are abundant signs that the public is now demanding acceptable results for their money from administrators and teachers just as they insist on winning results from coaches. The public is demanding that administrators and teachers hold up for public view their "win-loss" records — and to be held accountable for the results. In short, the public is reminding us what we are about, what our mission is, what schools, colleges and universities are for.

One way of evaluating the quality of an educational organization is an *internal* one such as the criterion-referenced assessments used in the Louisville Public Schools. Other examples are standardized achievement tests and "college boards." But such internal standardized measurements of quality must be very cautiously interpreted. If an institution's students consistently *exceed* national norms the institution has not necessarily done a superior job. Indeed, it might have done an inferior job compared to another institution whose students, on average, achieved *below* national norms. This anomoly is easily explained. Students coming from superior socio-economic backgrounds may score higher more as a result of nonformal than formal learning. For internal standardized evaluation to have meaning, it must first be determined what the overall average intelligence percentile ranking is of the school. Then by reconverting achievement and college board scores into percentiles a meaningful comparison can be made. If, for example, a school's sixth graders rank at the 60th percentile for the total score on the *Metropolitan Achievement Test,* under the prevailing practice, the teachers, principal and superintendent would proudly announce in a public relations bulletin what a superior job of instruction was occuring within the district. However, if it were found that these same 6th graders had a composit score on the *California Test of Mental Maturity* which placed them at the 75th percentile in mental ability, it likely would mean that the district had actually done an inferior job of instruction. Internal auditing means just that. It does not mean comparing one's own students with national norms in a vacuum. It instead means comparing learning results against learning ability. This is the true value of standardized tests — the ability to make such internal comparisons as means of auditing learning management results.

External evaluation of the quality of the educational job being done can be achieved through such comparative means as the percentage of entering students completing each grade level vis-a-vis like socio-economic communities, the fitness and relevance of skills to the needs of society, the citizenship actions; in short, how close to the measure of the defined "Educated Person" do the graduates fit.

These two different means for assessing a school system can lead to two different conclusions. The quality and efficiency of a school may be high according to its own *internal* standards. But if its teaching, judged by *external* criteria, is out-dated and irrelevant for its place and time, then its quality and efficiency must be considered unsatisfactory. If educational goals and objectives are to make any sense, and serve any useful purpose, they must be relative to the particular purpose, place and time of the student clientele's *future* needs.

The managers of educational systems must set their sights on adapting the educational curricula and standards to the realities of the situations they face, and, in doing so, they must try to harmonize the internal and external criteria of quality.

The obvious inference for the future is the emphasis on producing an *educable* person (a major criterion of an Educated Person) who can learn and adapt efficiently all through his life to an environment that is ceaselessly changing. If an educational system itself is not adaptable to changing environmental conditions it cannot expect to produce people who are.

Evaluation is the crux of accountability. It is through the evaluation function that effectiveness of the system is determined and accountability achieved. In short, an evaluation system as an accountability system establishes the requirement that we do that which we said we would do. This is achieved to the degree that congruance exists between system goals and system results. Just as a ship cannot sail without a map, an educational system cannot progress without a plan. The destination of both a ship and an educational system represent a goal, some desirable end result. Objectives represent intermediate stops toward a desired end goal. Because goals require a looking ahead a planning group is necessary, eg, a Council for the Future. Finally, as at the end of any journey, the result is assessed through evaluation. If the reader has understood these points, the goal of this chapter has been achieved.

Chapter 3

IMPLEMENTING GOALS AND OBJECTIVES

We expected people to come out from under the rocks and be creative, but we're beginning to see we can't force people to be free — Newman Walker

In the previous chapter the setting of goals and objectives was discussed. In this chapter the mechanics for achieving this will be outlined. The steps to be followed are as applicable to an individual as to a committee (eg, a Council for the Future). The basic steps to follow are as equally valid for use by a classroom teacher or counselor, an educational technologist or librarian, as for a dean or a principal, a president or a superintendent.

That in the 1st place there is need for educational change is self-evident if for no other reason than the fact that a quarter of our population reads below the 5th grade level; or if for no other reason than "schooling" has become separated from life.

To solve education's problems there is a need to focus on relationships and to see education as a whole, to focus on outputs as a ratio to inputs. In short, goals and objectives must be set and implemented. To accomplish this need requires the employment of a systems approach — an orderly approach for solving problems . . . a structured process based on a study of all the variables related to a problem.

The systems approach provides both a structure and a process. It provides communication links between the public and the board of trustees, between the trustees and the school administration, between the administration and the faculty, between the faculty and the students. This network, ideally, satisfies learning needs, conveys information, and helps to obtain the needed financial resources for the organization. Such networks function as part of a communications cycle involving a consumer and supplier of information.

It helps in implementing a successful change strategy for the initiator of change (goal setter) to think of himself not so much in his "role" as president or dean, superintendent or principal, teacher or counselor, educational technologist or librarian but instead more in the role of "problem solver." A problem solver depends upon the scientific method, not on the authority of his position. In the long run the problem solver, using the scientific method of the systems approach, is far more likely to succeed in implementing needed changes into the organization than one who tries to implement change through the authority of the position he holds.

However, good goal setting is generally not so much the product of one individual as it is the product of a group. The reason research shows that change *is* frequently the result of "strong" leadership is because of the failure of the leader of the organization to provide a vehicle for setting goals and objectives, change and evaluation. It was suggested in the previous chapter that Councils for the Future can serve as the requisite vehicle for organizational goal setting.

Setting and implementing goals requires problem solving. Generally, a representative group of affected individuals will not only suggest needed goals, but of equal importance can provide solutions for implementing them.

It is perfectly understandable that the reason so many promising innovations die after a chief executive leaves an educational organization is because the innovations (a *means* to achieve goals) were imposed through "strong leadership." Since the innovations were not the product of those affected by them, it is little wonder that the corporate body rids itself of the "foreign" product as soon as it can. Therefore, if a change is to "stick", it requires *early* involvement by those who are to be affected by it and by those who are to be responsible for implementing it.

Another basic error that change agents sometimes make is to confuse ends with means. "Ends" are goals while "means" are methods (eg, innovations, techniques, dollars, personnel). A classic example of this confusion is illustrated by Colonel Nicholson who confused the satisfaction of building a difficult bridge over the River Kwai with his responsibility to impede the building of the bridge in the first place as a captured World War II British officer.

Change and innovation are *not* goals. They are, instead, the *means* for achieving goals. Goals must *first* be set. Only then does it become time to seek out the most effective and efficient means for accomplishing the goals.

Certainly, anyone in an organization has the right and the responsibility to suggest goals, objectives, and means. But unless both the goals and the processes are acceptable to those affected, and those who are to be the implementers, the result will be aborted.

With these cautions kept in mind, there are seven distinct, sequential steps which are embodied in a systematic goal determination and impementation strategy: 1) diagnosing the problem, 2) formulating goals and objectives, 3) identifying constraints and needed resources, 4) evaluating alternatives, 5) selecting solutions, 6) implementing the selected solution, 7) feedback and evaluation.

Each of these steps will be discussed briefly below:

Step 1: *Diagnosing the problem.* A successful systematic goal-setting strategy begins with the recognition that the system is malfunctioning, or a better way exists to do an existing function, or something is not being done that needs doing.

The Louisville Public Schools' proposal for a federal grant to conduct a *Criterion-Referenced Assessment for Inner-City Children* illustrates particularly well a diagnosis of a problem facing nearly every city in the land to varying degrees:

CRITERION-REFERENCED ASSESSMENT
FOR INNER-CITY CHILDREN

Need

Problem Identification — The rigid, traditional, self-contained classroom approach of one teacher locked into a classroom of 30 to 40 children with little or no flexibility in scheduling or curriculum in many schools has generally stifled the teacher and stymied the potential creativity of many students. Teachers are cut off from mutual observation and the kind of healthy critiquing that contributes to professional growth. They are trapped in dull routines and trivial duties, such as collecting monies, filling out reports, taking attendance and shuffling paper.

Many children are trapped in a regimented, boring curriculum; many others are trapped in personality clashes with good-intentioned but insensitive teachers; and practically all lack sufficient individual attention.

Rote memory is still over-emphasized at the expense of meaningful learning. As a result, children show less and less enthusiasm for learning as they progress in our antiquated educational structure.

The over-worked teacher has little or no time to make home visits to secure parental cooperation. He is often caught in vicious counter pressures between insecure administrators and anxious parents. He spends more time as a disciplinarian than in developing his special creative potentials. As a result, conformity is all too often the measure of success.

The enthusiasm and idealism of beginning teachers is squelched by authoritarian leadership and stifling bureaucratic processes. As a consequence, these beginning teachers rapidly become frustrated factory workers who just put their time in to mechanically grind out a product.

Some of the faulty assumptions current in American educational practice and frequently present in the Louisville Public Schools are that

1.   what is taught is what is learned;

2.   students can be impersonally manipulated like objects;

3.   the ability to pass standardized examinations is an adequate measure of a student's performance;

4.   fear of failure motivates students;

5.   teacher's values are the only good values;

6.   children cannot be trusted to assume significant responsibility for their own learning;

7.   a good classroom is a quiet classroom; and

8.   coverage measures the amount learned.

New Approach to Problems — The Louisville District has proposed a major reorganization of the curriculum, instructional processes. staffing design, administrative structure and community participation concept of 14 Louisville schools — 1 senior high, 4 junior highs and 9 elementary schools.

Assumptions which undergird the program are that

1.   the school can and should be an enjoyable place for children to be;

2.   learning can and should be made interesting and exciting;

3.   teachers can and should develop a more personalized and trusting relationship with pupils;

4.   pupils can learn more meaningfully when they are actively involved in the planning of their learning activities;

5.   curriculum content can be significant to youth when it relates to issues and interests important to them;

6.   children can become more self-directed when given educational activities which they have helped to plan, carry out and evaluate; and

7. children can become more self-disciplined when they have shared in the development of their own school as a social system and have been helped to better understand their own behavior.

As can be seen, diagnosing problems takes time and money (staff salaries at least). Therefore, before a problem is diagnosed it must be decided to what extent it should be diagnosed in the first place. What is the genesis of the problem? Are there complaints — if so, from whom? If there are complaints, are they legitimate? Does a problem emerge from opinion makers and leaders or from chronic complainers? Has the problem arisen internally, externally, or both? When the problem solver(s) calmly, carefully, and objectively considers the elements of the problem he will be in a position to decide how much time, effort, energy, and money should be devoted to the matter. Some problems, or situations in need of improvement, have to be tolerated in a social system. The trick is to distinguish between the in- tolerable and the tolerable. This requires careful diagnosis. Fortunately, there now are management techniques and tools available to aid in distinguishing between trivial and real problems. These will be discussed in Part II of this book.

Step 2: *Formulating goals and objectives.* Having assessed the expectations of those within and without the organization who seek reforms and improve- ments, and having identified or separated the real from the imagined prob- lems, we are ready to search for solutions. Before we decide on a course of action, we have to decide explicitly what it is we are trying to do. In other words, we must know precisely what are our goals and objectives.

As has been illustrated, well stated objectives consist of three characteristics: 1) they are internally consistent with one another and compatible with organizational goals, 2) they are stated in operational or behavioral terms, and 3) they are comprehensive and output-oriented.

Using our Louisville Public Schools example again, we can see the formula- ting of objectives in action in a real situation:

Objectives

The specific objectives of the District's operational model are as follows:

1. At least 50% of the students in the 14 target schools will gain at least 1 full year in achievement in reading and arithmetic, and at least 75% will gain beyond expectation, based upon the past 2 years' performance, as measured by standardized tests — pre and post.

2.   At least 75% of the students in the 14 target schools will be present in school more often in 1970-71 than they were in 1969-70, and the 10% with the worst attendance records in 1969-70 will show significant improvement in attendance in 1970-71.

3.   The self concepts of at least 50% of the students in the 14 target schools will improve significantly, as measured by pre and post test data.

4.   Students enrolled in the 14 target schools will experience success in self-directed learning, as measured by the increasing number of optional assignments and projects completed during specified periods of the project.

5.   Students at the 14 target schools will develop more positive attitudes of citizenship, as measured by a 50% reduction in the cost of vandalism at target schools as compared to costs of the previous year.

6.   Students at the 14 target schools will learn to deal more constructively with authority, as measured by pre and post gain scores.

7.   Students at the 14 target schools will learn to settle personal disputes without overt hostile behavior, as measured by a 25% decrease in the number of conflicts with peers and staff throughout the project.

It will be remembered from the previous chapter that accountability for setting system-wide goals is the responsibility of the board of trustees while the achievement of the objectives necessary to reach these goals is the duty and the responsibility of the chief academic officer of the system with the aid of his staff. Caring citizenry will turn out their elected officials if they do not set goals consistent with what the citizenry demands. Likewise, a chief executive who is incapable of achieving significant system goals, through a series of support objectives, cannot be expected to last long in his job.

However, specificity through measurable objectives is far better than vague and ill-defined aspirations which leave everyone in the dark as to who is accountable for what.

A system's concern for the realization of human potential, of shaping human values, of creating Educated Persons reflects the goals of an educational system. Objectives help to assure the attainment of such goals.

Step 3: *Identifying constraints and needed resources.* Before launching any goal-setting effort, a chief executive and his staff need to be fully aware of the history and traditions which surround established practices. They need to acquire detailed knowledge of the resources needed to successfully implement a new program. Constraints or barriers may take the form of laws, established traditions, faculty attitudes, or any other force which works in behalf of maintaining the status quo. Resources take the form of money, people, facilities, materials, and information. Awareness of efforts elsewhere is necessary if alternative solutions to a problem are to be stipulated. "The task of information retrieval can be handled confidently and with a minimum of effort, if the searcher thinks about what he needs before he starts and plans an acquisition strategy which makes sense in terms of his needs." (12:77)

Continuing with our Louisville Public Schools example, Superintendent Newman Walker and his staff identified the constraints to be overcome and the resources needed in order to introduce massive changes. The constraints of size alone militated against significant change. There are 50,000 children (27,000 white, 23,000 black). Of the 50,000 students enrolled in the 70 schools 34 percent come from families with an annual income of $2,000 or less. In 1969, the year before Walker became superintendent, the system had the second highest dropout rate in the nation. Seventy-one percent of its students were achieving below the national averages.

To overcome the constraints, and to acquire the needed resources so as to make the changes clearly called for, Superintendent Walker and his staff employed three basic strategies:

1.   *Acquired additional funding.* By the spring of 1970 a dozen federal grants, in addition to such regularly appropriated funds as those granted under Title I of the Elementary and Secondary Act, were secured. Most of these funds were concentrated on the Focus-Impact project schools discussed in this and the previous chapter.

2.   *Initiated a massive program of humanistic education.* Convinced that insensitivity and unresponsiveness were the basic problems in schools, Superintendent Walker sought out the means to create schools where students could feel a positive sense of themselves and of their relations with others, and where teachers were committed to what they were doing because it had meaning for them.

Several 5-day retreats were one of the means chosen by Walker to implement the planned "humanistic" education program. Board members and administrators each attended one session. The retreat concentrated on helping board members and administrators get to better know each other and one another as persons, as individuals. Also, some of the principles of conflict management were introduced.

All the project teachers attended a paid 8-week summer training program designed to prepare them for the changes that laid ahead that fall. Like the administrative and board groups, teachers worked in small "process groups" which consisted largely of sessions intended to help teachers better understand their own behavior and how it affects those around them. Those involved in these sessions learned specific skills to communicate the feelings that motivated their behavior and received "feedback" on how their actions impressed others. Though some sessions dealt with curriculum changes and the building of teacher teams to work in individual schools, most operated on the assumption that if the teachers could be helped to treat each other and their students in a more open, honest fashion the schools would become more humane and more productive.

Psychologist Carl Rogers hearlded the Louisville Public Schools' approach to change as being "the boldest and most promising venture in education today." (3:52)

Rogers lauding of Louisville's "humanistic education" is particularly noteworthy in view of the fact that along with sensitivity training such emphasis is also placed on measurable performance objectives. Measurable performance objectives *is* a humanistic system for the simple reason that the system focuses on learning rather than on teaching — and that is what education is chiefly about.

3. *Initiated a feedback system.* It is not enough to introduce an innovation. It must be nourished along or "backsliding" will occur (just as it occured in Louisville). To overcome the inherent difficulties in most all innovations Superintendent Walker literally spent more time outside his office than in it. He had a telephone placed in his car so that he could accept calls, conduct business, and make minor decisions as he transported himself regularly to the schools of the district to meet with individuals and groups. Moreover, the system design of teaching teams, weekly reviews of progress, data flowing in on a scheduled basis to Dr. Larry Barber in the district's R & D office assured an ongoing results oriented program.

The key factors for overcoming most constraints and limited resources can essentially be summed up with three key words: "money", "imagination", and "involvement". Of the three, money is generally the least important. Nor does it take much imagination to identify an educational system's major problems — though it requires much more imagination to introduce the most workable innovations to solve a major problem. As was earlier emphasized, the chief problem in overcoming resistance to change lies in the failure to involve those in the solution who are part of the problem. Those who are affected by change *must* participate in that change if the change is not to be sabotaged or to enjoy only a short life.

Jerome Bruner, in analyzing the literature on learning, found that in a hundred years of research there are but three ingredients which cause us to learn: people do not learn unless they want to; people do not learn unless they are actually involved; people do not learn without reinforcement or feedback. Thus, we will not do what others want us to do without *motivation, participation,* and *reinforcement.* Nor can we get others to learn or accept our ideas unless the potential "customer" feels a need (motivation), is involved in the decision (participation), and receives feedback on results (reinforcement).

In sum, if setting and implementing goals and objectives is to be more than a paper exercise, it must consist of a system which meets the learning needs of the participants — community, staff, and students.

Step 4. *Evaluating alternatives.* Having successfully analyzed internal and/or community concerns, identified the underlying causes of those concerns, established specific goals and objectives, and identified possible barriers and needed resources, it is time to evaluate alternative means for achieving intermediate and terminal results. To do this requires, first, becoming aware of alternatives through the systematic review of appropriate information sources.

There are several important aids in retrieving alternatives: internal research, outside consultants, visits to other organizations similar to one's own, and reading. A survey of the literature is often the best beginning in choosing alternatives. This can now be accomplished with relative ease through the twenty Educational Resources Information Centers (ERIC) which acquire, screen, store, and disseminate up-to-date information on a wide range of topics to those who request it. Access to this information can be conveniently achieved by subscribing to two monthly publications offered by the U.S. Office of Education: *Research in Education* (Supt. of Documents, US Govt Print Office, Wash DC 20402) and *Current Index to Journals in Education* (CCM Info Corp, 909 Third Ave, NY, NY 10022). Between the two, some 26,000 articles and publications are reviewed annually. In addition to the ERIC clearinghouses and periodicals, there are 50 state Research Coordinating Units, several regional Educational Research Laboratories, and innumerable county or regional development centers (see R. Havelock *Educational Information Sources*. Educational Technology Publications, Englewood Cliffs, NJ 07632).

In the Louisville Public Schools example we have been using for illustrative purposes for the setting and the implementing of goals and objectives, it is obvious that considerable attention was given to the evaluation of alternative solutions. Internal research was conducted. Reading was done. Visits were made. Consultants were employed.

Step 5. *Selecting solutions*. Choosing from among the array of promising alternatives those solutions which seem to best meet the requirements set for the achievement of goals and objectives necessarily involves establishing criteria for comparative purposes. Feasibility, workability, and effectiveness represent 3 of the major criteria to be formally weighed in considering each alternative solution or combination of solutions.

Feasibility is largely determined by the constraints and needed resources specified under Step 3. Available dollars, staff, capabilities, state and federal regulations, community expectations, and like factors must be carefully considered. This often requires ingenuity, but ingenuity alone cannot make a solution feasible (see PPBS, Chpt. 6).

Workability refers to the extent to which a potential solution really is likely to work or not. Careful analysis must be made to determine if the proposed change can really deliver the expected benefits. The reliability of the procedure needs to be delved into. How carefully and sufficiently have the recommended steps been worked out must be ascertained (see PERT, Chpt. 5).

Effectiveness is often the most difficult criterion to employ, because of the time lag between a particular demonstration and the response. Though, in the final analysis, a subjective judgment must be made in choosing one or more solutions from an array of alternative solutions, there are objective aids to assist in making such decisions. They include such aids as *Simulation, Monte Carlo,* and *Queuing* (see OR, Chpt. 7).

In any event, an ultimate decision must be made at some point in the hierarchy. Where the decision is made, and by whom, will be dependent upon the nature of the decision. Major organizational decisions will be made by the board of trustees or their chief executive. Major institutional decisions usually will be made by the chief executive of the institution (president, or provost, or principal). Major department decisions will be made by deans or department heads. Major classroom decisions usually will be made by the instructor. The best decisions, in most instances, however, will be those which have resulted from representative group deliberations.

In the Louisville Public Schools example we have been using, it is evident that the use of T-groups (sensitivity training), team teaching (with differentiated staffing), and measurable performance objectives (also called "behavioral objectives," "instructional objectives," "measurable objectives," etc.) are but three of a number of alternative solutions which could have been chosen. Obviously, the decisions made there were based upon the conclusion that these three approaches likely held the most promise, among an array of alternative solutions, for attacking the complex problems of the district.

Step 6: *Implementing the selected solution.* Having settled upon a potential solution, the final decision-maker and his staff must now go about implementing the strategy and gaining acceptance for it in the system. As has been repeatedly emphasized, this requires early involvement of those who are likely to be affected by that procedure and by those who share the responsibility for its implementation. This, in turn, requires a clear and precise understanding of the participants' roles as well as the fact that risk-taking may be a necessary ingredient in the change process. Risk-takers must be given assurance that if failure should occur, the failure will not be a reflection upon those who have conscientiously done their best to implement the procedure.

In implementing the selected solutions in the Louisville Public Schools, Superintendent Walker, after the staff and the community were thoroughly familiar with the project, placed all the teachers then staffing the 14 Focus-Impact project schools into a district pool. The teaching positions were then opened to anyone in the system that wanted to apply — including the original teachers from the 14 affected project schools. A grand shuffle ensued as teachers voluntarily transferred from 1 school to another; in some places, the entire staff was replaced. As mentioned previously, those who staffed the 14 Focus-Impact project schools attended a paid 8-week summer training program. Continual follow-up and assessment occured throughout the school year.

In hindsight, it is generally admitted by the Louisville staff that the major error in the implementing process there was the faulty assumption that deep and complex changes sought could be achieved in so short a time (about 6 months lead time). Likely, an additional year of preparation by staff would have been better or to have begun with a fewer number of schools. The lesson of Louisville needs to be heeded. Adequate *preparation* time for implementing needed change is nearly as important as selecting the most promising solutions themselves.

Even though inadequate preparation time for implementation was allowed for at Louisville, there is no doubt that the selected solutions resulted in positive gains for the students as research findings show.

Step 7: *Feedback and evaluation.* Unless a change system has built into it a self-healing corrective feedback system, and a built-in audit plan for assessing terminal results, then the system is like a modern ship without radar. It cannot see the obstacles surrounding it nor is the course steady and true. By regular feedback, minor course corrections can be achieved. To wait until the end of a project before making an assessment may be too late to correct what otherwise might have been a successful choice of solutions.

In our "case study" of the Louisville Public Schools, it will be remembered from Chapter 2 that there was frequent feedback of results both vertically and laterally. There also was more formal assessments of progress toward goals and objectives made as shown below:

Feedback and Evaluation Procedures

General Design —

The design of the proposed project includes the following activities, which will be completed in the order of their listing:

1. A cadre of supervisors from the Departments of Instruction and Student Personnel Services will meet with principals, their faculties and instructional teams at the building level to produce instructional objectives for each instructional team. Supportive services of the Central Office will ensure that the objectives will be stated in behavioral terms, amenable to assessment techniques.

2. A group of administrative personnel from Research and Evaluation, Instruction and Organizational Development will develop paper-and-pencil tests and other assessment devices for measuring behavioral objectives advanced by the teams. This specialist group will be interdisciplinary in nature, including persons with competence in

   a. constructing valid tests,
   b. devising classroom observation schedules and other unobtrusive measures,

        c.   developing diagnostic tests in special instructional areas, and

        d.   devising assessment techniques for special education students and/or students with severe reading handicaps.

3. Workshops will be conducted for training teachers and guidance counselors in the utilization of the assessment techniques. Personnel will be taught

        a.   how the assessment techniques were designed to measure teachers' objectives;

        b.   how to administer the tests or utilize observation schedules; and

        c.   how to utilize the data to make decisions about instructional programs of individual students.

4. Assessment devices will be administered on two occasions: for an interim evaluation and for a final evaluation. At the interim evaluation, teachers will use the data to determine the extent to which the behavioral objectives which they built have been achieved. Devices will also be administered in control schools which have not based their instruction on the objectives used as criteria for test building.

They will also give feedback to the specialists on test construction according to the extent to which assessment devices

        a.   measured the stated objectives,

        b.   were appropriate measures of learning progress for students at all ability levels (culture-free and suitable for students with learning handicaps),

        c.   were easily administered and interpreted, and

        d.   could be used for instructional diagnosis and prescription

5. The specialist group on test construction will revise items according to the preceding teacher feedback and will conduct specific pilot studies of the indices for which a) mastery did not occur or was infrequent, and b) the range of mastery deviated from expectations of the specialist or teacher group.

6. Revised tests and other assessment devices will be administered for a second evaluation at the end of the school year in the project and control schools.

7. The specialist group, teacher and guidance personnel will evaluate the year-end data and revise assessment schemes. The revisions will be incorporated into a permanent System-wide assessment package which can be utilized and revised on a continuing basis. This package will include a pool of instructional objectives and appropriate assessment schemes categorized by broad cognitive and affective areas and classified by grade level.

Notwithstanding the shortness of time allowed for the planning of the implementation process, the first year results which came out of the Louisville Public Schools were encouraging. The downward slide in academic achievement of previous years was halted. Vandalism in project schools was down 11 percent compared to a 16 percent increase in non-project schools. Suspensions were down 70 percent in project schools but up 45 percent in other schools; dropouts in project junior high schools declined by 39 percent compared to a 4 percent decline in other junior high schools.

Figure 3-1 diagramatically shows the seven sequential steps requisite to setting and implementing well-defined goals and objectives.

Building a climate for needed change is not only a function of early involvement and capacity for change, but also a function of anticipated rewards. Rewards may take many forms. For most teachers, it is sufficient reward to see their students achieve beyond expectation. Because of the time lag frequently involved in observing significant behavioral changes in students, faculty derive little satisfaction from their efforts unless some more immediate feedback mechanism on student achievement is built into the change program. Other professional staff need similar feedback. More frequent measures of interim progress toward the achievement of a longer-term goal is an important *must* for facilitating the implementation of new programs (see MBO, Chpt. 13).

A candid analysis of that first year at Louisville given by Superintendent Walker (3:54) will serve to aid the would-be innovator as he plans for implementing change:

At the beginning, I had assumed that with the right kind of training people could implement an educational philosophy of

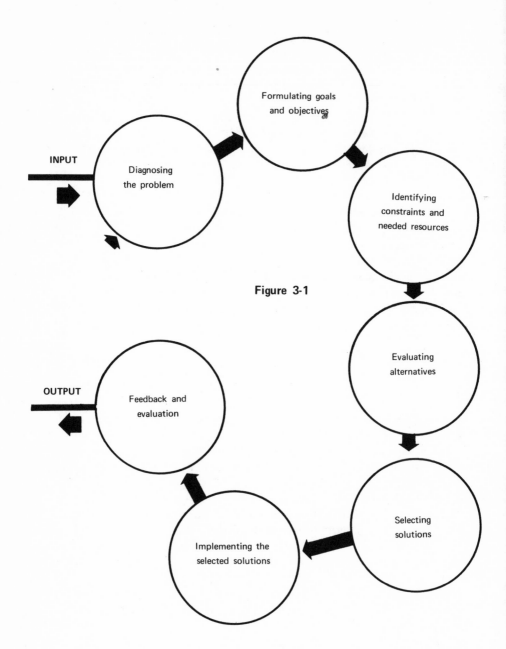

INPUT

Diagnosing
the problem

Formulating goals
and objectives

Identifying
constraints and
needed resources

Figure 3-1

Evaluating
alternatives

OUTPUT

Feedback and
evaluation

Selecting
solutions

Implementing the
selected solutions

humanism and freedom. What I didn't see was that the way
we went about that training only made the teachers and kids
and parents feel less human and less free. We had the right
content, but the process was contradictory. Humanism became a technology that people applied because we told them
to, not because it was their philosophy or way of life. From
now on, we won't be rejecting the personal growth emphasis
of T-groups, but we'll be trying to give people more power
over what happens to them. We think people will work on
what they own, on what's theirs. They may not come up
with what we want them to, but that's okay, as long as
they're aware of what they're doing and its consequences.
We're going now for a system of educational alternatives so
that people have a choice. That seems an obvious stance for
a system in transition, but it wasn't obvious in the beginning.

Part I has been concerned with the basic management principles in education. The principles enunciated include the need for accountability by the
setting of measurable or concise results oriented goals and objectives, and
by implementing them through a humanistic systems approach. Part II will
present some sophisticated management techniques, tools and theories which
can aid the educational manager in these processes.

PART II

MANAGEMENT THEORIES, TECHNIQUES, AND TOOLS

Chapter 4

THE DELPHI TECHNIQUE

Law 1: When in doubt take no action whatsoever unless and until sufficient evidence is uncovered to warrant an action — Richard W. Hostrop

It is beyond the scope of this book to do little more than to acquaint the reader with some of the more important management theories, techniques, and tools. The bibliography, however, offers to the reader suggested titles which discuss others and which describe in-depth particular ones discussed in Part II. And the glossary provides a further aid to understanding.

Theories, techniques, and tools make up the technology of management. And technology is the sum total of those activities which, in the aggregate, enable man to carry out almost any imaginable manipulation or modification of his external (material) or internal (behavioral) environments. Technology is used as the cutting edge of a knife to slice through the "cake of resistance" to needed change. It is human thought, then, rather than physical matter which is the true material of technology. Material things as the wheel and lever, the book and computer, may be described as human thought and knowledge made tangible. Management, thus, can be thought of as having to do with the ordering of the possessions of the mind by combining human and material resources in such a way as to achieve predetermined goals and objectives. Some of these theories, techniques, and tools which aid in achieving these results are discussed on the pages of Part II.

The Delphi Technique

To aid the decision-maker, or a group of decision-makers (eg, a Council for the Future), in setting and implementing more rational goals and objectives, management has available to it a most useful method — the *Delphi Technique.*

The Delphi Technique is a method of assessing group opinion by individuals through responses to a series of successive questionnaires, rather than through a series of group meetings. This approach provides an organization with a more objective means to 1) assess the range of ideas about goals and objectives, 2) give priority ranking to these goals and objectives, and 3) establish the degree of consensus about the goals and objectives.

Given good leadership, a discussion among experts can usually produce some kind of "group opinion," but the opinion is likely to be a *compromise* rather than a *consensus*. The compromise opinion often reflects the thinking of the more prestigious experts in a group, or the experts who are the most verbal, or simply those who can talk the loudest. However, the opinion of these experts may be no better or more valuable than the less prestigious or less extroverted members of a group. Moreover, in determining what is, what should be, or forecasting what is to become there is need for some idea of the range of opinion that a group of experts can offer and some indications of the kinds of reasons that back up their various specific declarations.

A consensus would ideally give just this information, plus a statement of the "majority view." In discussing a problem, presumably, a group of experts will contribute to one another's understanding of the issues and difficulties involved, and their personal opinions will be refined as a result of this interchange. It is, therefore, important for the experts to interact, and this seems to imply some sort of group discussion (with all the time-consuming elements involved). But, on the other hand, it is most difficult to obtain concise judgments from a group without distorting or submerging the individual opinions and rationales of its members.

In the early 1950s a research group headed by Olaf Helmer of the RAND Corporation devised the Delphi Technique (named for Apollo's oracle at Delphi in Greece) as a means of circumventing problems associated with group opinion. The method consists of a set of procedures for eliciting the opinion of a group of people, usually experts, in such a way as to reduce the undesirable aspects of group interaction. The Delphi procedure may be described as follows:

1. Participants (who usually remain anonymous to one another) are asked to list their opinion on a specific topic in the form of brief written statements to prepared questionnaires, such as recommended activities or predictions for the future.

2. Participants are then asked to evaluate their total listing against some criterion, such as importance, chance of success, etc.

3. Next the statements made by the participants are received and are clarified by the investigator.

4. Each participant then receives the refined list and a summary of responses to the items and, if in the minority, is asked to revise his opinion or to indicate his reason(s) for remaining in the minority.

5.   The statements made by the participants are again received by the investigator who further clarifies, refines, and summarizes the responses.

6.   Each participant then receives the further refined topical list which includes both an updated summary of responses and a summary of minority opinions. Each participant is also given a final chance to revise his opinions.

7.   Finally, the investigator receives the last round of the questionnaires which he then summarizes in a final report. The successive, individual and independent process of requestioning of each of the experts, combined with feedback supplied separatley from each of the other experts, *via* the investigator, is designed to eliminate misinterpretation of the questions and the feedback, and to bring to light knowledge available to one or a few members of the group but not to all of them. An example should make it clear how this set of procedures works to generate a *consensus of opinion*:

Figure 4-1

ROUND 1 QUESTIONNAIRE

Probe Category:	Panel Member:						Division:		
	DESIRABILITY			**FEASIBILITY**			**TIMING**		
1. List below all anticipated events (indicating source) which likely will have a significant effect on the organization in the above category.	Needed Desperately	Desirable	Undesirable but Possible	Highly Feasible	Likely	Unlikely but Possible	Year by which the probability that each event will have occured = P		
2. Evaluate each predicted event with respect to the three factors at the right in view of the anticipated events.							$P = .1$	$P = .5$	$P = .9$

Round 1: In the first round of questioning, each expert is asked to list developments he believes will occur in his field, say, within the next half century. An expert in curriculum might predict that within 50 years there will no longer be any standardized curriculum anywhere, but rather individual curricula for each individual learner. Another expert might predict that community learning centers, using and expanding the traditional public

Figure 4-2

ROUND 2 QUESTIONNAIRE

Probe Category: 001 - Curriculum   Panel Member: 001   Division: Instruction

Event Number		Panels Evaluating	Familiarity	Desirability	Feasibility	Probability of Event	Dates
0001	There will no longer be any standardized curriculum anywhere but rather individual curricula for each individual learner	03, 05 06	1. Fair 2. Good 3. Excellent	1. Needed 2. Desirable 3. Undesirable	1. Simple 2. Possible 3. Unlikely	+0.7	.1 = '79 .5 = '85 .9 = '90
0002	Community learning centers, using and expanding the traditional public library facilities, will receive more of the knowledge construction dollar than on-campus construction	02, 05 06	1. Fair 2. Good 3. Excellent	1. Needed 2. Desirable 3. Undesirable	1. Simple 2. Possible 3. Unlikely	+0.6	.1 = '88 .5 = '12 .9 = '50

Figure 4-3

ROUND 3 QUESTIONNAIRE

Probe Category: 001 - Curriculum   Panel Member: 001   Division: Instruction

Event Number	Event Description of Potential Occurrence	Panels Evaluating	Consensus or Discordance to Date	In your opinion by what year does the Probability of Occurrence reach		If your 50% estimate falls within either the earlier or the later period indicated below, briefly state your reason for this opinion
0001	It is not likely that a standardized curriculum will exist anywhere, but rather individual curricula for each individual learner	03, 05 06	Consensus is that it will occur; there is disagreement as to when.	50%	90%	Why before 1988? ___ Or, why after 2012? ___
0002	Possibility that more tax funds will go to support creation and expansion of public libraries into community learning centers than in to school and college expansion.	02, 05 07	Consensus is that it will occur; there is disagreement as to when.	50%	90%	Why before 1988? ___ Or, why after 2012? ___

library facilities, will receive more of the knowledge construction dollar than on-campus construction. The investigator(s) then edits these predictions to reduce irrelevant predictions, to improve clarity, and to avoid distortions of intent and meaning. The investigator then prepares a questionnaire for the second round.

Round 2: Each expert is given a composite questionnaire which asks him to estimate certain numerical quantities, eg, the date by which there no longer will be a standardized curriculum for a given group of learners, or the predicted date when more tax monies will be spent on community learning centers ("libraries") than on school and college construction. By asking for such simple numerical estimates, as shown in the example in Figure 4-2, the investigator can easily summarize the responses in a simple statistical fashion. Note in Figure 4-2 that each panel member is assigned a code number (here, 001) by which he may be identified if further contact concerning his evaluations are necessary. The panels represent groups of experts from a particular specialty area. Note, eg, that the expert in our panel believes he has excellent familiarity with curriculum problems. Note that he expects Event 0001 to occur and that the event will occur between 1979 and 1990 with the most probable date being 1985.

Round 3: The digested information from the second round of questioning is then re-edited and fed back to each of the experts; they are all asked to scrutinize their first responses. In addition, if an expert's first response fell *outside* the median range of responses (.1 - .9), it is customary, when practical to do so, to ask him to express his reasons for his "extreme" opinion. To continue with the examples given, the questionnaire for the third round might appear as shown in Figure 4-3.

Experience has shown that obtaining reasons from respondents whose opinions fall outside the median range achieves two things:

    1.   It permits the investigator to refine his question. By taking into consideration some of the more lucid reasons given for the more extreme responses, the investigator can reword or modify the question so that the range of response will narrow itself down.

    2.   It permits the investigator to state the minority opinions, and to feed this information back to the whole group on a fourth round of questioning.

Almost always a number of experts change their estimates after rethinking the question, and the consensus narrows as a result.

Round 4: Once the investigator has digested the new estimates, and calculated the new consensus on the year of estimated achievement, he can approach his experts with a still further refined questionnaire for the fourth round. Figure 4-4 shows what this questionnaire might look like. (Note the refinement in the description from Figure 4-3). If it seems desirable to do so, the questioner can refine still further the results of this version and go on to a fifth or even a sixth round. Experience, however, has shown that the technique seldom requires more than 4 rounds and, conversely, never less than 2.

Figure 4-5 illustrates how the future probes might appear in final published form. The composite evaluation by all panelists questioned indicates that:

1. On a scale ranging from + 1.0 (highly desirable) to − 1.0 (highly undesirable) the numerical composite median evaluation for Event 0001 is +.8 and for Event 0002 it is +.6 indicating that panel members believe these events should happen.

2. On a scale ranging from + 1.0 (highly likely) to − 1.0 (highly unlikely), the numerical median of the evaluation of feasibility is +.6 for both events. Thus, the panel of experts believe both events are not faced with overwhelming obstacles towards being achieved.

3. The numerical average of estimates of the probability that the event will occur sometime is +.7 for Event 0001 and +.6 for Event 0002 on a scale ranging from + 1.0 (highly probable) to − 1.0 (highly improbable).

4. If Event 0001 does occur, the most likely date for it to happen is 1988 (the median .5-date); the period of expectancy ranging from 1983 (the median .1-date) to 2000+ (the median .9-date). If Event 0002 does occur, the most likely date for it to happen is 1997, within an expectancy range of from as early as 1990 to as late as sometime in the 21st century.

The Delphi method, thus, achieves a true consensus without sacrifice of important opinion and background information, and avoids the difficulties in small group discussion and the impracticalities of large group discussions. The investigator helps the experts toward a consensus by rewording his questions, and the experts help themselves toward a consensus by re-thinking the problem in the light of divergent estimates.

The method has worked quite successfully in a number of diverse situations. For example, expert respondents have been asked to estimate such a known

Figure 4-4

ROUND 4 QUESTIONNAIRE

		Panel Member: 001			Division: Instruction

Probe Category: 001 - Curriculum

Event Number	Event Description of Potential Occurrence	Panel Evaluating	Majority Consensus to Date	Minority Opinion	Record Your Estimate
0001	It is unlikely that a set curriculum will exist anywhere, but instead there will be tailored curricula for each individual learner.	03, 05 06	By 1985 A.D.	Will take longer, or even never occur, because each individual needs to have assured to him the rudiments of general education founded in the liberal arts. Elementary-age students cannot be expected to have tailor-made curricula for each of them because of their lack of maturity.	50% - Year ___ 90% - Year ___
0002	Probability is that more tax funds will go to support creation and expansion of public libraries into community learning centers than in to school and college expansion.	02, 05 07	By 2000 A.D.	Will take longer, or even never occur, because significant creation or expansion of either libraries or educational institutions is unlikely since most new learning spaces will result from use of existing business and social institutions and home study via computer consoles and other educational technology.	50% - Year ___ 90% - Year ___

Figure 4-5

FINAL REPORT

Probe Category: 001 - Curriculum

Division: Instruction

Event Number	Event Description	Panels Evaluating	Desir- ability	Feas- ibility	Prob- ability	Probability Dates					2000 and Beyond		
						1975	1980	1985	1990	1955	.1	.5	.9
0001	It is unlikely that a set curriculum will exist anywhere, but instead there will be a tailor made curriculum for each individual learner beginning about age 10.	03, 05 06	+.8	+.6	+.7								
0002	It is probable that more tax funds will go to support the creation and expansion of public libraries into community learning centers than in to school and college expansion. The *rate* of increase will be more pronounced than actual. Emphasis will be on informal learning using existing home and community facilities.	02, 05 07	+.6	+.6	+.6								

quantity as the number of oil wells in Texas in 1960 — a figure that the respondents could not have possibly been expected to know precisely. In a majority of the cases, after a few rounds of questioning, the median or consensus moved close to the actual figure.

The possible variations of the technique are endless. Large projects have usually required the help of data processing equipment; and, in principle, Delphi serves as a method of cybernetic arbitration. Large educational organizations have found it profitable to bring experts on-line to a computer program designed for the Delphi Technique. But the technique can be used and is used far more frequently without the aid of computers and sophisticated computer programs. Many projects lend themselves to the Delphi Technique by the individual administrator, teacher, and others with great effect.

Delphi provides not only a means for forecasting the future but for investigating matters of the historical past. It also provides a means for assessing "what is" (organizational conditions) and "what should be" (goals and objectives).

The Delphi Technique has many practical uses in education. As has been illustrated, it can be used for forecasting future curricular developments which can have a profound effect upon teacher training programs, educational purchases, building construction, and a host of related effects. Administrators can use the Delphi Technique for such purposes as determining in a sophisticated way what the faculty believes the administration should *really* be doing, for forecasting future enrollments, for setting educational goals and objectives, etc. Teachers can use the technique in such imaginative ways as having their students assess certain conditions of life in times past — followed by research as to what was the actual case. Counselors can use the method as an aid in improving counseling services by having students and teachers serve on Delphi panels which ask of them "what is" and "what should be" in regards to counseling services. Librarians in a similar way, can improve their procedures through such sophisticated probing. Educational technologists can probe the future so that building design and hardware purchases are realistic to the needs of the 21st century. These are but a very few of near endless examples of how the Delphi procedure can be used to determine "what was," "what is," "what should be," and "what is to become" so as to improve the educational process in and out of the classroom.

Delphi provides a means whereby a spanking new institution can ascertain its course of direction in its early planning stages so as to be in consonance with the community it is to serve. One such notable example is GSU (Governors State University) located in Park Forest South, Illinois. The Delphi Technique was utilized for just this purpose. Exhibits 4-6 and 4-7 show the letter of President Engbretson and the first questionnaire sent out to more than a thousand individuals and offices whom GSU officials believed could provide particularly valuable input.

Exhibit 4-6

GOVERNORS STATE UNIVERSITY
P.O. Box 316
Park Forest, Illinois 60466

October 27, 1969

Dear Friend:

Plans for a new type of university were launched on July 17th, 1969 when Governor Ogilvie signed Governors State University into existence. The university, which will be located in Park Forest, Illinois, is unique in that it will be a senior division university, offering only third and fourth-year and master's programs. It is specifically designed to serve community college transfer students who will be commuting from Chicago and neighboring communities.

Governors State University is also unique in that it is intended to be an innovative, future-oriented, and public service minded institution. Its instructional units will probably include liberal arts, applied and health sciences, business and public service, and education. Governors State University anticipates planning to meet the educational needs of students and society not only in the '70's but in future decades as well.

While we are still on our early developmental planning stages, we are seeking opinions on better ways to use our educational potential. We believe that planning an institution such as Governors State University should reflect the best thinking of socially concerned individuals from government, education, business, industry, and the arts — from the local to the national level.

The technique we will be using to gather opinions is called the Delphi Technique. It was developed in the early 1950s by Olaf Helmer and his colleagues at the Rand Corporation. The technique is based on the premise that it is possible to influence the direction of future trends by proper planning, based on informed, intuitive judgments. While individuals never meet face-to-face, their opinions are collated and refined in a series of successive questionnaires. Feedback on the opinions of others is provided, thus permitting individuals to change their minds on particular issues, if they wish.

The procedure is as follows:

1) A first questionnaire calls for a brief list of what are considered to be major goals or recommended targets for action by the institution.

2) On a second mailing each individual receives a copy of a collated list of responses and is asked to rate each item by its importance and probability of success.

3) Later, a third and final mailing may report on the consensus of opinion, if any, on the items rated. Individuals may then be asked to either revise their opinions or to specify reasons for remaining outside the consensus.

The Delphi Technique, which has been used extensively to predict what *will* happen in the scientific, political, and technological areas, is now being increasingly used in education to predict what *should* happen. Even when group consensus cannot be reached, important issues can be clarified.

Your participation will be sincerely appreciated. Names will not be used in published tabulations and all participants will receive reports of the final results. Approximately ten minutes in each of the three above steps is needed. The first questionnaire is attached to this letter.

Won't you please help us plan this new university to serve the people of the State of Illinois?

Cordially,

/s/ William E. Engbretson

William Engbretson
President, Governors State University

Enclosure

Exhibit 4-7

*Name_____**Position**_____

Address_____

GOVERNORS STATE UNIVERSITY DELPHI QUESTIONNAIRE "A"

The purpose of this questionnaire is to elicit suggested goals, purposes and developmental targets which, without the support your recommendations can provide, might not be considered for adoption during the critical planning phases which are immediately ahead. Please consider that Governors State will be built as a *totally new* senior institution on what is now farm land immediately adjacent to the southern edge of metropolitan Chicago. Therefore, suggestions with regard to any phase of institutional development are appropriate.

Please be as concise as you can about the targets you suggest we direct ourselves to. You may respond by completing the following expressions with phrases of your choosing.

Governors State University Should Be:

1. Responsive to_____

2. Built For: (a)_____
               (b)_____

3. Organized To: (a)_____
                (b)_____

4. Open To: (a)_____
              (b)_____

5. Selective In_____

6. Demonstrative of: (a)_____
                    (b)_____

*All responses are confidential. The names of respondents will in no instance be reported. A promit response would be appreciated.

The second instrument, "Questionnaire 'B'," was prepared by first studying the responses to Questionnaire "A" and then employing them to guide the writing and assemblage for the new instrument. Thus, the 51 items generated for Questionnaire "B" were prepared directly from the responses given to Questionnaire "A." One thousand two hundred five Questionnaire "Bs" were mailed out to the 8 panels surveyed (external community leadership, academic operation management, faculty, college admissions, public education, external associations — education and certification, students. Five hundred forty seven responses (45.4 percent) in the self-addressed and stamped envelopes provided were returned. GSU officials found it necessary to only send out the two questionnaires, "A" and "B," to determine the information they were seeking. Exhibit 4-8 shows President Engbretson's second letter and Exhibit 4-9 shows Questionnaire "B."

Exhibit 4-8

GOVERNORS STATE UNIVERSITY
P.O. Box 316
Park Forest, Illinois 60466

January 2, 1970

Dear Friends:

This fall we addressed a letter to you and others in which you were told about the development of Governors State University, a senior college and graduate school to be located south of Chicago in Will County, Illinois. Many responses to that letter have been received and are greatly appreciated.

A new Delphi-oriented instrument has been developed on the basis of the first several hundred responses. The instrument contains brief summaries of goals suggested for Governors State University. While statements do not appear exactly as made by respondents, an effort has been made to include the intention or content of each statement as originally made. The purpose of this new instrument is to seek opinions on the relative priorities to be assigned to the assembled goals.

The instrument, enclosed with this letter, calls for your selection of one of five priority levels for each item: (H) highest, (AA) above average, (A) average, (BA) below average, and (L) lowest. Since most, if not all, of the listed goals are of considerable contemporary importance, it is essential that you discriminate between them. Your responses should cover the complete range of the scale — from highest to lowest. Please feel free to change any of your opinions after completing the instrument.

Since we are faced with an early deadline for the beginning of architectural planning, we urgently request that your response be forwarded as promptly as possible. We appreciate your cooperation and would like to thank you again for your assistance in planning Governors State University. We will be pleased to send you a summary of the total response to this questionnaire, if you wish. A space for this request has been provided at the close of the instrument. Please make any appropriate corrections in title or mailing address.

Cordially,

/s/ *William E. Engbretson*

William E. Engbretson
President, Governors State University

Enclosure

Exhibit 4-9

GOVERNORS STATE UNIVERSITY NEEDS SURVEY
QUESTIONNAIRE "B" — PRIORITY SURVEY

On the right side of each item below CIRCLE the *one* symbol that most closely approximates the level of priority which in your opinion should be assigned to each of the listed goals.

Circle: H. . . . . for highest priority
Circle: AA . . . . for above average priority
Circle: A . . . . for average priority
Circle: BA . . . . for below average priority
Circle: L . . . . for lowest priority

Remember to use ratings on the lower end of the scale — preferably as often as those on the higher end.

A Goal of Governors State University should be:

1. to assure continuation of the liberal arts tradition in education. H AA A BA L

2. to select a faculty which has diverse backgrounds and attitudes. H AA A BA L

3. to provide work-study programs in urban and inner city areas. H AA A BA L

4. to involve the citizens of nearby communities in decision-making about university development. H AA A BA L

5. to assure that teaching will be the most re-   H   AA   A   BA   L
   spected role for a faculty member.

6. to admit students on the basis of their   H   AA   A   BA   L
   interests and desires more than on the
   basis of their academic performance or
   aptitude.

7. to support the faculty in its efforts to under-   H   AA   A   BA   L
   take research aimed at extending human
   knowledge.

8. to assure receptivity to change by building in   H   AA   A   BA   L
   automatic change mechanisms in all curricular,
   instructional, and institutional systems.

9. to allocate percents of enrollment for minority   H   AA   A   BA   L
   groups or groups having low socio-economic
   status.

10. to assure freedom in the personal lives of all   H   AA   A   BA   L
    individuals in the campus community.

11. to strongly emphasize undergraduate teaching   H   AA   A   BA   L
    and learning.

12. to be receptive to and to encourage experimen-   H   AA   A   BA   L
    tation with new ideas for educational practice
    at all levels.

13. to develop strong programs of interscholastic   H   AA   A   BA   L
    participation in forensics, athletics, etc.

14. to encourage innovation at all stages of institu -   H   AA   A   BA   L
    tional planning and development.

15. to provide for continuous long-range planning   H   AA   A   BA   L
    for the total institution.

16. to make available activities and opportunities   H   AA   A   BA   L
    for intellectual and aesthetic stimulation
    outside the classroom.

17. to stimulate the local population and help it   H   AA   A   BA   L
    be a part of the university community.

18. to produce educational programs pointed   H   AA   A   BA   L
    toward new and emerging career fields.

19. to stress community service as a defined part   H   AA   A   BA   L
    of faculty commitment and load.

20. to provide an architectural climate conducive   H   AA   A   BA   L
    to learning.

21. to produce an institution which contributes to the solution of social problems. H AA A BA L

22. to encourage loyalty to the university, its faculty, and administration. H AA A BA L

23. to seek commitment of faculty and administrators to established objectives. H AA A BA L

24. to undertake systems development and analyses as guides for institutional development. H AA A BA L

25. to assure that the needs of superior or outstanding students are met. H AA A BA L

26. to facilitate individualized movement of students through the curriculum. H AA A BA L

27. to assure academic freedom for faculty and students. H AA A BA L

28. to select a student body which is representative of the various ages, races, and aptitudes in our society. H AA A BA L

29. to provide for freedom of student expression and to clarify and protect students' rights. H AA A BA L

30. to broadly apply cost criteria to curricular and instructional alternatives. H AA A BA L

31. to assure that independent, tutorial, and small class instruction will be available. H AA A BA L

32. to concentrate on the use of mass media and instructional technology. H AA A BA L

33. to provide for the educational needs of the people of the State of Illinois. H AA A BA L

34. to involve non-school agencies in the educational programs of the university. H AA A BA L

35. to develop plans for curricular and instructional evaluation for all programs. H AA A BA L

36. to recruit and reward faculty members who are highly proficient at research and scholarship. H AA A BA L

37. to undertake institutional research by which to formulate and revise plans. H AA A BA L

38. to provide educational and cultural opportunities for all adults in the surrounding area. H AA A BA L

39.	to strongly emphasize the development of graduate curricula and graduate learning.	H	AA	A	BA	L
40.	to provide instruction in human relations and good government for all students.	H	AA	A	BA	L
41.	to develop plans for curricular and instuctional evaluation for all programs.	H	AA	A	BA	L
42.	to assure that work experience or specially assessed performances may be substituted for specific course requirements.	H	AA	A	BA	L
43.	to encourage open and honest communication among faculty and administrators.	H	AA	A	BA	L
44.	to encourage shared, decentralized decision-making about university programs.	H	AA	A	BA	L
45.	to model Governors State University in the established patterns of the more highly successful contemporary senior colleges.	H	AA	A	BA	L
46.	to meet the paramount educational needs of junior college graduates who are baccalaureate bound.	H	AA	A	BA	L
47.	to provide strong technical programs to meet the needs of individuals.	H	AA	A	BA	L
48.	to provide opportunities for advanced level adult continuing education.	H	AA	A	BA	L
49.	to involve students in curricular and instructional evaluation.	H	AA	A	BA	L
50.	to assure individuals the opportunity to be represented in decision-making which affects them.	H	AA	A	BA	L
51.	to prepare an environment conducive to informal, comfortable, human relationships.	H	AA	A	BA	L

___
___ Yes, I would like to receive the summary of the total response to this instrument.

Name _____

Title _____

Address _____

Note: All responses are confidential. The names of respondents will in no
instance be reported.

ETS (Educational Testing Service) has pioneered a number of test intruments which are based upon the Delphi principle for external and internal assessment of "what is" and "what should be" (eg, the *Institutional Goals Inventory*). It was ETS which was contracted to conduct the GSU goals survey. However, as has been illustrated by forms and examples in this chapter it is not necessary to use a commercial firm for such purposes if competent staff with sufficient time are available within the organization to conduct such *must* program planning.

In addition to providing the means to intelligently forecast the future, to plan new organizations (and subunits), and to use for curricular purposes, as has been illustrated, there are still other notable uses for Delphi. The procedure provides the means for dispassionately determining "what is" as well as "what should be." It also provides a means for determining important goals and objectives sought by the constituencies of long-standing institutions as well as for those planning new ones. It provides a means whereby everyone's "voice" can be equally heard within the same group. It is a means for unmasking the vocal minority and uncovering the will of the majority. The technique also frequently results in a residual, positive side effect by helping to create a sense of community internally and good-will for the organization externally since the opinions solicited touch, if not all, a large number of relevant group members. All of us like to have our opinions solicited. We like to participate in those organizational plans which do or can affect us.

Involvement in inputting to goals and objectives, which represent the potential solution to significant and important long-range problems, can also be effectively used with subgroups within the organizational or institutional structure as well as for the structure as a whole.

The Delphi Technique, thus, is a means whereby a better determination can be made about uncertainties over planning or issues by means of a consensus from many individuals and/or groups. It provides a means for objectively assessing the will of a group (as well as subgroups) in policy making. It also provides a protective armor of dispassionate facts when highly vocal and militant minority opinions are expressed which otherwise might be construed by upper educational management as majority opinion in absence of objective evidence to the contrary. Certainly, the results from Delphi-based surveys should not serve as an excuse to ignore minority opinions. But seldom should minority views be given disproportionate weight in policy making.

The Delphi Technique provides educational management with an important means for making decisions based upon more objective data than today's crude "common sense" decision-making method. Seldom can the wheat be separated from the chaff by such a "method." Certainly, the Delphi Technique is not a panacea for curing all of education's ills nor is it a very helpful method for making quick decisions. But it does provide management with a means for replacing such "fire-fighting" emphasis with a "fire-prevention" emphasis. It is a means for providing an organization with a genuine sense of direction. It is a means for peering into the past and forecasting the future. Finally, it provides a means for determining what is and what should be. An educational organization which has these characteristics is one that is managing events, rather than having events manage it.

Chapter 5

PERT

Law 2: Take no action which unnecessarily antagonizes any individual or group — **Richard W. Hostrop**

The Delphi Technique provides educational managers with a means to achieve a consensus on what was, what is, what ought to be, and what probably will be. In short, as we have seen from the previous chapter, Delphi is a procedure for *setting* authoritative goals and objectives. *PERT* (Program Evaluation and Review Technique) can assist in *implementing* the goals and objectives set.

PERT was pioneered by Du Pont engineers during the mid-1950s to deal with situations where completion times were uncertain. As a result they were able to reduce idle equipment time in a synthetic rubber process by more than 35 percent and thereby increase annual production by about a million pounds. Thus PERT is a probability system which seeks to reach goals and objectives in the shortest possible time with minimum cost. The technique also, not infrequently, is known as CPM (Critical Path Method).

PERT has been successfully used for such widely varying activities as building construction, scheduling a Broadway play, constructing the Polaris submarine, putting a man on the moon, establishing a new 2-year college, developing new curricula, etc.

What we do in our jobs and when we do it depends on what others have done or should be doing, and our work today determines the work that others will be doing in many other places tomorrow. In other words, we all function as parts of elaborate networks, and our own effectiveness relies on the effectiveness of others with respect to time, cost, and quality of output.

A *network* is the foundation of the PERT system. It shows the plan estab-lished to reach program goals and objectives, interrelationships and inter-dependencies of program elements, and priorities of the elements of the plan. In short, the network is a graphic representation of the program plan.

A network is composed of events and activities. *Events* represent the start or completion of an activity and do not consume time, personnel, or resources. Events are instantaneous points in time when an activity has been started or completed and usually is represented by a circle. *Activities* consist of work processes which lead from one activity to another and are usually represented by arrows. *Dummy Activities* — those which do not consume time or resources — are represented by dotted arrows. An example of a simplified network is shown in Figure 5-1.

After a network has been constructed, and its logic approved by its users, the time to complete each step is estimated. *Three* time estimates are made for the expected duration of an activity. These 3 estimates are known as Pessimistic Time, the Most Likely Time, and the Optimistic Time.

The *Pessimistic Time* assumes that anything that can will go wrong, short of an unforeseen calamatious event. It takes into account the most adverse conditions including the possibility of failures occurring which require new starts. The time estimate has no more than 1 chance in a hundred of occurring.

The *Most Likely Time* is that which, in the estimator's judgment, the activity will consume under normal circumstances.

The *Optimistic Time* estimate is the least amount of time the activity will take under the most optimum conditions. It assumes that there is not more than 1 chance in a hundred of the task being completed by the time given.

Time estimates assume that material and human resources will be available on a normal basis or as approved in the project proposal.

It is *essential* that estimates of activity duration time be secured from the person responsible for the accomplishment of an activity rather than un-informed higher authority.

Time estimates initially ignore calendar dates to avoid possible estimator biasing toward some "desirable" date. Instead, time estimates are based on a 5-day work week and are established as a given number of *work* days or by weeks and 10ths of weeks. A time estimate of 0.1 week would be equivalent to ½ of a day; an estimate of 0.2 would be equivalent to 1 day; and so forth. At the end of the network calculation an estimated calendar completion date is made.

After the 3 time estimates have been secured, *Expected Elapsed Times* are calculated for each activity using the following formula:

$$t_e = \frac{o + 4m + p}{6}$$

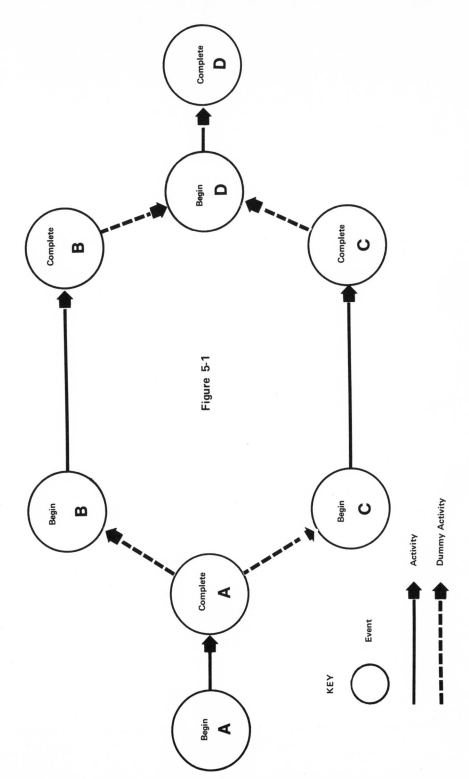

Figure 5-1

KEY

Event

Activity

Dummy Activity

89

In this formula t_e is the Expected Elapsed time, o the Optimistic time, m the Most Likely time, and p the Pessimistic time.

Let us assume, by way of illustration, that a chief curriculum officer decides on March 1 that he wishes to have prepared a teachers' guidebook concerned with the teaching of ethnic studies. He estimates from experience that the most optimistic time that can be expected to have such a curriculum guide prepared would be 90 working days; the most realistic, 120 days; the most pessimistic, 180 days. Hence, total values entered in the formula are:

$$o = 90$$
$$m = 120$$
$$p = 180$$

The calculation of the problem produces the following result:

$$t_e = \frac{90 + 4(120) + 180)}{6}$$

$$t_e = \frac{90 + 480 + 180}{6}$$

$$t_e = \frac{750}{6}$$

$$t_e = 125 \text{ days}$$

After the Expected Elapsed time has been computed for an activity, one should also obtain an estimate of variability of time estimates associated with it. The range of time spread is represented by the standard deviation (σ) of the activity times. The formula for finding the standard deviation is:

$$t_e = \frac{p - o}{6}$$

substituting the values in the above example,

$$p = 180$$
$$o = 90$$

$$t_e = \frac{180 - 90}{6}$$

$$t_e = \frac{90}{6}$$

$$t_e = 15 \text{ days}$$

The obtained value can be used to estimate the probability of an acitivity being completed within a range of estimated times employing normal curve concepts. For example, a 68 percent chance exists that the development of the curriculum guide will be completed within 15 days either side of the Expected Elapsed time (t_e) of 125 (ie, 110-140 days); a 95 percent chance that it will be completed within 30 days either side of t_e (ie, 95-155 days); and a 99 percent chance that the activity will be completed within 45 days either side of t_e (ie, 80-165 days).

Beginning with the current date, calendar date estimates are made. In our illustration, the curriculum director finds that the *Ethnic Studies Teachers' Curriculum Guide* cannot realistically be expected to be completed before late in the fall because of the spring and summer recess. (Calculations show that only about a 5 percent chance of completion exists before school is out.) If the completion of the curriculum guide is of such urgency that it should nevertheless be readied by fall, then a decision will have to be made if those scheduled to work on the guide can be employed during part of the summer to complete it. "PERTing" the problem provides the curriculum director with soundly based time estimates to go to his superordinate with for such a decision (a decision, though, which normally should have been decided earlier at yearly goal setting time!)

In order to help improve the estimate of Optimistic, Most Likely, and Pessimistic times, and to better schedule human and material resources available, networks of events and activities should be constructed for the task. Suppose that the task of preparing an "Ethnic Studies Teachers' Curriculum Guide" involves five steps and that the first two steps A and B may be performed simultaneously, steps C and D depend on completion of Step A, and step E depends on steps A, B, and C as represented in Figure 5-2.

Suppose further that step A's Most Likely time estimate is 60 work days, step B 10 days, step C 40 days, step D 30 days, and step E 25 days. This information can be incorporated into a more complete network as illustrated by Figure 5-3.

The first question to be asked after the events and activities have been established, and time estimated via networking, is to determine what is the

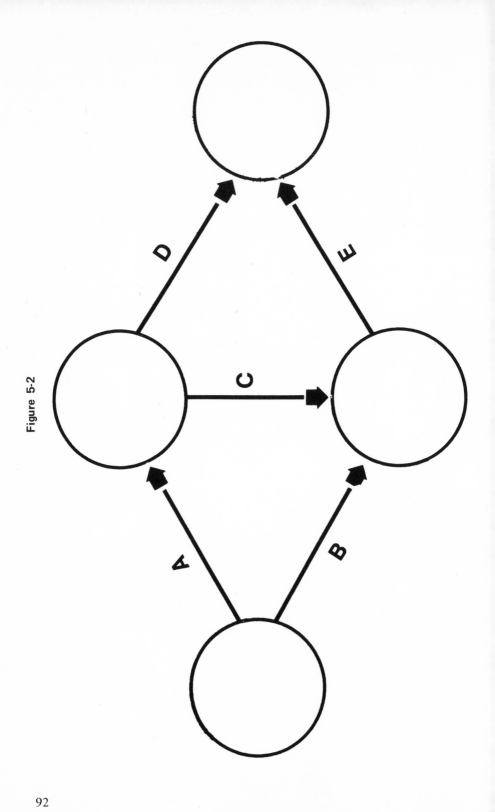

Figure 5-2

92

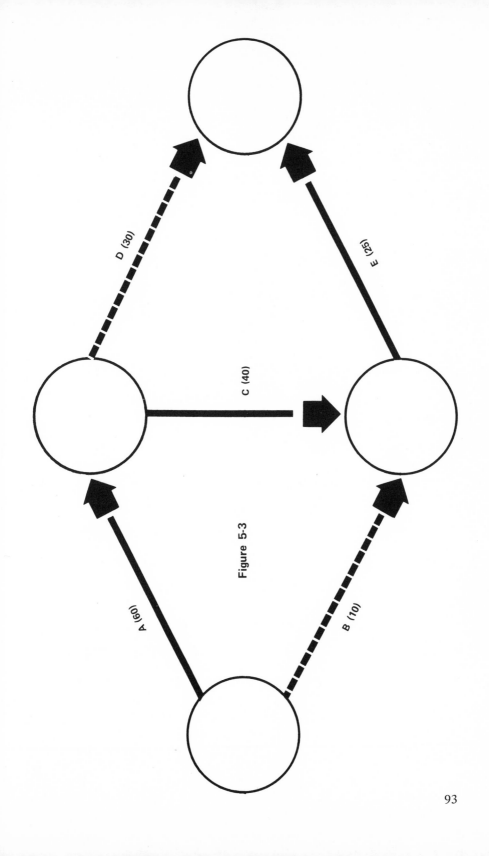

Figure 5-3

93

shortest way through the network — ie, the *critical path.* In this instance, direct inspection points to the sequence A-C-E which takes a total of 125 days and is indicated by a heavy line (sometimes two parallel lines) as shown in Figure 5-4.

A-C-E is the critical path. It has special significance in that it focuses attention on those steps which determine the completion time of the process. Steps B and D are "slack" steps (indicated with partial dotted lines) which allow some leeway and need not be as strictly monitored. B, for example, could take as long as 100 work days without delaying the process (equal to the time of A plus C) and D could take as long as 65 days after A was completed (C plus E) and still not delay the overall process. But for the director of curriculum to meet his Most Likely (or t_e) schedule, the critical path steps A, C, and E must be completed on time, and if the schedule of completion time is to be shortened, these are the steps to streamline.

As should now be evident, PERTing not only saves time and optimizes resources but frequently saves money as well. Personnel are employed at the time needed (eg, only during the time represented by solid lines as in Figure 5-4). This basic *PERT/COST* application helps to break down costs for each activity as shown in Figure 5-5. Such arraying aids in determining if the result is worth the cost and if certain costs can be reduced or even eliminated without substantially affecting the end result.

The PERT procedure can be applied to almost any project where logical planning is required.

Repetitious activities, such as student registration procedures, are not the kinds of projects for which PERT is most useful. But a project designed to develop a *new* registration procedure, to be ready *by a certain date,* would be.

Generally, PERT becomes a highly desirable tool when there is a task whose completion will take at least two months and one in which the network consists of at least 10 distinct events.

Simplified procedures for establishing the first original network should be employed. Experience has shown that using large sheets of newsprint, chalkboard, or large sheets of acetate covered cardboard and grease pencil are useful organizational tools. The employment of "activity" cards in the preparation of networks is also helpful. This procedure consists of identifying each project activity on a separate 3" x 5" card. The cards are then arranged

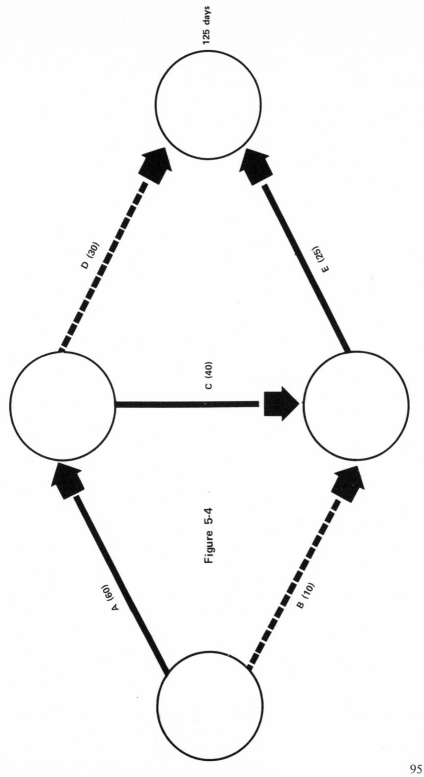

125 days

D (30)

E (25)

C (40)

A (60)

B (10)

Figure 5-4

95

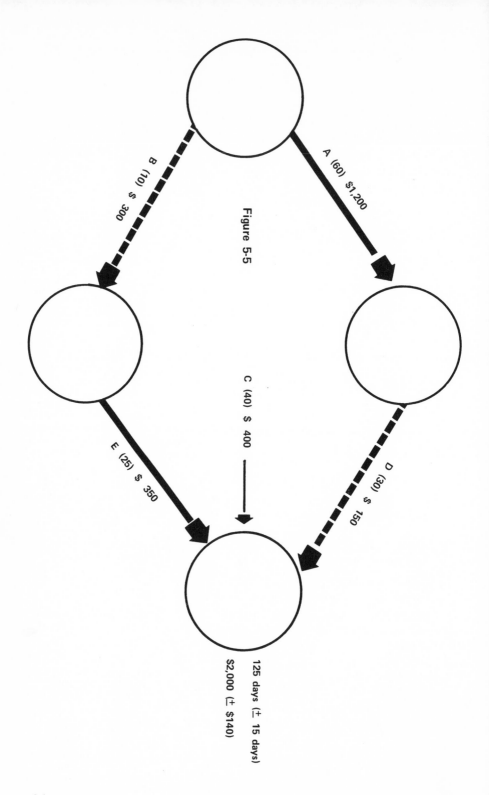

Figure 5-5

A (60) $1,200

B (10) $ 300

C (40) $ 400

E (25) $ 350

D (30) $ 150

125 days (± 15 days)
$2,000 (± $140)

on a large table, working *backward* from end objective to project start. This provides a means whereby the activities can be moved freely about in order to ensure the establishment of proper dependencies and interrelationships for each necessary event to occur. When the final placement of cards has been made, a hand copy of the network can be prepared, using the spaces between cards as activity lines and the cards as events in circular form as start and end points. Exhibit 5-6 shows a sample Activity Card.

Figure 5-6

ACTIVITY CARD

Prev. Event No._____   Succ. Event No._____

ACTIVITY_____

    Optimistic time (o)   _____

    Most likely time (m)   _____

    Pessimistic time (p)   _____

    Expected elapsed time (t_e)   _____

Figure 5-7 shows what a more complex PERT network might look like prior to calculation of time and costs for each step. Note that in this instance the objective must be achieved by June 1. This means that sufficient time, funds, and the right numbers and kinds of personnel must be provided so as to attain the objective by the mandated date.

Exhibit 5-8 graphically illusrates a model form used to display not only time estimates, but cost and personnel estimates as well. Subsequently, *all* are subject to t_e and σ calculations. Readers are invited to make the t_e and σ calculations for each *total*. Answers are provided at the end of the chapter.

In a complex network, exceeding approximately 30 activities, the use of a computer is generally called for. There are a number of PERT computer programs designed for educational applications and a competent programmer can design a tailor-made one for any given PERT situation.

In sum, the PERT procedure helps to efficiently and effectively implement established goals and objectives.

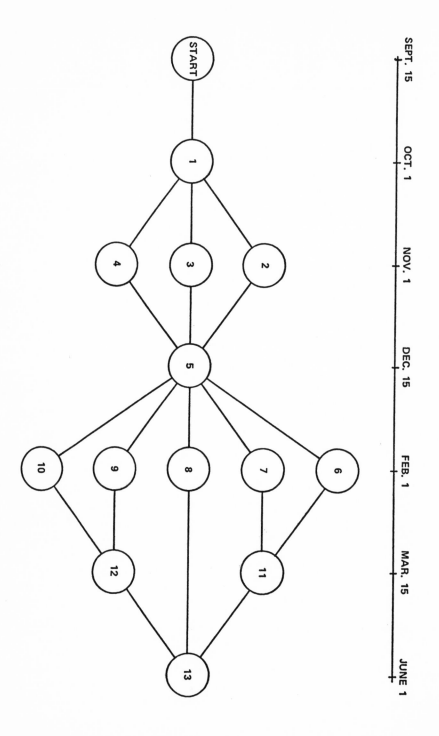

Figure 5-7

IMPLEMENTATION

SEPT. 15   OCT. 1   NOV. 1   DEC. 15   FEB. 1   MAR. 15   JUNE 1

98

Exhibit 5-8

Objective: Orientation Program for New Students   **Task Leader:** "Mary Smith"   **Date:** May 15, 19____

No.	Task Elements	Time (weeks)			Money			Personnel			Comments
		P	M	O	P	M	O	P	M	O	
1	Review the	2.0	1.0	0.2	50	25	0	10	4	2	Library may have some information but doubtful there is enough.
2	Visit other institutions who have such programs	3.0	1.0	0.4	1,000	200	40	10	2	1	The best program I have heard of is out-of-state, but 2 fairly good ones are nearby. Nearby ones will be visited first.
3	Etc.										
4	Etc.										
5	Etc.										
End	Total	20.0	12.0	10.0	2,000	650	350	12	4	2	

Answers to the totals given in Exhibit 5-8:

		Time	Money	Personnel
t_e	=	13 weeks	825 dollars	5 individuals
σ	=	$\pm$ 1.66 weeks	$\pm$ 275 dollars	$\pm$ 1.66 individuals

Chapter 6

PPBS

Law 3: Take action when inaction would unnecessarily antagonize an individual or group – Richard W. Hostrop

As has been shown, the Delphi Technique is a procedure for *setting* goals and objectives, and PERT is a means for *implementing* them. *PPBS* (Planning – Programming – Budgeting – System) provides a method for determining the *costs* of program goals and objectives. PERT focuses on the *parts* of overall goals and objectives, PPBS focuses on the interdependencies and the *total*. Figure 6-1 illustrates these conceptual interdependencies and the total inter-relationships of program budgeting.

Figure 6-1

THE CONCEPT OF PROGRAM BUDGET

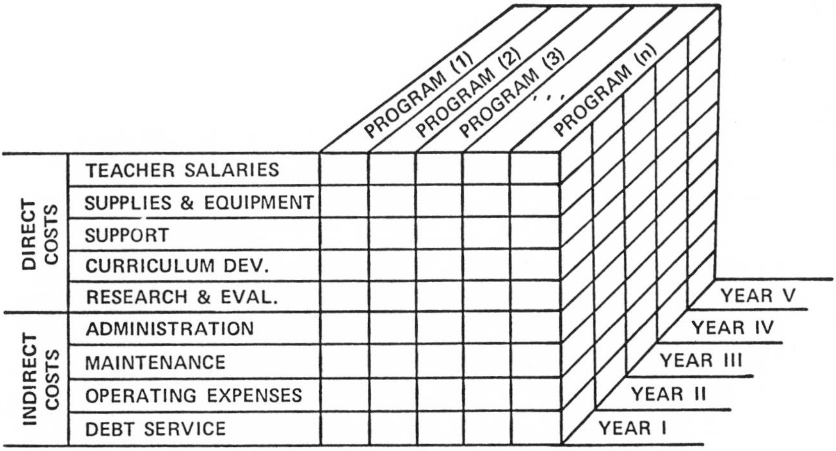

PPBS (frequently just PPB) is an approach to cost-effectiveness which seeks to make the best use of available resources in the attainment of system goals through budgeting on a program rather than on a line-item basis.

PPBS provides managers with a management tool to aid in more effective decision making. It is a means whereby the public and the decision makers can have communicated to them what the schools are doing in terms of programs, cost of programs, and success of programs.

PPBS begins with the identification and defining of goals and objectives. It then groups the educational system's activities into programs that can be related to each objective. This requires grouping by end-product rather than by functional administrative organization. PPBS looks at *what* is produced — output — in addition to *how* it is produced (which can be called consumption of input). This procedure contrasts with the traditional budget found in most educational systems where costs are assembled by types of resource inputs or line-items and by organizational categories. PPBS focuses attention on the competition for resources within programs, thus forcing careful review of relative effectiveness. Figure 6-2 graphically shows PPBS implementation procedures.

A program is any activity or proposal that can be defined in terms of student, faculty, space, or financial resources. A program might be as specific and immediate as a new course in ethnic studies, or the acquisition of a cyclotron for a physics department. Or it might be as pervasive as a long-term project to better prepare future librarians in a school of library science to cope more effectively in providing library services in the inner-city of large metropolitan areas.

PPBS provides the means for better determining the resources needed to carry out plans for improving the design of the programs used to reach the goals and objectives chosen. PPBS does not choose the goals and objectives nor does it decide upon the criteria for determining whether or not goals and objectives have been achieved. Moreover, while it is intended to provide information as to the resources going into a program, it does not say whether they are too little or too much or just right. If the objectives of a program are greatly exceeded, it *might* suggest that less resources are needed; if they are grossly underachieved, it *might* indicate that more resources should be allocated to the program. Outcomes *might* also mean that the program should be changed or that more realistic goals and/or objectives be chosen.

Figure 6-2

IMPLEMENTATION STEPS FOR PPBS

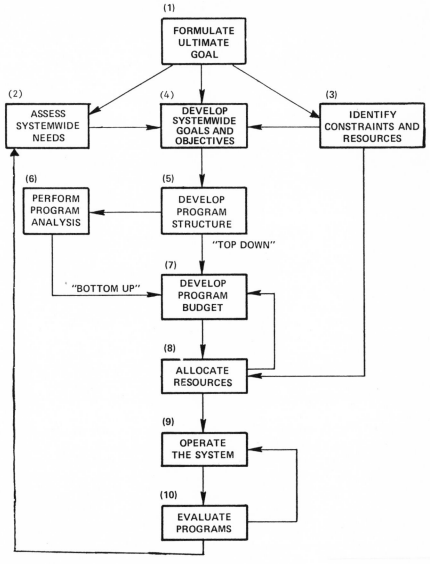

Once a program is defined, approved, and funded, the Planned Program Budget System is used to set up the necessary budgetary and accounting controls. These controls are coded so that any related transaction can be identified with it. Expense data (payroll, purchases, and encumbrances) are retrieved during day-to-day administrative computer processing, and totals are accumulated by program to keep tabs on the expenditure versus the program budget status.

While the computer is not directly involved in program budgeting, PPBS would be impractical without it. The computer can maintain basic files on students, faculty, space, and financial data. The computer can draw together the profiles; it can handle the forecasting of resource needs; and it can process accounting transactions each month so as to total up expenditure data for each program.

It is vital to successful program budgeting to always keep the emphasis on primary academic services. Support services which are not facilitative of academic services can be identified, and thus can be eliminated under PPBS.

The aim of program budgeting, obviously, is to fund the department plans as effectively as possible, taking into consideration the relative program priorities at the department, institutional, and organizational levels.

Good PPBS procedure calls for a quarterly updating of student, faculty, space, and fiscal position to reflect the current situation.

Once each year, January being a particularly good time, profile data is used to forecast the continuation of program budgets. This process is a combination of linear programming techniques (space), simulation models (students, finances) and department, institutional, and organizational judgment (professional staff). The assumption is that nothing will change except student enrollment totals and staff, space, and finance requirements affected by the enrollment changes. In this phase of budgeting, there is no anticipation of, or allowance for, new and/or improved programs – or elimination of existing ones.

Student enrollment forecasts are produced by district, by institution, by level, by subject, and by course. The computer works with this data and with staff profiles. Space needs of each department are forecast. The computer works with expenditure and financial profile data, takes into consideration workload factors, cost of living changes, and then forecasts the continuation needs for personnel services, equipment, and operating expenditures by department, institution, and system.

Budgeting of a new program, or a program improvement, begins at the department level with a request from the department head. A request form describes the program, indicates whether it is a new program or an improvement on an existing one, and explains how the program contributes to the implementation of a system's *Five-Year Plan* (see "intermediate goals," Chpt. 2). The department head ranks the program budget request on a priority scale. The institutional head ranks all requests according to priorities of the institution. The system head does likewise for the system as a whole. Exhibit 6-3 illustrates such a program request form.

Exhibit 6-3

PROGRAM REQUEST

Program description:
(new or existing one)

Describe how this program will, if approved, contribute to implementing the system's Five-Year Plan:

List additional budget needs if request is approved:

	Personnel Services	*Equipment*	*Space Needs*
Numbers:			
Kinds:			
Support Services: (eg, travel, supplies, etc.)			
Total dollars needed:			

PROGRAM
GRAND TOTAL: $

Rank the program proposal as to necessity in order to implement the system's Five-Year Plan: (Circle one)

    1. Essential   2. Highly desirable   3. Desirable

Justify your ranking:

Name of Submitter	Title	Department	Date

In a typical line-item budget there is no way to tell what are the programs of the organization or their costs. Nor can it be told what the items listed are expected to do in any concise way. The budgeted line-items are simply under such broad categories as administration, instruction, supplies, maintenance, and debt retirement. In short, it is nearly impossible to establish program and individual accountability with a line-item budget. By contrast, a PPBS budget clearly establishes what a program is expected to do and what its costs will be. Program and individual accountability are easily established.

By way of illustration of the PPBS principles previously enunciated, a sample eighth grade reading program in the PPBS format is presented in Exhibit 6-4 below.

Exhibit 6-4

The Middle Reading Program
1-1-12-3

THE READING PROGRAM TERMINAL OBJECTIVES

Study Skills

1. By the end of the eighth grade, the student completes one written research composition with 90% technical accuracy using criteria specified within an eighth grade English text.

2. Given a series of eighth grade questions, the student selects the most appropriate book location in the library with 90% accuracy.

3. Given a selected list of titles, the student identifies the category within the Dewey Decimal System in which the book belongs with 90% accuracy.

4. Given a selection with ten underlined words, the student uses a dictionary to discover (1) correct pronunciation, (2) specific meanings, (3) part of speech, and (4) etymology, with 90% accuracy.

5. Given a map, atlas, chart or graph, the student answers relevant questions with 90% accuracy.

6. The student arranges a list of random words in alphabetical order according to the first four letters of each word with 100% accuracy.

7. Given a topic for research, the student identifies and locates three different types of reference materials in the library within 20 minutes.

Exhibit 6-4—*Continued*

8. Given a variety of eighth grade selections, the student identifies the literature type (essay, poetry, drama) with 80% accuracy.

9. Given eighth grade reading selections with a variety of literary devices, the student selects appropriate literary definitions with 90% accuracy.

10. Given a variety of eighth grade selections, the student identifies the author's intent and mood with 90% accuracy.

11. Given an eighth grade basal-reader selection, the student identifies the main idea and significant details and summarizes in written or oral outline form with 90% accuracy.

12. Given an eighth grade reader, the student skims to find ten specific factual details within five minutes with 90% accuracy.

13. Given a variety of eighth grade poetry selections, the student identifies the basic idea with 90% accuracy.

14. A student lists ten famous authors and identifies a major literary contribution of each author with 90% accuracy.

FUNCTIONAL

Comprehension

1. Given a variety of paragraphs, the student discards irrelevant materials with 90% accuracy.

2. Given an eighth grade paragraph to which conclusions of predictions must be supplied, the student selects the most logical conclusions or predictions with 90% accuracy.

3. Given a selected list of eighth grade questions, the student evaluates the validity of source materials and is able to select the most appropriate with 90% accuracy.

4. Given a variety of eighth grade paragraphs, the student selects the appropriate reading speed category with 90% accuracy.

5. Given a variety of eighth grade paragraphs, the student selects the appropriate propaganda technique with 90% accuracy.

6. Given a list of eighth grade paragraphs, the student selects the most appropriate motive derived from the characterizations with 80% accuracy.

Management Theories, Techniques, and Tools

Exhibit 6-4—_Continued_

Skill Development

1. An eighth grade student reads and pronounces with 90% accuracy ten lists of eighth grade words selected from a basal reading test.

2. An eighth grade student correctly applies analysis skills 90% of the time in reading and pronouncing a selected list of nonsense words.

3. The student predicts with 90% accuracy the meaning of words using context clues on a standardized vocabulary test.

4. The student reads silently 350 words per minute with 75% comprehension in an eighth grade basal reading test.

5. The student reads orally with 90% accuracy and 75% recall the eighth grade paragraph on the Gilmore Oral Reading Test

PPBS BUDGET SHEET

Program Title: Reading-Middle   **Program Level:** VI   **Program Number:** 1-1-12-3

PROGRAM EXPENDITURES

Expenditures	1975-76	1976-77	1977-78	1978-79	1979-80
Personnel	$36,504				
Services					
Supplies/materials					
Equipment					
Other	544				
Direct Total	$37,048				
Allocated Indirect Costs					
Total					
Source of Income					
Cost per Student: $37,048 562	$ 66				

EXPENDITURE DETAIL

	1975-76	1976-77
Salaries: 22% of 7 teachers' salaries		
One full-time equivalent teacher (21 periods/wk)	$36,504	
Fixed Charges: retirement, permanent fund, insurance	544	
	$37,048	

As the preceding shows, PPBS focuses on program objectives and their costs. Traditional line-item budgets do not reveal objectives, and program costs cannot be determined. Line-item budget costs are related to functional *inputs,* PPBS costs are related to program *outputs.*

Program budgeting is an approach which can improve the pace, scale, and conditions of education wherever it is used. It is a means for maximizing limited resources and for making qualitative decisions. It is a means for "visualizing" goals and objectives, and a way to manage education for results.

Chapter 7

OR

Law 4: 'Telegraph' a contemplated controversial action before taking the action to determine if the action is really worth the likely reaction –
Richard W. Hostrop

Delphi helps us to set goals and objectives. PERT helps us to implement them. PPBS shows us what each will cost. And *OR* (operations research) enables us to *analyze and evaluate* our proposed means for implementing them before taking real action.

Though operations research was developed by English scientists and mathematicians as early as 1938, in conjunction with World War II needs, it was not until 1959 that OR techniques were attempted in the field of education. This was some 10 years after the economic sector had first extrapolated the war time concepts for peace time use. The Rand Corporation was the group to first see the applicability of OR techniques in education. Some of its members became intrigued with such educational problems as how to optimize the transportation routes of school buses in the interest of cutting costs. Other educational applications of OR procedures are discussed below.

While characteristics vary somewhat between OR models, the following 3 characteristics are common to most OR models:

     1.   The models take the form of an equation in which a measure of the system's overall performance is equated to a relationship between a set of controlled and uncontrolled aspects.

     2.   Users must be able to explicitly state both those variables which may be controlled and not controlled.

     3.   All objectives must be quantifiable.

OR tools are of considerable aid in analyzing a problem and developing alternative solutions. They can find and bring out the underlying patterns in the behavior of an educational system and its environment, including those that have hitherto lain beyond the educational manager's field of vision or range of imagination. They can thus bring out alternative courses of action. They can show which factors are relevant (ie, facts) and which are irrelevant (ie, mere data). They can show the degree of reliability of the available data and what additional data are required to arrive at sound judgment. They can show what resources will be needed in any alternative courses of action, and what contribution from each component or function would be required. They can be used to show the limitations of each possible course of action, and the risks and probabilities of each. They can show what impact a given action would have on other areas, components, and functions. They can show the relationship between input and output and the location and nature of "bottlenecks." Finally, they can tie together the work and contribution of each function or component part with those of all the others and show this total impact on the behavior and results of the entire educational system.

In essence the tools of OR are tools of information, and of information-processing, not of decision-making. They focus on possible alternative courses of action. They thus make possible decisions with a high degree of rationality with respect to futurity, risk, and probability. This is the kind of information each manager needs as he sets out to achieve the objectives of his department so as to contribute to achieving the goals of the educational system as a whole.

OR are tools of systematic, logical, and mathematical analysis and synthesis. Thus operations research is a "system." In this chapter 3 system tools of operations research, having particular applicability to education, will be discussed. They are: *programming, simulation,* and *queuing theory.* A library example will particularly be emphasized to illustrate these 3 tools at work. From this focused example the reader should be able to extrapolate the principles to his own particular situation in any given educational area.

OR as a System

As the reader continues to read, it should ever be borne in mind that what has preceded, and what follows throughout this chapter and the remainder of the book, is part of a total systems approach. Particularly in Part II the systems approach can be seen as a framework for organizing complex problem situations for readier solutions.

It will be recalled from Part I that a system is a collection of pieces or elements which are related or dependent in some way. Consequently, it is useful to consider the whole set as an operational entity. A key word in systems analysis is *connectivity,* or relationships between elements. It is apparent, then, that systems are a fundamental part of any orderly process of thinking, since one must relate ideas in order to achieve a rational framework.

To show that systems analysis is a point of view, consider an ordinary fork. By itself, as a piece of formed metal, a fork is not a system, because no parts or relationships have been defined. A fork is a system, however, if it is interpreted as part of a place setting or when actually in use as an eating tool. Other simple illustrations of systems are children cutting with a pair of scissors or a boy using a fishing pole, line, leader, hook, and sinker to fish. Other complex systems which illustrate the interconnectedness and interdependencies of systems include the limbs and organs of the human body — or the processes in hospitals, schools, and libraries.

Using a library as an example of a system, it is clear that a library must function as an integrated whole toward accomplishing goals and objectives which are designated for the total system. Although it is difficult to quantify an all-inclusive performance measure, specific objectives and their measurements should be established. Thus, as one system example, the objectives of library circulation, cataloguing, and reshelving is a subsystem of a library system designed to minimize loss of user time within the limitations of resources available.

As stated earlier, operations research is a collection of mathematical models for the solution of various types of complex problems. Alternate titles, sometimes used interchangeably, such as *management science* or *decision theory* have slightly different connotations from *operations research,* but all usually share certain important characteristics in common as listed below:

1.   The problem is mathematically formulated and uses quantitative measurements for explicit variables.

2.   An attempt is made to optimize or improve a set of one or more numerical values which represent the solution to a problem.

3.   The scope is sufficiently broad to encompass a significant segment of the total problem environment. Interaction among several important decision variables is included in the model formulation.

4.   Models take a systems point of view because they look at the relationship of different variables upon each other; this often implies a team approach or the interaction of several types of expertise.

Among the many different techniques which are collected under the heading of operations research, programming, simulation, and queuing theory are extremely useful to educational managers. Each of these management techniques are described briefly below.

Programming

A manager must *program* the resources which he controls in order to optimize the goals of his organization within the environmental realities of his situation. In programming techniques, quantitative variables or activities are chosen which 1) express a reasonable range of strategic choices, 2) lend themselves to measurement of objectives, and 3) are limited by fixed conditions in the environment. Measurements of activity levels may be in such units as dollars, space, size, weight, utility, or time.

Consider the case of a library which receives a given dollar budget to perform an academic service. The library decides to measure its total service by the amount of annual circulation (14:169-71). Activity variables are assigned to each different class of reading materials and/or customer services. An algebraic expression called the *objective function* adds the various activities in terms of their effect on circulation. Thus objective functions quantify goal attainment in programming models. A set of algebraic expressions, called *constraints,* relates strategy combinations of activities to environmental limitations. For example, library service activities must be associated with budgetary dollars, supply of trained personnel, available space, and limits of user demand. Among strategy choices within a given budget would be *trade-offs* between more volumes and additional or faster services. If within reasonable ranges, the impact of any activity can be separated out from the impact of other activities (eg, twice as many books take up twice the space), then conditions are satisfied for an important subclass known as *linear programming* or LP.

The mathematical key in linear programming is the linear equation. This is an equation which is drawn on a graph. The basic idea merely requires that its user know what the problem is and be able to state it in a way so that experts can shape the model. In simple, straight line problems any professional can solve his own problem (eg, twice as much space will be needed for twice as many books). Mathematicians or systems analysts, with the aid of a computer, can solve the more complex problems.

Since a routine solution procedure is available for LP, but not for most other types of programming, a librarian must attempt to formulate his problem in accordance with the 3 linear conditions cited at the beginning of this section. The library LP illustrated above will determine the quantities of each service activity so as to maximize circulation for given budget, personnel, or other limitations.

Linear programming has such further educational applications as scheduling students into classes; determining optimal numbers and hours of counselors, custodians, cafeteria workers; and where to locate additional educational facilities, etc.

Simulation

A *simulation* is an OR technique for reproducing or abstracting out, through a computer or role playing, a model of a system, subsystem, component, operation, or environment for predictive or instructional purposes.

Simulations can aid in the very important and frequently asked question by managers, What would happen if . . . . ? Answers to simulated situations reduce the need for voluminous management reports. Simulating "what if" situations leads to greater contact between line managers at all levels and between these managers and the staff managers.

Simulation, as an OR technique, permits the manager to learn from his mistakes without having to experience the consequences of those mistakes. It provides a means for bringing order and predictability out of seeming chaos of multiple variables. A unique advantage is the ability to forge ahead in time; and if the model is realistic, this glimpse of possible futures permits an educational system to evaluate and choose the most favorable of the many alternatives open to it. We have seen that the Delphi Technique is a means for *setting* goals and objectives. A simulation provides the means for *evaluating* how realistic, or even how desirable, certain goals and objectives may be — given the constraints of available funds, personnel, space, and time. Simulations make it possible to select *alternative* paths which hold particular promise for achieving system, institutional, and departmental goals and objectives.

Simulation is not a theory, nor is it even a solution technique in the usual sense; rather it is a methodology for experimentation and prediction. The actual definition of the word "simulate," is "to assume the appearance of, without the reality" according to *Webster's Collegiate Dictionary*. Webster's definition captures the essence of the technique.

Having captured the appearance of reality in a model we want to "run" the model through time. Usually a large number of "dry runs" can be made in a fraction of the time required for one cycle of the "real thing." From a problem-solving standpoint it is necessary to observe the behavior of the system over time. Simulation, then, increments time in terms of the variables and relationships of the system. In this way the simulation plays out the scenario which is representative of reality. The decision maker can thus watch a replica of reality "pass by" and utilize what is learned as a basis for actual decisions.

In our primary example a few hours work on a library financial budget with a piece of paper, pencil, and adding machine may *simulate* many years of actual financial life. All planning is a form of simulation, since the future has not yet taken place. In our library example there is a special problem because the future is uncertain as to both quantities of library materials and relationships. One way to cope with this is to try out different combinations of possibilities by running multiple simulations. Suppose in the preparation of a library budget there are 5 possible levels for appropriation of funds, 3 different salary proposals, and 5 levels of service demand for each of 6 different classes of books. In order to represent all possible combinations of these factors 234,375 different budgets would have to be calculated. Such calculations would be out of the question by hand, although they might be feasible on a large computer. Even so, this illustration shows that it would not take much variety in combinations of uncertainties to exceed the capacity of even the largest computers. *Monte Carlo* is a simulation technique which can reduce such multiple simulations to a reasonable level.

Monte Carlo is named for the famous gambling casino in Monaco since this type of simulation procedure employs chance methods of selecting particular values for variables. It is a means whereby statistical sampling of value combinations of variable inputs replaces a simulation run for every combination. By accepting some statistical risk of error, a library manager may *infer* behavior of his variable budgets from a Monte Carlo sample. In our example, the library manager must assign *probability* distributions of values for each of 8 variables (appropriation, salary, and 6 classes of books). The output of his Monte Carlo simulation will show the probability distribution of values for resulting strategies and control items in the budget. The budgeter has succeeded in quantifying and systematizing his original uncertainties.

Although Monte Carlo simulation requires a great deal of computation (which can be done by a computer), it is a powerful tool for organizing and optimizing the behavior of complex systems.

Another example of the use of the Monte Carlo simulation in an educational setting is the perennial problem of ascertaining in advance the probability of course selections by high school and college students — with all the attendant implications for numbers of teachers needed, class size, location of classes, number of class periods, times to be scheduled, etc.

Other examples of computer-based simulations include such "what if" problems as simulating curricular changes in order to estimate the implications for staffing and facilities. PERTing, preparing budgets in the PPBS format, determining such items as the effect of certain policy variables relevant to decision making, and the functional relationships between policy variables and output variables are other examples of computer-based simulations.

Thus, the use of computer-based simulation techniques by educational systems and individual institutions makes it possible to 1) project future conditions, needs, and outputs, 2) test the implications of new policies as related to intermediate and long-term goals, and 3) explore the effects of proposed changes on other components of the system — all in advance of making "real" decisions.

It should also be noted that not all simulations require powerful computers and sophisticated programmers. This is particularly true of the learning manager, ie, the teacher. Though there are computer-based learner-oriented simulations, particularly for business and economic courses, most *instructional* simulations are noncomputer based. Moreover, there are a number of commercial noncomputer based simulations appropriate to all levels of education — elementary school through graduate education.

Examples of noncomputer based simulations are to be found particularly in history and the social sciences. Most of these simulations require *"role playing."* The participants assume parts and "act out" their roles in accordance with the "rules" of the game. This is why simulations are sometimes known as *Gaming* or *Game Theory.* Among such noncomputer based simulations are the political science games of *NAPOLI* and *INTERNATION,* the economic geography game of *Trade and Development,* and the U.S. history game *The Kansas/Nebraska Act.*

Unlike acting role players have no set lines, but instead are usually presented with a complex problem which they attempt to solve. As a result, participants gain insight into the complexity of human relationships (affective domain) as well as acquiring information (cognitive domain). Research has shown that the value of instructional simulations "appears to lie in their ability to clarify abstract relationships by presenting them on a more concrete level which students can experience directly, and in their power to influence students' attitudes." (17:20)

Role playing simulations also lend themselves particularly well in such real life educational activities as assessing and improving student teaching performance and intern counseling performance. The capabilities of potential administrators can likewise be assessed and improved by simulating problem situations and studying their responses. As Don Bushnell says, "It is a short step from training administrators to the use of simulation for the actual operation of school systems."

Potential and practicing administrators can simulate collective bargaining sessions, student demands of various kinds, preparing for trustees' meetings, and the like.

Potential and practicing teachers can simulate the conditions of the "open classroom" by assuming both student and teacher roles. Teachers can assume other teaching roles such as "lecturer" or "systems designer" (teaching and learning via measurable performance objectives), etc. And teachers, like administrators, can use simulation techniques to better comprehend the strengths and weaknesses of collective bargaining.

Besides computer-based and role playing simulations there is one other type of simulation widely used for educational purposes, *psychomotor* simulations. Two brief examples will serve to illustrate: the use of driver education and flight training simulators used in advance of actually driving or flying.

In sum, simulation techniques provide the manager with a means of "seeing" some of the consequences of proposed decisions before taking them. It aids the manager to answer the very important question, "What if . . . ?" It provides students with the opportunity to "experience" historical events, notable current events, running a business, or to learn psychomotor skills. It provides a means for administrators and teachers to crawl inside each other's role, as well as their students, in addition to their own. Thus, simulation techniques can provide a means to gain insight and skills without the risk that action in a real situation would entail.

Queuing Theory

The third, and last, OR technique this chapter discusses is *queuing theory*. This theory deals with the nature of waiting lines, particularly, but not exclusively, as such lines relate to people. It is an important member of a class of models which are used to minimize the total of 2 sets of costs which move in opposite directions. In education 1 set of costs generally pertains to financial expenditures, the other to human costs of lost time or learning.

Queuing theory can aid in solving such problems as how to optimize the ratio between waiting time of commuters and parking attendant personnel costs at university parking lots; defining optimal levels of storage of food for cafeterias and of custodial supplies for bathrooms and maintenance purposes; defining optimal staffing levels for various hours of cafeteria, custodial, and book store personnel; and other similar situations where queues cause "hurry up and wait" problems.

Two important parameters of any queuing system are the average number of *arrivals* for service per time period and the average number of *services* which could be completed per time period. It is, of course, impossible to schedule service to precisely match arrivals because individual arrivals vary unpredictably from the average. Thus idle costs, as in a school or college cafeteria, cannot be totally eliminated, but rather only minimized. Given a cafeteria (or any other queuing environment) with a particular combination of *average arrival rate* (symbol λ) and *average service completion* rate (symbol μ), the question is, how many serving stations will result in the least total system cost? In practice this question is answered by calculating costs and income in hourly units and then determining the cost/profit ratio. For example, in analyzing costs of operating a cafeteria it is not enough to just calculate the sum of the cost of a cashier station per hour times the number of serving stations. The cost of waiting customers (and those who leave before getting served!) must also be added per hour. The latter is the cost of lost good will plus lost time per customer per hour times the average number of customers in the system (symbol $\angle$). Customers "in the system" are the sum of those waiting and those being served. If the statistical distribution pattern of arrivals and services is known, it often is possible to compute $\angle$ mathematically from given λ and μ .

OR at the Ohio State University Library

Charles L. Hubbard, Gerald Johoda, and Robert Torter worked on a problem common to many libraries — public as well as academic — viz, to determine the optimal number of duplicate volumes which should be available for high demand readings (15:52-53). In public libraries this high demand is for "best sellers," in academic libraries it is assigned readings and reserve books. Alternately, the model developed provides rationing rules for coping with high demand for other library resources, eg, audiovisual materials and equipment — and personnel.

Multi-channeling queuing was used to determine expected times in a reading program, and from this a policy for social cost minimization was developed.

In a library queue, *arrivals* are readers who seek a high demand volume. *Serving stations* are the number of available duplicate copies of a volume in high demand. A *service* consists of reading a desired or required book.

It was found at the Ohio State University Library that $\angle$ (average number of readers in the system) based upon λ (average number of readers arriving per hour for a particular high demand reading book) and μ (average number of nonwaiting persons who complete this reading per hour) were not being well served. There was too much waiting for high demand volumes. This fact, in the view of the investigators, resulted in too many lost learning opportunities. They concluded that the "cost of reader time has generally been neglected in library planning, whereas it is actually the most significant decision variable."

In support of the investigators' conclusions they found examples of "impatient" behavior by readers. Some potential readers would not join a queue if more than X number of persons were also waiting. There is a "discouragement factor" which increases the probability of reader refusal to wait as the length of a queue increases. Then there is "complete reneging" by some potential users who refuse to wait at all if the book desired is not available immediately. "Impatient" readers may return later or never come back. Thus, in the latter instance, there is the serious imperative of how to prevent lost education. If a reader has not had his need met, will he come back at all? Shifting a bit, by way of another illustration, if a student voluntarily comes for counseling help but all counselors are busy, will he come back? How much learning loss or mental health loss can society afford are sober questions which educators must give serious attention to. The application of queuing theory is one relatively inexpensive way for mitigating potential learning and mental hygiene losses — and other kinds of losses.

At Ohio State University, as a result of the queuing study, library personnel were in a position to better schedule the time of their staff, to make additional purchase of high demand volumes, and to establish closer partnership relationships with the teaching faculty.

The Ohio State University Library queuing study also has important implications for planning new library facilities, and other facilities, where queuing is a factor, eg, cafeterias and book stores, and location and number of counseling offices.

In this chapter we have discussed 3 OR techniques: programming, simulation, queuing. These 3 decision-making models have significant educational implications as well as applications. These 3 elements of systems analysis will become increasingly important in the immediate years ahead. Educational managers will have to acquire a systems point of view in face of today's traditional "common sense" view. But as managers shift from the traditional to the new, as they begin to use such system models as Delphi, PERT, PPBS, OR, MIS, etc., present practice should operate alongside new practice until the new practice is clearly understood and accepted as the better way. Old practice serves as a "fail safe" practice even when it is little more than a "rule of thumb" practice.

Finally, a word about the influence of electronic computers is necessary to view the whole subject of systems analysis in perspective. Extensive calculations are required for many useful programming, simulation, or queuing models for large systems. This is why OR sometimes is referred to as a "computer-oriented decision-making system." To make complex OR calculations it thus takes a "systems analyst," a computer programmer, and a computer.

Though most academic managers will not require sophisticated system analysts' skills, nor sophisticated programming skills, it will be necessary to acquire a modern systems point of view. The acquisition of a systems point of view is not difficult to acquire once educators become familiar with its logic and its theories, its techniques, and its tools.

Chapter 8

MIS

Law 5: When it appears necessary to take a possible controversial action, delay taking such action as long as possible so as to be sure that the controversial action really is necessary and desirable; if so, then use the delayed time to optimize the decision by refining the means for achieving the desired result – Richard W. Hostrop

MIS (Management Information System) can be defined as "an organized method of providing management with information needed for decisions, when it is needed and in a form which aids understanding and stimulates action." (26:32) From this definition we can see that Delphi, PERT, PPBS, and OR are some of the aids which make management information systems possible. But in themselves they do not represent a *total* management information system. MIS strives to integrate these, and other procedures, into a total and unified system.

Levels of Information

In an educational environment information is needed at 3 levels and can be divided thusly: 1) information for operation, 2) information for control, and 3) information for management decisions and planning. These 3 functions of information somewhat parallel the 3 functions of management: *administering, planning,* and *leading.*

The lowest level, *information for operations,* consists of the information needed for clerical functions – payroll, financial transactions, student records, and the like. Here good administration is needed.

The middle level, *information for control,* involves information needed to implement administrative decisions and policies. Two examples will serve to illustrate. It is decided that no department shall exceed its supplies budget. Information concerning each department's expenditures for supplies is maintained on a current basis, and controls are established and operate in such a way that orders for supplies in excess of budgeted amounts are automatically rejected. Or student performance minimums are established for promotion from one class to the next with the information used to control student promotion. Effective administration and planning can ensure the adequacy and implementation of information for control.

The highest level, *management decision and planning,* requires the skills of a good planner and, more often than not, a good leader as well. To illustrate, if the chief executive officer determines from planning reports that operating funds will increase the subsequent year by only 3 percent, but student enrollment is projected to increase by 9 percent, he and his board are faced with some very difficult decisions — especially, if in addition, the faculty is demanding a 7 percent increase in salaries and a 5 percent reduction in class size. The planner must simulate various factors to determine the effects of such constraints and such proposals — including, of course, investigating various possibilities for securing additional funds. This single complex illustration shows the very real need for gathering as much information as possible, and then use such OR techniques as simulation to determine the effects that such inputs will have on the outputs of the total organization. This will affect such decisions as what is offered to the faculty in the process of negotiations, what alternative "trade-offs" may be put forth, eg, *increased* class size rather than a reduction of class size, and a salary increase of perhaps 4 percent rather than the 7 percent asked.

An information system designed to serve as an aid to management in operating, controlling, and for decisions and planning has 2 main features:

1.   A data acquisition and storage system to maintain orderly records on variables important to the decision making process and a convenient recall system to make information dervied from the file accessible to the decision-maker.

2.   A logical structure to identify what variables are to be maintained in the file, the computations to be made on these variables, and how the results of these computations are to be used in the decision process.

The logical structure, called a *model of the process,* is central to the design of a management information system. Likewise, except for the most simple situations (an enrollment of under about 500 students), a computer is mandatory to retrieve the information management needs.

ADP

ADP (Automatic Data Processing), a term almost synonymous to the layman for the computer, has revolutionized technological societies. Because of its central importance to MIS we pause to focus on this remarkable "idio-savant."

Invented in 1945, introduced for scientific and engineering use in 1951, in a form designed for business applications in 1954, and used for educational purposes beginning circa 1960, the computer, in less than 20 years, now accounts for the dollar equivalent of more than 10 percent of all new plant and equipment expenditures in the United States! (6:31)

The electronic computer and, in particular, the information theory and technology that have made it possible, represent one of the most important technological advances of our times. These technologies make it possible to build machine systems for handling information for any purpose we wish. It is this − the fundamental nature of the innovation − that makes the computer such an important example of technological change, profoundly affecting business, industrial, military, and educational management decision making.

Significant improvements of ADP (sometimes also called EDP for Electronic Data Processing) are continually occurring: eg, pneumatic card-transport systems; improvements in optical scanning devices making it possible for direct machine reading of documents; improvements in voice-input and response devices; more sophisticated visual display devices; greater use of electronic light pens on plasma screens for modeling and response purposes; newer peripheral devices expressly designed to facilitate the exchange of information between the computer system and its human users. In short, the computer desk console, with complementary peripheral devices, will become nearly as common by the year 2000 as the manager's telephone is today. Similar consoles will be found in homes not too many years later.

Properly programmed, ADP automatically provides key management personnel not only with exception reporting (See MBO, Chpt. 13) but with *adaptive dissemination* − a system which has on record a profile of each manager indicating the kinds of events he should know about and the functions for which he is responsible. Adaptive dissemination provides a powerful means for implementing the *situational theory of management* − approaching situations from an orderly and scientific basis rather than from a "rule of thumb" basis. (See Management Theory, Chpt. 10)

ADP focuses on programs rather than on traditional departmental boundaries. Decision makers, thus, are given the opportunity to consider problems in their entirety rather than as segmental pieces.

ADP enables processes from originator to receiver to be reduced cost-wise and time-wise. But one example of things to come is a Japanese newspaper company which now transmits its newspaper directly into the home by television.

What all these new ADP developments mean is work that today seems economically out of reach will, in a very few years, be uneconomic if conducted in any other way.

The MIS manager, heading up the data processing department, must be included in the councils of top management itself so as to ensure that management decisions are based upon the best pertinent management information available.

Educational managers, themselves, will become programmers made possible by ADP languages now available much like every day language.

ADP programs now incorporate self-correcting features permitting the machine to recognize its own malfunctions, correct them, or to select a different path to solve a problem.

There now are heuristic and self-organizing systems that allow machines to develop their own problem solving methods best suited to the management analysis of a given problem at hand. In some instances the decision making is made by the computer. Increasingly, machines are "thinking" in the accepted meaning of the word.

As has already been suggested, to successfully PERT beyond approximately 30 activities, the use of the computer becomes necessary insurance to assure accuracy and to minimize time required for preparation. To prepare the multi-varied calculations of a budget in the PPBS format, or to compute for an OR model, demands the aid of ADP equipment. To effectively manage an educational system with an enrollment much beyond 500 students also demands ADP aid.

It is essential that every professional educator obtain rudimentary knowledge of ADP systems as a means for making better management decisions. This knowledge is essential not only in order to better understand the nature of PERT, PPBS, OR, and other computer-based management techniques and tools, but to better comprehend the use of the computer in the basic instructional areas as well. Administrators and faculty must become thoroughly familiar with the cost/benefits of CAI (Computer Assisted Instruction) and CMI (Computer Managed Instruction).

The instructional and counseling aspects of ADP systems will become publicly more visible in the years ahead than the planning and decision making aspects of ADP. Project PLATO, developed at the University of Illinois, shows great promise for bringing instructional costs down via use of the computer to a competitive level with the cost of teachers, and, in some instances, of increasing learning and retention as well. (11:6-7)

Though computers are not likely to ever completely replace teachers they, nonetheless, will be able to provide not only highly individualized but highly personalized teaching. Teachers who do not teach like a machine will not be replaced, administrators who do not administer like a machine will not be replaced; but those who do will and ought to be. What has occurred in Palo Alto and Urbana, and what likely will occur elsewhere, is greater cybernation— greater integration of human and nonhuman resources, working in complementary tandem to achieve system goals and objectives.

Finally, it is to be realized that ADP is the tool of MIS; and PERT, PPBS, and OR are some of its techniques. MIS serves to integrate the theories, techniques, and tools of total information for optimal use by decision-makers.

Inaugurating an MIS Program

It is not possible to develop an MIS program unless managers themselves are willing to devote time to the effort. MIS cannot be inaugurated by systems and information technologists working by themselves, or only with personnel at the operations level. The development requires a joint effort of management personnel and information specialists. Only management — the decision-makers — know what decisions it must make and what information it needs for decision making. Indeed, as William M. Zani says, "An effective system, under normal conditions, can only be born of a carefully planned, rational design that looks down from the top, the natural vantage point of the managers who will use it." (27:95) This means that unless there is interest and participation by the chief executive in developing a management information system there is little likelihood that a viable management information system can be developed in an organization. This becomes especially evident as one looks at the specific steps necessary for the successful development of MIS in an organization:

1.   Objectives of the MIS system are specified.

2.   Fixed MIS system requirements are specified.

3.   The MIS system is developed as efficiently as possible to fulfill the organizational goals and objectives.

4.   Compromises are made as necessary.

5.   The MIS system is tested.

6.   MIS revision is made as necessary.

7.   MIS is implemented.

8. MIS is evaluated.

9. Steps 1-8 are reviewed quarterly.

Though not wholly discretè steps, in general, the tasks should be performed in the order indicated. Figure 8-1 shows how a once inaugurated management information system serves to coordinate the activities of an educational organization.

Figure 8-1

MIS AS SYSTEM COORDINATOR

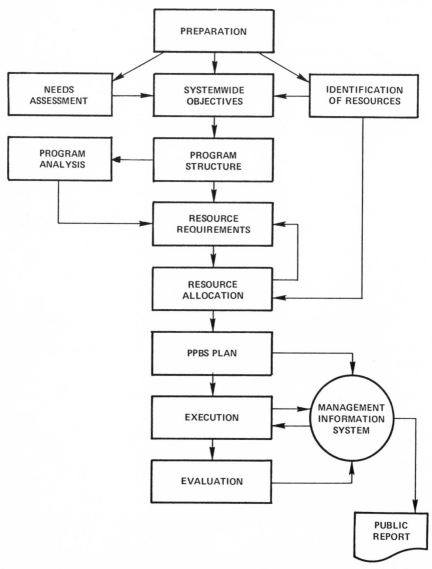

Managers at various levels of an organization require different items of management information even though the actual development of MIS must begin at the very top. The chief executive requires information of a type that is not required of anyone under him for making decisions concerning the educational system, or the institution, as a whole. Yet, *some* of the information he needs is also needed by lower level managers. Information which is needed is not always held in common. Still there must be interfacing between all levels of managers so that all information available to an organization can be plugged into as needed. The manager of instruction's information needs are somewhat different than the manager of students, and usually considerably different than the manager of business. Counselors, educational technologists, librarians, and teaching faculty have still different kinds of information needs even though, obviously, there are close linkages. To ensure appropriate linkages and interfacings each superordinate must insist on MIS summaries from his immediate subordinates.

The fact that there are close associations of information needs throughout an educational structure requires a *unified* management information system. Thus, there must be a common agreement as to data elements with respect to numbering, titling, summary description, and additional definitions and/or comments. Uniform element numbers are used throughout the system, and the MIS structure typically is organized around 6 major information areas: Student Related Elements, Staff Related Elements, Curricular Components, Facilities, Finance, Major Equipment. Preferably, the organization's MIS will tie in to a larger external group, eg, a consortium so that data gathered can be compared with like educational organizations. WICHE (Western Interstate Commission for Higher Education), headquartered in Boulder, Colorado, is one of the more notable examples of a consortium whose major effort to date has been to introduce MIS among its members. An extract of a WICHE document is shown in Exhibit 8-2. This exhibit is an example of a form designed to assure uniform element numbers, titles, summary descriptions, and additional definitions and/or comments for ready computer retrieval. The "USES" columns simply refers to various consortium needs with respect to reporting. Consortium arrangements aid participants to compare notes so as to help improve one another's MIS. Moreover, it provides a means for highlighting wide deviations from the norm for analysis as to the probable cause of such deviations.

The preceding suggests that an educational system contemplating a modern management information system would do better to observe developed systems in similar organizations rather than make an extensive feasibility study of its own.

Exhibit 8-2

DATA ELEMENT DICTIONARY
STUDENT RELATED ELEMENTS SECTION
Personal Data

_____ (Date)

Page: ___1___

No.	Data Element Title	Summary Description	Additional Definition and/or Comment	Uses			
				TU	H	III	IV
1.	Student Name	Legal name of student		T			
2.	Student Number	A number to uniquely identify each individual student	The student number will uniquely identify each student in attendance at a given institution. When the student number is coupled with a number uniquely identifying each institution of higher education, it will be possible to uniquely identify each individual student among all students in the nation. The student number may be a social security number.	T	R		R
3.	Social Security Number		May serve as a student number. Highly preferred.				R
4.	Sex			T	R	R	R
5.	Date of Birth	Month, Day, Year of Birth		T	R	R	R
6.	Citizenship	An indication of whether the student is or is not a U.S. citizen.		T	R	R	R

Data Requirements for Management Decisions

Some further examples of data information banked in a computer will suggest the kinds of information that can aid the decision-maker in making decisions. There are 3 areas to be considered:

Data relating input to output is information needed by every manager. There will be different emphases by the nature of each manager's function. Still, there are certain common input/output concerns by the mere fact of common organizational goals and objectives. Some examples include:

the cost per student per year in particular fields of study or grade levels

the cost per diploma or degree in particular fields of study

the cost of adding students to a particular field of study

the cost of programs at particular levels of quality

the cost of expanding existing programs or institutions

the cost of establishing new programs or institutions

beneficial side effects on the system itself

relationship between inputs and their associated costs and outputs and their associated benefits

relationship between costs and sources of funding

values added to the student, knowledge, and society

Information system and subsystems are identifiable even though an educational system can be considered as a single information system. Subsystems should be developed separately with integration provided where subsystems overlap. The data of all subsystems must be defined with management use in mind, and the data should be stored in such a manner that data in all of the subsystems may be readily retrieved and related to each other. The major information subsystems appear to be the following:

Information components related to *output*

Instructional Program

Research Program

Community Services Program

Information subsystems related to *input*

Student Records

Personnel Records

Facilities

Major supporting equipment

Finance

Identifying and measuring output may include such quantitative and qualitative student outputs as the following:

Instructional Program

A.D.A. or F.T.E. students

student credit hours

student contact hours (by level)

academic awards (diplomas, degrees, certificates)

quantitative measures of academic achievement

rate of academic promotion or of employment

peer judgments

characteristics of first employment

degree of success in employment

rate of acceptance of students as transfers to higher institutions of education

rate of participation in academic, community, civic, and political affairs

degree of conformance to institutional objectives

rate of salvage of disadvantaged learners

rate of salvage of "unemployables"

rate of admission to apprenticeship programs

degree of user satisfaction with the institution

rate of graduates placed in national fellowship programs

rate of elections of graduates to learned societies

Research Program

research findings and application (new knowledge and technical advancement)

awards for research findings

social contributions of research

Community Services Program

solutions to community and regional problems: economic, industrial, social (research output can apply here, also)

cultural enrichment programs (concerts, film series, art exhibits, etc.

issues programs (speakers, forums, panels, debates, etc.)

avocational offerings (hobbies and special interests)

MIS is in its early stages in education, so therefore still "crude." However, even crude analysis provides the promise of being highly beneficial by pointing out probable consequences of alternatives. In other words, it is better to be "crudely right than precisely wrong."

Difficulties with regard to human relations are a greater block toward the establishment of MIS than are the technical difficulties. To resolve the relationship between operating systems and management information systems there must be *communication.* The next chapter addresses itself to this most important topic.

Chapter 9

COMMUNICATION THEORIES

Law 6: When a controversial action is necessary, take the minimum action necessary to accomplish the desired result — Richard W. Hostrop

Notwithstanding the fact that communications has been a subject of study of philosophers, psychologists, sociologists, semanticists, and human relations experts since the first quarter of the century there clearly is *diminishing* communication within organizations and between groups and individuals in society.

As information explodes communication seems to implode in direct proportion. Witness relations between white and black, rich and poor, young and old, faculty and administrators. Contrast these relationships of today to those prior to the introduction of television on a mass scale circa 1950. Modern information systems have made the world smaller, but more hysterical at the same time; it took weeks for the Americans to know what was happening in the Napoleonic wars, and months to learn about a flood or famine in India — now information simultaneously presses down on us in microseconds, and the sheer concentration of disaster makes the media seem so "sensational."

We can vividly see how this information explosion has occurred if we plot the accumulation of information on a historical continuum beginning with the birth of Christ. The first doubling of information occurs in 1750; the second in 1900; the third in 1950; the fourth only 10 years later, in 1960; and the fifth in the mid-1960's. In other words, while it took 1,750 years for man to double his knowledge the first time after the birth of Christ, it took only 5 years for him to similarly double his knowledge from 1960 to 1965! In the past 20 years mankind has acquired more scientific information than in all of previous history. And 90 percent of all the scientists that ever lived are alive and working today. The information explosion is so vast and so far-reaching that the importance of grasping and keeping up with it at some points becomes indistinguishable from one's career. (13:1112)

Though television has been most responsible for the information explosion, the publishing industry and computers have added their weight to the mass of information that threatens to bury us. Not that information is not desirable — for it certainly is — but what the abundance of information does is to *increase* the communication problem. It makes communication both more urgent and even less tractable.

The preceding facts point up the imperative for organizations to manage information rather than to be buried by it, to communicate rather than to orate.

Our failure to effectively communicate with one another is poignantly pointed up by the felt need for intensive groups of various kinds (T-groups, encounter groups, sensitivity training, sensory awareness groups. . .). The popularity of such groups attests to the failure of our attempts at effective communication.

Despite the sorry state of communication in practice, we have nevertheless learned a great deal about it. However, rather than emerging out of studies about communication per se, our knowledge of communication theory are largely by-products of studies in other disciplines. Though we may never completely understand all elements making for effective communication we do know some things which are worthwhile with respect to *managerial communications.*

What we know of communication in organizations consists largely of what does *not* work and, sometimes, why it does not work. What seems the blunt truth is that most of what passes for communication in most organizations — whether business, labor unions, government agencies, or educational systems — is based on assumptions that have proven to be invalid — and that, therefore, these efforts cannot have results. Knowing what does not work gives a glimpse at a few things which *do* work.

Communication Principles

Peter F. Drucker summarizes what we have learned about communications through doing mostly the wrong things, in 4 cardinal principles:

1. Communications is perception.
2. Communications is expectations.
3. Communications is involvement.
4. Communications and information are totally different though totally interdependent. (9:4-5)

Communications is perception. An old philosophical question posed by the mystics of many religions — the Zen Buddhists, the Sufis of Islam, and the Rabbis of the Talmud — asks: "Is there a sound in the forest if a tree crashes down and no one is there to hear it?" The mystics of old always answered, "No." They knew that there is no sound unless someone perceives it. Sound is created by perception. Sound is communication. Though seemingly trite, the correct answer to this age-old question has profound implications for modern management.

1.   First, it means that it is the *receiver* who communicates. The person who emits the communication does *not* communicate. He utters. Unless there is someone who hears, there is no communication. There is only noise. The utterer may speak and write, sing or whistle, but without a receiver he communicates nothing. *No one can communicate anything.* One can only make it possible, or impossible, for a receiver (technically a perceiver) to perceive.

2.   We know that perception is experience, not logic. Therefore, one always perceives a configuration, not single specifics, a total picture, not part of a picture. This means that facial expressions, gestures, body posture, tone of voice, cultural and social setting — in short, the total environment — cannot be dissociated from the spoken language. In fact, without such referents, the spoken word has no real meaning and cannot effectively communicate. One cannot communicate a word without the whole man coming with it.

3.   We also know that one can only perceive what one is capable of perceiving. Stimulus cannot become communication without understanding. One has to talk to people in terms of their own experience, that is, one has to use an electrician's metaphors when talking to electricians, and so on. One can only communicate in the receiver's language and terms used must be experienced-based. It, therefore, does very little good to explain terms (eg, electrical) to people if the terms are not of their own experience. Such unfamiliar terms simply exceed their perception capacity.

The connection between experience, perception, and concept formation (cognition) in the learner, whether child or adult, is not separate. We cannot perceive unless we also conceive. Likewise, we cannot form concepts unless we can perceive. To communicate a concept is impossible unless it is within the perception of the receiver. Ergo, in communicating, whatever the medium, the 1st question has to be, "Is this communication within his range of perception — can he receive it?"

The "range of perception" is partly physiological and, thus, largely determined by the physical limitations of one's own body. But when we speak of communications the most important limitations on perception are usually affective and cognitive rather than physical.

That perception is conditioned by what we are capable of perceiving today is well known. Disagreements and conflicts are not so much over answers as simply over incongruities in perception between individuals and groups. One of the best examples of incongruity in perceptions is the old story about the blind men and the elephant. It will be recalled that every one of them, upon encountering the strange beast, felt one of the elephant's parts — his hide, his leg, his trunk — and each reported an entirely different conclusion to which each tenaciously held. There was no possibility of communication between them until each verified the experience of the other. This old tale illustrates why there is no possibility of communications unless we first know what the receiver, who is the true communicator, understands and can perceive.

Communications is expectations. As a rule we perceive what we want to perceive. We see largely what we want to see, and we hear largely what we want to hear. The unexpected and unwanted is usually not received at all. It is ignored or misunderstood, that is, misseen as the expected or misheard as the expected. This *selective-exposure hypothesis,* as it is known, is considered to be the single most important finding of communication research.

Scores of confirming research on the selective-exposure hypothesis have revealed that the human mind attempts to fit stimuli and impressions into a frame of expectations. The mind vigorously resists any attempt to make it "change its mind," ie, to perceive what it does not want to perceive. Thus, the hypothesis implies that as the intended communication becomes increasingly discrepant from the would-be receiver's preconception, the more resistance he will put up so as to neutralize or minimize its attitude change effect. To overcome the resistance to expectancy of perception nothing short of a "shock signal" will do. The use of gradual, incremental steps will not work.

Before we can effectively communicate, we must, therefore, know what the receiver expects to see and hear. Only then can we know whether communications can utilize his expectations — and what they are — or whether there is a need for a "shock of alienation," for an "awakening" that breaks through the receiver's expectations and forces him to acknowledge that the unexpected is happening.

Communications is involvement. Communication always makes demands. It always demands that the receiver become somebody, do something, believe something. It always appeals to motivation. If the communication fits in with the aspirations, beliefs, and values of the receiver, it is effective. But if the communication goes against an individual's aspirations, purposes, and values it is likely to be firmly resisted if received at all. Though it is a rare existential event it is possible for communication to bring about a conversion in personality of an individual through changing his aspirations, beliefs, and values (a vivid example is "the drug scene"). But since this infrequently happens there are few instances of communication unless the message can be keyed to the receiver's own values, at least to some degree.

The most effective communication process to prevent or resolve conflicts and problems, to give purpose and direction, is through the use of *dyadic* groups (groups of two), eg, doctor and patient, lawyer and client, shop foreman and union stewart, administrator and teacher, teacher and student.

Groups of two show markedly *dissimilar* characteristics to *similar* groups of larger size. Dyadic groups are markedly low on showing disagreement and unfriendly behavior but markedly high on showing tension and asking for information of the other. They appear to take extra care to avoid conflict and to persuade one another gently. In groups of larger sizes, either of 2 conflicting members can appeal to other persons in the group to combine with them or act as impartial judges. The pressure of a coalition or the pressure of somewhat impersonal group norms can be brought to bear. But in an isolated group of two, each member of the pair is unusually vulnerable to the other. This vulnerability to each other frequently resolves mistrust, leads to mutual understanding, and improves the likelihood of goal realization. This human phenomenon has extremely important implications for managers. When a manager senses a conflict with a superordinate, subordinate, or peer, with a student or a member of the community, more often than not, a quick arrangement for a tête-à-tête will mitigate, if not resolve, a conflict.

There is considerable merit for superordinates to employ elements of *Rogerian nondirective therapy techniques* in both dyadic and larger groups. The Rogerian method (so named for psychologist Carl R. Rogers) employs all the communication principles summarized by Drucker to varying degrees. In this method the superordinate makes every effort during the discussion to maintain an equalitarian relationship with the other person or persons; to basically be as positive and supportive as possible; to agree without compromising own principles whenever possible; to show friendly behavior. Such an approach aids the subordinate(s) to see himself and his position more clearly and to cause him to make these adjustments necessary to give himself a positive self-image. This "working through" also tends to make him feel positive about the superordinate because he is constantly accepted and reinforced in his attempts to express his feelings and to work toward a position that is in harmony with both his and the organization's goals. The superordinate keeps bringing the process back to the "early phase of nearly all problem-solving cycles" where friendly behavior and exchange of information predominate. The subordinate(s) does most of the talking but the superordinate talks a moderate amount. He also provides a sensitive, positive feedback on every remark of the subordinate he nonhypocritically can.

The superordinate especially concentrates on *repeating back* his interpretation of what a subordinate has said to serve as a mirror for the subordinate and to ensure that his own interpretation of the point presented is accurate. Only in this way will true, mutual understanding occur.

Communications and information are totally different though totally interdependent. Communication is perception, information is logic. Information, standing alone, is impersonal rather than interpersonal. The more information is freed from the human component of emotions, expectations, perceptions, and values the more valid, reliable and valuable does it become.

Communications are subject to gross biases and faulty perceptions. The problem, therefore, is how to glean pure and untainted information out of interpersonal relationships. All through history, the problem has been how to isolate the information content from an abundance of perception. Because of the conceptual work of the logicians, especially the symbolic logic of Bertrand Russell and Alfred North Whitehead, and because of technical advances made in automated data processing storage and retrieval, we now have an opposite problem. Now we have the problem of handling information per se, devoid of any communication content.

The requirements for effective information are the opposite of those for effective communication. Information is always specific whereas communication is always perceived as a configuration. The best information is economical in content. Anything beyond what is essential can mask the essence of what is needed. Embellishment does not enrich, it impoverishes.

Information presupposes communication. Information is always encoded. To be received, let alone to be used, the code must be known and understood by the receiver. Therefore, before communication can begin between the emitter and the receiver each must use the "common language" appropriate to the discussion — eg, "pedagese."

The logical implications of the 4 postulates of communication as perception, expectations, involvement, and communication as different from information, though perhaps simple and obvious, are at odds with current practice in organizations. Indeed, notwithstanding the fact that communication is at the very heart of our work as educators our communication skills are among the least developed of all professions.

Communication in Organizations

What, then, can our knowledge and our experience teach us about communication in organizations, about the reasons for our past failures, and about the prerequisites for success in the future?

1.   From time immemorial we have attempted, and continue to attempt, to communicate *downwards* — from superordinate to subordinate. This has not worked, nor does it work, nor will it ever work no matter how hard and intelligently we try to make it work. It has not worked nor will this practice ever work for the simple reason that it focuses on what we as the superordinate want to say (eg, superintendent to principal, principal to teacher, teacher to student). This procedure assumes, in other words, that the emitter communicates. But we know that all he does is utter. *Communication is the act of the receiver.* Past practices in all our formal "management" training programs (including teaching as well as administration courses) have largely concentrated on ways and means of assisting the "trainee" to become a more effective and capable communicator. But all one can communicate downward are commands (See Theory X, Chpt. 10). One cannot effectively communicate downward anything connected with understanding, let alone motivation. *This requires communication upward,* from those who perceive to those who want to reach their perception (eg, principal *to* superintendent, teacher *to* principal, student *to* teacher).

Managers still need to work on clarity in what they say and write. However, how we say something can only come after we have learned what to say. And this cannot be found out by "talking down to," no matter how well it is being done. Administrative bulletins, faculty bulletins, student bulletins, and the like, no matter how well done, will be a waste unless the writer knows what the receivers can perceive, expect to perceive, and want to do. They are a total waste unless they are based on the receiver's rather than on the emitter's perception.

2.   "Listening" is not enough either. Research findings by the Human Relations School of Elton Mayo reveal that listening alone is ineffective as a means of communication.

Certainly, listening is a prerequisite to communication. The superordinate should instead of starting out with what he wants to get across first find out what subordinates want to know, are interested in, are, in other words, receptive to. But the classical human relations prescription of being first a "good listener" is not adequate, and it cannot, by itself work. This fact may account for the reason why listening is not being widely used despite the popularity of the slogan — where it has been tried, it has failed to work.

Listening assumes that the subordinate can communicate whereas his superior cannot. This he obviously cannot do. Listening can result in as much misunderstanding and miscommunication as talking. Neither talking alone nor listening alone take into account the fact that *communication is involvement.* Listening does not bring out subordinate's desires and preferences, his aspirations and values. Listening may explain the reasons for misunderstanding. But it does not lay down a basis for understanding. These factors account for the fact that extrapolating certain aspects of the Rogerian method of nondirective therapy, previously discussed, to management is soundly based.

The preceding is not to say that listening is undesirable, any more than the futility of downward communications furnishes any argument against attempts to write well, to say things clearly and simply, and to speak the language of those whom one addresses rather than using one's own jargon. Indeed, the realization that communication must begin with the receiver rather than the emitter is fundamental to the concept of listening. But listening is only the starting point.

3.   Moreover, more and better information does not solve the communication problem. Rather, the more information the greater the communication gap is likely to be.

The more effective the information process the more impersonal and formal will it become, the more will it separate human beings. The consequence of impersonal and formal information systems is a dependence upon prior agreement on meaning and application, that is communications. Without communications, information is relegated to mere data. In absence of direct, personal face-to-face relations with other people communication cannot occur. Therefore, an effective MIS manager is even more concerned with the establishment of viable communication links and interfaces than efficient information links and interfaces.

The Information Explosion is the most compelling reason for improving communications. Information is responsible for the widening communications gap all around us — in the academic sector between boards of trustees and their chief executive, between administrators and faculty, between faculty and students (and between both of them and the administration). In other sectors conflicts exist between management and labor, blacks and whites, young and old, and so on. Information flows like a flood out of the television tube and the computer, but without a commensurate increase in communications.

Communications at Work

We now know that for true communication to have a chance it must start with the receiver of communications rather than from the emitter. In a hierarchical system communications must start upward. Downward communication cannot, does not, and will not work. Only *after* upward communications have successfully been established will downward communications have a chance. Downward communications must largely be reaction rather than action, response rather than initiative.

But we also know that it is not enough to listen. Upward communications must first be focused on something that *both* receiver and emitter can perceive, focused on something that is common to both of them. Moreover, it must be focused on the motivations, values, beliefs, and aspirations of the intended receiver.

One proven example of facilitating the communication process is for the superordinate to request his subordinates to think through and present to him their own conclusions as to what major contribution to the organization — or to the unit within the organization — the subordinates feel they should be expected to perform and thus be held accountable for. It likely will be found that what each subordinate comes up with is not what the superordinate expects. But the first aim of this exercise is to precisely bring out the divergence in perception between superordinate and each of his subordinates. The result is a perception which can be focused on what is real to each pair. To realize that they see the same reality differently is itself communication. (See Management Appraisal, Chpt. 14)

Second, in this approach, the intended receiver of communication, the subordinate in this one-to-one, face-to-face interaction with his superordinate, is given access to different levels of experience which will aid him to better understand decision making. Further, the subordinate is aided in better understanding problems associated with establishing priorities, the conflict between what one likes to do vis-à-vis the demands of a situation, and above all else understanding and accepting the need for being held accountable for a decision.

Discussion between subordinate and superordinate on the job perception of the former usually has several favorable results. The subordinate gains an understanding of the complexity of the superordinate's position and the realization that the complexity is not of the superordinate's making, but is inherent in the situation itself. Likewise, the superordinate gains an appreciation and understanding of his subordinate's perceptions and interests which can frequently be capitalized on, especially for ad hoc tasks. Finally, even if a "goodness of fit" (see Contingency Theory, Chpt. 10) cannot be fully achieved so that the perception of the subordinate's job by each is one and the same there is at least a realization where the differences lie — and why. Thus, greater sensitivity by the superordinate should result in the noncongruent areas of the subordinate's job duties and responsibilities and hence more effective results should be able to be brought forth.

Another example, that has had excellent results in an organizational situation, in which communication has been traditionally absent, is the performance appraisal coupled with the appraisal interview. Performance appraisal at the management level today is standard practice in large business and industrial organizations. But in education, formal performance appraisal is sporadically used. Moreover, the kind of performance appraisal used in the economic sector (to be discussed in Chapt. 14) is practically nonexistent in education. We know that most people want to know where they stand. One of the most common complaints of employees in organizations is that they are not being appraised, are not being told whether they are doing well or poorly, or what they can do to be more effective in their work.

Though "evaluation" forms may be filled out and sometimes given to an employee, an accompanying appraisal interview is infrequent. The exceptions are in organizations in which performance appraisals are considered more a communication's tool than a rating device. Where performance appraisal interviews are conducted implicit is, "What has this individual done well?," followed by "And, therefore, what should he be able to do well?" The interview then should be able to elicit "And what would he have to learn or to acquire to be able to get the most from his capacities and achievements?" With positive focusing, weaknesses are then seen as limitations to what the subordinate himself can do well and wants to do, rather than as defects. A proper conclusion to a properly conducted appraisal interview is not on what the subordinate should do so much as on what should the organization and superordinate do to capitalize on the subordinate's strengths and to minimize the effect of his weaknesses. In short, a successful appraisal interview ends with a communication which has meaning for *both* subordinate and superordinate.

The start of communication in organizations must be to get the intended receiver himself to try to communicate. To reiterate, this requires a focus on 1) the impersonal but common task, 2) on the intended receiver's achievements, aspirations, and values, and 3) the experience of accountability. Research has also revealed that communication will be considerably facilitated if the superordinate makes it a point to be seen often by his subordinates informally and in helping ways.

Communication in organizations demands that masses, whether they be employees or students, share in the responsibility of decisions to the fullest possible extent. (See Theory Y, Chpt. 10.) They must understand because they have been through it, rather than accept a decision because it has been explained to them. Effective communication is only in direct proportion to the involvement of those to be affected by any given decision. To be excluded is to be part of the problem, to be included is to be part of the solution.

The traditional defense of paternalism (Theory X) has always been "It's a complex organization; it needs the expert, the man who knows best." But paternalism, as research into motivation, learning, and perception has revealed, really can only work in a simple world. When people can understand what "Pater" does because they share his experiences and perceptions, then Pater can actually make the decisions for them. However, in our own exceedingly complex society, there is need for *shared* experiences in the decisions, or there will be no common perceptions, ergo, no communication, and, hence neither acceptance of the decisions, nor the ability to carry them out. The ability to understand presupposes prior communication. It presupposes agreement on meaning. The "Father knows best" syndrome, associated with an uncommonly large number of school administrators, is particularly resented by teachers. Since teachers have been entrusted with the professional responsibility of managing from 30 to 300 different young people each week, they feel entitled to full participation in professional decisions. We have seen what has happened since circa 1965 when teachers have not been given the opportunity to meaningfully participate in professional decision making. Once isolated and scattered, teacher strikes are no longer so isolated nor scattered. The chief issue of these strikes is frequently as much, or more, concerned with teacher involvement in professional decision making as over "bread-and-butter" issues. Indeed, the danger in some places now is not over the question whether teachers are to be involved in professional decision making but to what extent are *administrators* to be allowed to participate. To exchange one kind of autocracy for another can be no improvement. Instead, mutual respect and cooperation is needed. The theory and principles of communication are designed to facilitate this mutual respect and cooperation.

Exhibit 9-1 shows a communication system that was ratified by the academic staff of Prairie State College — a public, 2-year, comprehensive community college.

As Exhibit 9-1 shows, the communication system was designed to ensure broad participation by all elements of the college community, and to ensure that communication flowed upwards. This was accomplished by assuring initially that the chairman of each committee be a member of the faculty and to have the majority of members on each committee a member of the faculty.

Administrators serve as secretaries to each committee since they have secretarial help more readily available to them; but more importantly, this secretarial role results in faster action by the administration in support of faculty needs.

Exhibit 9-1

18 September 67

To: Academic Staff

From: Richard W. Hostrop and Glenn Schmitz

PROPOSED COMMUNICATIONS SYSTEM

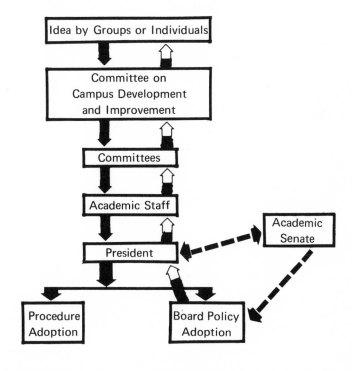

Ideas for campus development and improvement can be submitted by any group or individual in the College Community to the Committee on Campus Development and Improvement.

Exhibit 9-1—*Continued*

The Committee on Campus Development and Improvement is not a decision making body, except as decisions relate to the establishment of standing and/or ad hoc committees to meet the expressed needs of groups or individuals in the College Community. The CCDI will be responsible for selecting Committee members, following up of ideas that have been submitted to committees, receiving the minutes of committees for distribution to the College staff as a whole, assisting in the preparation of academic staff meeting agendas to insure that items which have gone through Committee reach the staff, and other activities which will assist in facilitating communications. The CCDI will insure that each idea or suggestion for campus development or improvement will be considered.

Finally, the CCDI will keep minutes of their meetings and a log of all ideas submitted, date of submission, where idea was considered and final disposition of the idea.

Committees which are formed will have a majority of faculty. A faculty member will be Chairman and an Administrator will be Secretary. Each committee will have one, but not more than one, Administrator. The foregoing procedures might be changed or modified depending upon expressions received by the Academic staff. The CCDI's final operating procedure is to be approved by the Academic staff as a whole before the first idea or suggestion is considered by them.

The Committee on Campus Development and Improvement will consist of seven members. They will include the following:

1	Administrator	(appointed by the President)
1	Student	(President of the Student Body)
1	Non-academic staff	(elected by the non-academic staff)
4	Faculty	(selected by the faculty)

It is requested that each faculty member register his preference as to what the qualifications of the selected faculty should be. The following qualifications have been suggested:

- ☐ Two senators and two new faculty
- ☐ Three senators and one new faculty
- ☐ Two division Chairmen and two faculty
- ☐ Three faculty and President of the Academic Senate
- ☐ Suggestion for some other combination (write in)

Exhibit 9-1—*Continued*

Please return any comments you might have on the proposal and your faculty membership preference to Mrs. Webber, non-academic library clerk in the Library no later than 1:00 p.m. on Tuesday, September 19th. Dr. Hostrop and Mr. Schmitz will pick up the returns at that time, will review the returns and will report the results at the next Academic staff meeting.

COMMENTS:

Finally, it is noteworthy that the final proposal to the academic staff was sent out under the joint auspices of the president of the college and the president of the academic senate as a *mutually* approved document.

In sum, there will be no communication if it is conceived as going from "me" to "you." Communication only works from one member of "us" to another. Communication cannot exist without cooperation, cooperation cannot exist without dialogue. Therefore, there can be no communication without dialogue. Communication is not a *means* of organization. Communication is a *mode* of organization.

Communication is the most important aspect of managing education for results. As a social instrument, education is wrapped up in the process of communication. Thus, education is communication and communication is education.

What has preceded, and what follows in the remainder of this book, assumes the reader's understanding that each topic presented is thoroughly permeated with communication as an integral and viable part of the topic.

Chapter 10

MANAGEMENT THEORIES

*Law 7: Communicate contemplated controversial actions beforehand to
superordinate and appropriate subordinates; communicate necessary
unavoidable surprise actions to them as soon thereafter as possible —*
Richard W. Hostrop

To make information useful there must be communication. To make communication effective it must be theory based. Without theory there is no
praxis. Management theories can transform information into communicative
action. In this chapter 4 theories of organizational management will be discussed: Theory X, Theory Y, Contingency Theory, and Situational Theory.
Each are in use to varying degrees depending upon the type of organization
and the characteristics of their decision-makers.

Theory X

Those in business and industry were among the first to recognize the need for
an altered concept of human nature in order to increase the effectiveness of
human organizations. The late Douglas Murray McGregor of the School of
Industrial Management at the Massachusetts Institute of Technology was to a
large extent the originator and the chief spokesman for many of these altered
views of the best way to employ the creative resources of human energy.

McGregor did not allow himself to fall into any semantic traps. He merely
called the conventional view "Theory X." The conventional, classical management point of view (Theory X) views the average person as lacking in ambition, as disliking work, and of preferring to be treated this way, so as to be
able to avoid responsibility.

The consequence of this conventional view is that people have to be persu-
aded, rewarded, punished, controlled, and their activities must be directed
toward organizational goals.

McGregor, in his writings (19), pointed out that most people who are treated
in this way play out the role expected of them in conformance with the expectations of Theory X — not as a consequence of inherent human nature,

but rather of the nature of the organization's philosophy, policies, and practices.

Though education probably has never operated quite as stringently under the assumptions of Theory X vis-à-vis the economic sector, nevertheless there are ample evidences that education has far from been immune from Theory X assumptions. Indeed, even today, there are enough evidences of Theory X assumptions operating in education as to be disquieting. Militant faculty unionism has not infrequently been one major outward consequence of Theory X application. Administrators who operate their educational organizations under Theory X assumptions can expect unionism to come where unionism does not now exist, and strikes to occur where unionism does exist. Of course, unions have been formed and strikes have occurred even where an enlightened administration did and does exist. But one thing is certain, faculties will not put up with the perceived paternalistic assumptions of Theory X, even when perceived as benign, any longer, anywhere.

But it is not only some administrators who treat faculty as if they "lacked ambition," as "disliking work," of "preferring to be treated this way" so as to be able to "avoid responsibility." Many faculty are equally guilty in relationship to their students. There are thousands of authoritarian classrooms across the national landscape. They are identified by the traditional factory system of education "in which the students are the depositories and the teacher is the depositor." In this necrologic "banking" system "instead of communicating, the teacher issues communiques and makes deposits which the students patiently receive, memorize, and repeat." (10:58)

Probably the single best example of Theory X assumptions at work today in our national life is in the military system. But, even here, some startling modifications of Theory X assumptions have occurred since circa 1970.

There may have been some valid reasons, if not valid assumptions, as to the desirability of operating under the assumptions of Theory X prior to the arrival of today's service-oriented society (as measured by greater GNP from services than from the production of goods). But if there ever were any valid reasons in the prior industrial and agricultural eras for operating economic and social institutions under the assumptions of Theory X, these reasons now seldom exist. . . . though admittedly, Theory X assumptions may occasionally be valid in certain individual cases under certain unusual conditions.

Theory Y

The classical Theory X management-by-directives approach in the economic sector began to be replaced by the "Theory Y" management-by-participation approach circa 1950 as the American economy began to move out of the industrial era into the new "service" era (also called "post industrial" era and "super industrial" era). Education, as the handmaiden of business and industry, also began to make a similar shift — but some 10 years later.

McGregor pointed out that people were treated as they were under Theory X assumptions under the mistaken notion of what is cause and what is effect. In light of what McGregor considered to be a mistaken notion, he offered Theory Y as a more accurate set of assumptions about human nature and motivation.

The assumptions of Theory Y are that people do not hate work; that people do not have to be forced or threatened; that motivation, potential for development, capacity for assuming responsibility, and readiness to direct behavior toward organizational goals are all present in most people. Management does not put these attitudes there. A responsibility of management, McGregor felt, is to create a climate in which people recognize and develop these human characteristics for themselves since people will only commit themselves to an organization to the extent that they can see ways of satisfying their own ego and development needs.

We can see Theory Y administratively at work in a number of enlightened educational systems and institutions. Most of the major universities of our land have operated their governance structure under Theory Y assumptions for years. This has been true, too, of the majority of 4-year colleges, and is becoming increasingly true in the 2-year colleges. Greater autocracy exists in secondary than in postsecondary education, but still there is strong movement there for greater collegiality, for more meaningful participation in the decision making process by those who are to be affected by the decisions made.

Where school governance practices tend to still be more Theory X than Theory Y oriented are in our elementary schools. The reason seems to be two-fold: elementary school teachers teach more hours per week than their professional counterparts in secondary and postsecondary education which leaves them with less time and less energy to demand a greater voice in decisions which affect them, and, secondly, the "plantation" chauvinism that has been allowed to thrive in elementary schools in which approximately 85 percent of the faculty are female but approximately 85 percent of the administrators are male. Yet, strangely, the situation is nearly reversed when the relationship between faculty and students is examined at the various levels of education. That is to say, as one ascends the educational ladder the more apt students are likely to be treated under the assumptions of Theory X rather than Theory Y. In secondary and postsecondary education the banking concept of education reigns supreme:

the teacher teaches and the students are taught

the teacher knows everything and the students know nothing

the teacher thinks and the students are thought about

the teacher chooses and enforces his choice, and the students comply

the teacher acts and the students have the illusion of acting through the action of the teacher

the teacher chooses the course content, and the students (who were not consulted) adapt to it

the teacher lectures, the students take notes, with the ideas passing through the brains of neither

student learning opportunities are neatly packaged lecture notes and a textbook, with the library standing not as a generic book, but as a study hall and social lounge

the teacher is the Subject of the learning process, while the students are mere objects

Certainly, there are notable exceptions to the perhaps too harsh preceding illustrations of Theory X in certain secondary and postsecondary classrooms. But the fact remains that though secondary and postsecondary faculty enjoy far more participation in determining the conditions of their working milieu than their colleagues in the elementary schools, the same participatory experience is not generally afforded their students. With "university without walls," "open education," "more options, less time," and similar educational ventures occurring, radical changes in secondary and postsecondary education are happening – and none too soon.

Where the bright implementation of Theory Y principles is occurring is in many of our elementary schools in the instructional area. Elementary education is getting well from its past "narration sickness" unlike its cousins. There has come a realization that "authentic education is not carried on by 'A' *for* 'B' or by 'A' *about* 'B,' but rather 'A' *with* 'B,' mediated by the world – a world which challenges both parties, giving rise to views or opinions about it." (10:82) This problem-posing education bases itself on creativity, and stimulates a true praxis upon reality. We see this learner-centered, Theory Y-based education in our better "open classrooms."

The principles of Theory Y at work in the instructional area of a school can be notably seen in the elementary schools of North Dakota and the infant schools of England whence the open classroom concept came. In such schools, the teacher is a true learning manager and the principal a true school manager. And Theory Y is systematized from principal through student and back again.

For the anti-dialogical, Theory X banking instructor, the question of content simply concerns the program about which he will discourse to his students; and he answers his own question, by organizing his own program. But for the dialogical, Theory Y problem-posing instructor-student, the program content of education is neither a gift nor an imposition — bits of information to be deposited in the students — but rather making organized, systematized, and developed "pure" information available to students who want to know more about any given thing. Each individual student, rather than the instructor, then synthesizes this information which he makes real for himself.

What needs to be done in education is to more widely implement Theory Y principles in the classrooms of secondary and postsecondary education, and in the governance structures of elementary school education. In short, the dialogue of education must be the practice of freedom — both inside and outside the classroom.

The premise of sound *educational* management which this book rests on is Theory Y — but with the added refinements of *Contingency Theory* and the *Situational Theory of Management*.

Contingency Theory

In 1969 Paul R. Lawrence and Jay W. Lorsch presented a refinement of McGregor's management theories. They called their approach to organization development "Contingency Theory," which they defined as "the fit between task, organization and people." (16:2)

The theoretical assumptions undergirding the Contingency Theory emphasize that the appropriate pattern of an organization is *contingent* upon the nature of the work to be done and upon the particular needs of the people involved. The assumptions of Contingency Theory are:

1.   Human beings bring varying patterns of needs and motives into the work organization, but one central need is to achieve a sense of competence.

2.   The sense of competence motive, while it exists in all people, may be fulfilled in different ways by different people depending on how this need interacts with the strengths of the individuals' other needs — such as those for power, independence, structure, achievement, and affiliation.

3. Competence motivation is most likely to be fulfilled when there is a fit between task and organization.

4. A sense of competence continues to motivate even when a competence goal is achieved; once one goal is reached, a new, higher one is set.

An important implication of the Contingency Theory is that managers must not only seek a fit between organization and task, but also between task and people, and between people and organization. Thus, an organization functions best which tailors itself to fit the task *and* the people. If achieved, more effective performance and a higher sense of competence results. Reinforcing feelings of competence by providing the climate for successful performance is a more consistent and reliable motivator than salary and benefits — "nothing succeeds like success."

In sum, any adequate theory of motivation and organization has to take into account the contingent relationship between task, organization, and people.

The Situational Theory of Management

Theory Y emphasizes the importance of creating conditions in which individuals are able to participate in the solution of problems (learning). The Contingency Theory adds a refinement by emphasizing the importance of creating conditions in which individuals are able to exhibit competence (success). The importance of the Situational Theory of management lies in its highlighting the importance of management *individualizing,* rather than generalizing, its approaches to organizational situations.

The situational approach to management is a basic, logical process which has been adapted to all areas of management theory as a means to provide a more orderly and scientific basis for approaching problem solving, decision making, and action in all areas of management.

Fundamentally, the situation approach boils down to a basic management process:

1. Diagnose any given situation to define its basic problems and parameters, to clarify management objectives, and to identify a solution technique.

2. Study the facts of the situation to isolate the key factors affecting decision making.

3. Develop alternative courses of action.

4.   Evaluate each alternative to determine which one best meets the specific requirements of the situation.

5.   Convert the evaluation into action that will effectively further the educational system's goals and objectives.

Using this approach, a manager can draw freely on every area of management theory and research. Thus, Situational Theory is a *unifying* concept within management thinking. It applies what seems to be the best theory and research information available to any given situation rather than try to fit *every* situation under the umbrella of a *single* theory. In some instances Theory X may be the only valid assumption which can be acted on — but this would be a most rare valid assumption insofar as professional educators are concerned. The Contingency Theory is more useful insofar as educators are concerned. Educators are highly motivated to do even better when their competencies are formally and informally recognized. The Contingency Theory, with its emphasis on the contingent relationship between task, organization, and people, is also of value to educators by nature of the complexity of problems educators face, yet, perhaps not of as great a value in this aspect as would be true in some other sectors of society in which the personnel have more heterogeneous functions to perform. Theory Y would seem to be of particular value to educational managers with its assumptions that individuals like to participate and work. What the Situational Theory does for us is to remind us that there is not a one way, or an only way, of organizing for every situation.

Research has shown that certain types of workers actually respond best to firm, autocratic leadership. Others, as in professional education, respond best to democratic leadership. Research further shows that participative management does not work best in all situations, though it does in most educational ones.

Situational Theory begins first with the situation rather than the personnel involved. The situation is analyzed rather than the individuals per se. Once the situation has been boiled down, the basic management process begins as shown at the beginning of this section. Though this approach makes greater demands on decision makers than a neat, single approach would, the result is to merge theory with practice. This merging usually results in the best possible decision being made under any given set of conditions.

Management Theories at Work in Education

To act on the theories discussed in this chapter requires that managers *really* get to know those they work with. It requires getting to know what individuals can do well, what they enjoy doing, what their strengths and weaknesses are, and what they want and need from their profession (or studies in the case of students). It then behooves the manager to create an organization designed to cope with situations rather than one designed only to handle housekeeping chores. The *only* excuse for an organization is to maximize the chance that each individual, working with others, will achieve growth from his job. People cannot truly be motivated externally. That door is locked from the inside. What a good manager *can* do is to create a climate in which individuals will motivate themselves. This is done by permitting educators to participate in the decision making process. This is done by superordinates reinforcing the competencies of subordinates through genuine recognition and praise. When educators are permitted to participate, and are given deserved recognition, they will help their educational system and/or institution achieve its objectives and goals — objectives and goals in which they had a hand in setting.

With respect to students, we see Theory X operating where the lecture/text and chalk/talk method prevails. We see Theory Y and Contingency Theory operating in open classroom learning situations. Finally, we see Situational Theory at work where case studies and role playing simulations are employed.

Theory X, Theory Y, Contingency Theory, and the Situational Theory of management provide the *modus operandi* by which various organizations operate. Within the modus operandi is the link of communication which ties people together in an organization. The theories themselves are *communication theories* of the first order for they set the very conditions and rules by which communication is to occur.

Part I emphasized the need for setting goals and their support objectives. Part II has introduced some of the theories, techniques, and tools for setting and implementing goals and objectives. Part III will discuss concrete principles and practices by which managers can manage more effectively so as to achieve system goals and objectives.

PART III

MANAGEMENT PRINCIPLES AND PRACTICES

Chapter 11

MANAGEMENT IN EDUCATION

*A human soul without Education is like marble in the quarry, which shows
none of its inherent beauties till the skill of the polisher fetches out the
colors, and discovers the ornamental clouds that run through the body of
it. Education draws out to view every talent and virtue which without such
help would never be able to make their appearance* – Anon

Illustrations of management at work have been presented in Part I and Part II.
It has been pointed out that where precise descriptive goals and measurable
objectives have *not* been set, administration rather than management exists.
Where such aids as Delphi, PERT, PPBS, OR, MIS, and communication and
management theories are *not* being used, administration rather than management exists. Conversely, where these elements do exist, management rather
than administration exists.

The distinction between administration and management can be further
illuminated by their functions. Administration pertains to directing, organizing,
and executing. Management, on the other hand, has 3 aspects in which administration is but *one* of its functions. Besides *administration,* management
is equally involved in *planning* (conceptual thinking) *and leadership.* In short,
the functional responsibilities of management alone determine the success or
failure of an enterprise.

Management at Work

As but one illustration of the assertion that it is management alone that
determines the success or failure of an enterprise, the *Avis Car Rental Story*
is particularly noteworthy. In 1962 after 13 years Avis had *never* made a
profit. Three years later, under a new chief executive, Robert Townsend, the
company had grown internally (not by acquisitions) from $30 million in sales
to $75 million in sales, and had made successive annual profits of $1 million,
$3 million, and $5 million. Even more revealing is the fact that Townsend
kept the same management team that had been at Avis before his arrival. He
only brought in 2 outside people, a lawyer and an accountant. Townsend
says, "I ascribe it all to my application of Theory Y." (25:141) There are
notable examples of similar, effective managerial leadership in the education

sector: eg, Newman Walker (K-12), Robert Lahti (2-year college), James Dixon (4-year College), Father Theodore Hesburgh (university), Harold Grant (counseling), Robert Heinich (educational technology), Kenneth Shaffer (libraries), and Samuel Postlethwait (teaching).

The Nature of Management

The emergence of management in the 20th century as an essential, a distinct and a leading institution is a pivotal event in social history. Peter F. Drucker has said, "Rarely, if ever, has a new basic institution, a new leading group, emerged as fast as has management since the turn of the century. Rarely in human history has a new institution proven so indispensable so quickly; and even less often has a new institution arrived with so little opposition, so little disturbance, so little controversy." (8:3-4) Plainly, the time for management has arrived.

The skilled manager provides the dynamic, life-giving element in every enterprise. Without such leadership the "resources of production" (teachers in the educational enterprise) are inhibited resources able to provide only limited production.

Management is rooted in the very nature of democratic Western institutions. It expresses the belief in the possibility of creating a near utopian society through systematic organization of economic and social resources. Management is the instrument specifically charged with making the resources productive.

Despite its crucial importance, its high visibility, and its widespread acceptance, management is the least known and least understood of our basic institutions. The public and even faculty often do not know what their managers (administrators) do, are supposed to be doing, how they act and why, whether they are doing a good job or not.

The term "management" or "administrator" is often seen as little more than a euphemism for "the boss." Another view is someone who directs the work of others and, therefore, "does his work by getting other people to do theirs." But these views do not describe what management is and what it does. An analysis of management can only be described and defined through its function.

Management is the specific organ or instrument of an enterprise. The reason for its existence is to supply economic goods and services in the economic sphere, to prevent and deliver destruction in the military sphere, to provide an organized means for worship in the religious sphere, to facilitate learning in the educational sphere, to "referee," balance justice, and to provide social services in the governmental sphere. Management, in any of these given spheres of society, must always have every decision and action based first of all on its raison d'être. Otherwise management has failed to deliver. By-products must be considered incidental to economic performance, defense capability, facilitating religious fulfillment, learning mastery, or balancing equities for the "good life" for all. Good management focuses on ends, out-puts, results — not inputs, activity, processes. Management can only justify its existence and authority by the results it produces.

Managing education for results. The foremost definition of management is that it is the *specific* instrument of an enterprise used to achieve positive end results. In education this means that every act, every decision, every delibera-tion of management has as its first dimension a learning results dimension. For *learning is the single common product of every dimension and every level of education.*

However, this apparently obvious definition of management leads to con-clusions that are far from being obviously or generally accepted. It implies both severe limitations on the scope of management and manager (and should be), and yet a major responsibility and opportunity for truly creative action.

Though management can never be an exact science for the simple reason that humans are not constant materials, nevertheless the work of a manager can be systematically analyzed and classified; there are, in other words, distinct pro-fessional features and a scientific aspect to management. Nor is managing a school district or building, a college or university, or a classroom or a library just a matter of hunch or native ability; its elements and requirements can be analyzed, can be organized systematically, can be learned by any profes-sional in the educational enterprise. This book assumes that a manager can improve his performance in all areas of management, including the managing of a school district, school building, a college, a university, a classroom, a counseling center, or a library. Improvement can be achieved by a manager at any level through the systematic study of principles and their applications, the acquisition of organized knowledge, and the systematic analysis by the manager of his own performance in all areas of his work and job. Indeed, nothing else can contribute so much to his skill, his effectiveness, and his performance. And underlying this proposition is the conviction that the impact of the manager on modern society and its citizens is so great as to require of him the utmost self-discipline, responsibility, creativity, and high standards of public service as to be expected of a true professional. And yet the ultimate test of effective management is measurable performance. Achieve-ment demonstrated through *measurable* results rather than knowledge remains, of necessity, both aim and proof. In short, management is more a practice than a science or a profession, though containing elements of each.

The scope and extent of educational management's authority and responsibility, as has been pointed out, is limited largely to learning results. But it is also true that in order to discharge its educational responsibility management must exercise substantial social and governing authority within the enterprise – authority over the "raw products," its students, in their capacity as essential components of the enterprise. It is also a fact that because of the importance of the educational enterprise, management has inevitably become one of the leading groups in today's society. Since management's responsibility is always founded in learning performance, however, it has no authority except as is necessary to discharge its learning responsibility (and the important adjuncts of research and community services). To assert authority for management over the citizen and his affairs beyond that growing out of management's responsibility is usurpation of that authority. Furthermore, educational management can only be one leading group among several. It has partial rather than total social responsibility – hence, partial rather than comprehensive social authority.

Though management's scope and potential are limited, it nevertheless also embodies a major responsibility for creative action. For management has to *manage.* And managing is not just passive, adaptive behavior; it means taking action to make the desired results come to pass.

Though it is always important to adapt to changing economic and social conditions rapidly, intelligently, and rationally, managing goes way beyond mere reaction and adaptation. Explicit is the responsibility for attempting to shape the educational environment in anticipation of changing economic and social needs of the citizenry. While man can never really totally "master" his environment, since he is always held within a tight vise of constraints, it is management's specific job to make what is desirable first possible and then actual. Management is not just a creature of the environment; it is its creator as well. And in education only to the extent to which it masters the learning circumstances, and alters them by conscious, directed action, does management really manage. To manage a school district or a school building, a college or a university, a classroom, counseling center, or a library therefore means to *manage-by-objectives* so as to be capable of achieving measurable results toward the achievement of system goals and objectives.

Exhibit 11-1 visually summarizes the multi-faceted functions of management. It provides a unified concept of managerial functions and activities. It makes clear the distinctions between administering, planning, and leading – the 3 functions of management.

Management Efficiency and Productivity

It should again be noted that the *internal* efficiency of an educational system is defined by the relationship of its output to its inputs. And *external* productivity is defined as the ultimate benefit accruing to students and society from earlier educational investments (inputs). The challenge to management is to choose just the right array and amount of each input (teachers, paraprofessionals, materials, techniques, and the like) so as to achieve the maximum amount of learning using the minimum amount of time and money.

Unlike the economic sector, educators until about 1970 almost totally resisted incentive pay of any kind. Merit pay, differentiated staffing and the like have been resisted not only by professional staff in the United States but nearly everywhere else except in Yugoslavia. Yet, the concept of accountability for educational results mandates that teacher organizations look anew at incentive rewards. Already there are teachers in Arizona, Michigan, and elsewhere who have entered into internal performance contracts with their top management for measurable learning results. The results have been paid for in cold, hard cash.

Performance contracting is not the only scheme in which educators have been prodded to demonstrate accountability for educational results. In 1972 the nation's first operational educational voucher plan went into effect in Alum Rock, California. Like performance contracting, educational vouchers are designed to provide educational alternatives which show promise for increasing efficiency and productivity.

Still another scheme for increasing efficiency and productivity is the year-round school, particularly the "45-15 plan," first initiated on a total system-wide basis in Romeoville, Illinois in 1970. The 45-15 plan has made it possible for staff to work from 9 to 12 months at proportionate pay. The plan has resulted in fewer teachers being employed, thus reducing a variety of fixed charges. It also has meant cutting long-term indebtedness by a third since one-third fewer classrooms are needed through year-round utilization of existing facilities.

Yet another scheme being given serious consideration by a number of educators are the number of years of required schooling there should be. Persuasive arguments have been put forth for a 10-year common school curriculum leading to a high school diploma, and a 3-year curriculum for a bachelor's degree. Advocates believe there would be no real learning loss by certain eliminations, some tightening up, and a careful restructuring of the remaining educational offerings.

Exhibit 11-1

R. Alec Mackenzie,
"The Management Process in 3-D,"
Harvard Business Review,
November-December 1969.
Reprinted with copyright permission.

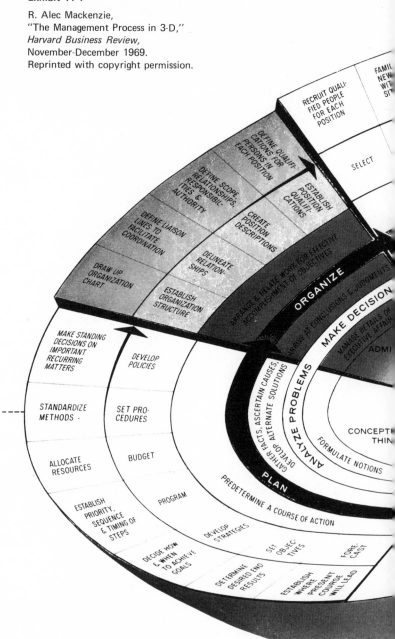

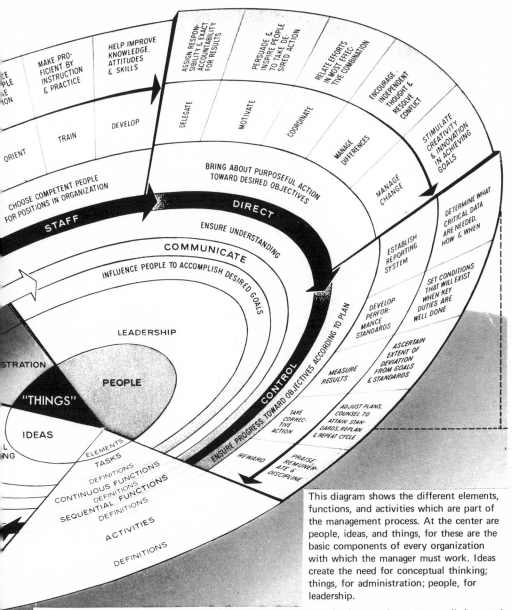

MAKE PROFICIENT BY INSTRUCTION & PRACTICE

HELP IMPROVE KNOWLEDGE. ATTITUDES & SKILLS

ASSIGN RESPONSIBILITY & EXACT ACCOUNTABILITY FOR RESULTS

PERSUADE & INSPIRE PEOPLE TO TAKE DESIRED ACTION

RELATE EFFORTS IN MOST EFFECTIVE COMBINATION

ENCOURAGE INDEPENDENT THOUGHT & RESOLVE CONFLICT

ORIENT

TRAIN

DEVELOP

DELEGATE

MOTIVATE

COORDINATE

MANAGE DIFFERENCES

STIMULATE CREATIVITY & INNOVATION IN ACHIEVING GOALS

CHOOSE COMPETENT PEOPLE FOR POSITIONS IN ORGANIZATION

BRING ABOUT PURPOSEFUL ACTION TOWARD DESIRED OBJECTIVES

MANAGE CHANGE

STAFF

DIRECT

ENSURE UNDERSTANDING

DETERMINE WHAT CRITICAL DATA ARE NEEDED, HOW & WHEN

COMMUNICATE

ESTABLISH REPORTING SYSTEM

INFLUENCE PEOPLE TO ACCOMPLISH DESIRED GOALS

SET CONDITIONS THAT WILL EXIST WHEN KEY DUTIES ARE WELL DONE

DEVELOP PERFORMANCE STANDARDS

LEADERSHIP

ASCERTAIN EXTENT OF DEVIATION FROM GOALS & STANDARDS

STRATION

PEOPLE

"THINGS"

MEASURE RESULTS

CONTROL

ADJUST PLANS, COUNSEL TO ATTAIN STANDARDS, REPLAN & REPEAT CYCLE

IDEAS

TAKE CORRECTIVE ACTION

ENSURE PROGRESS TOWARD OBJECTIVES ACCORDING TO PLAN

L

NG

ELEMENTS

TASKS

PRAISE, REMUNERATE & DISCIPLINE

REWARD

DEFINITIONS

CONTINUOUS FUNCTIONS

DEFINITIONS

SEQUENTIAL FUNCTIONS

DEFINITIONS

ACTIVITIES

DEFINITIONS

This diagram shows the different elements, functions, and activities which are part of the management process. At the center are people, ideas, and things, for these are the basic components of every organization with which the manager must work. Ideas create the need for conceptual thinking; things, for administration; people, for leadership.

Three functions—problem analysis, decision making, and communication—are important at all times and in all aspects of the manager's job; therefore, they are shown to permeate his work process. However, other functions are likely to occur in predictable sequence; thus, planning, organizing, staffing, directing, and controlling are shown in that order on one of the bands. A manager's interest in any one of them depends on a variety of factors, including his position and the stage of completion of the projects he is most concerned with. He must at all times sense the pulse of his organization. The activities that will be most important to him as he concentrates—now on one function, then on another—are shown on the outer bands of the diagram.

Principles of Educational Systems

There are 7 basic principles associated with applying a systems analysis as a strategy for maximizing learning output while minimizing input costs. They are:

1. *The principle of individual differences* tells us that students vary enormously with respect to individual aptitudes, rates of learning, and ways of learning; hence each individual will learn best when the means and conditions of learning are flexibly adapted to his particular pace and learning style. Conversely, when a teaching-learning system is extensively used which tacitly ignores these wide individual differences, the educational efficiency of the system is bound to militate against optimum conditions. Teachers, in particular, as managers of learning, govern this principle.

2. *The principle of self-instruction* says that every student, whatever his aptitudes, has an inherent curiosity and capacity for learning a great deal on his own, provided he is properly motivated and guided, and is given access to the full range of the Generic Book (all of man's learning possibilities) in attractive and digestible form. Conversely, the student who is lock-stepped into a system in which every student "digests" the same content from the same book at the same time will be dehumanized; his natural curiosity to learn will be suppressed and even destroyed if he is exposed over long periods to conditions which cause him to associate "learning" with dullness, monotony, and irrelevance. Psychologists have long ago learned that he who learns best takes an active part in the learning process. This is why the "open classroom" and programmed instruction are especially effective. The classroom manager, the teacher, chiefly governs the principle of individualizing learning.

3. *The principle of combining human energies and physical resources* states very simply that the work accomplished by a human being (teacher or student) can be greatly increased by placing sufficient and better tools and technologies at his disposal, and teaching him how to use these to best advantage. Conversely, if teachers continue to "talk and chalk" and "lecture and text" as has largely been true for half-a-millenium or more, then we cannot honestly expect much further improvement to come from formal schooling — the net learning gains are likely to occur at a faster rate from nonformal education, eg, television. But teachers are far from being responsible alone for this condition. Administrators are responsible, in conjunction with teachers, in providing in-service training programs on learning how to effectively and efficiently combine human and physical resources in the most optimum way to maximize student learning. Administrators are responsible for providing the necessary materials and to ease the interaction of students into the

external environment (field trips, resource persons, work-experience programs and the like).

4.   *The principle of economies of scale* reminds us that large scale operations usually result in less cost per student than small scale operations even when more expensive facilities and equipment are involved. What may be prohibitively expensive on a small scale (eg, one small institution renting a computer) may be economically feasible on a large scale (eg, several small institutions joining together in renting a computer). What the optimum size may be for any activity must be carefully audited using sophisticated research tools. Boards of trustees and administrators are chiefly responsible for the results of this principle.

5.   *The principle of division of labor* says that if people with differing kinds and degrees of special interests and competencies break a complex job into its component parts, and if each person then handles the parts that best match his interests and skills, each performs at his highest productivity, and the net result will be greater. Conversely, those who try to manage a complex task alone are unlikely to achieve an optimum result. The implications of this principle are equally valid for both administrators and teachers. It means for most complex administrative problems that a task force is more likely to come up with an optimum solution than a single administrator attempting to solve the problem alone. It means, for example, that team teaching is more likely to maximize learning results than the traditional self-contained classroom approach.

6.   *The principle of concentration and critical mass* refers to the fact that it is wasteful to embark upon certain learning objectives unless they are going to be pursued beyond some minimum point of intensity and continuity, short of which the effort will have little, if any, worthwhile "pay-off." Conversely, concentrating and critically massing resources and efforts toward achieving a predetermined objective beyond some minimum point of intensity is likely to result in a worthwhile pay-off. Though both administrators and teachers need to apply this principle, it typically involves activities more often for which administrators are to be held accountable.

7.   *The principle of optimizing* states that whenever several different components are combined in a productive "system," it is never possible for every component to be used to its theoretical maximum productivity, but the optimum overall results will be achieved when the components are combined in such proportions as to use the scarcest and more expensive components most intensively, and the more abundant and less expensive ones less intensively. Optimizing an educational system or subsystem involves a process of "trade-offs" designed to achieve the best combination of good learning results

on the one hand, and tolerable economic costs on the other. The optimum arrangement from a purely economic point of view rarely coincides with the optimum arrangement from an educational point of view; thus in practice the most satisfactory compromise must be sought. Converse practice can result in maximum learning at prohibitive cost, or, even worse, maximum savings at the cost of little learning. The principle of optimizing is largely under the control of administrators. They, therefore, are largely responsible for the results flowing from this principle.

The preceding 7 principles have been known and used in practice by a growing nucleus of school systems beginning about 1960. Some of the practical results flowing from these principles involve the following:

Reduction of school construction costs

Redeployment and more intensive utilization of available space

Sharing of expensive school facilities and specialized personnel

Lengthening of school hours

Inaugurating year-round schooling

Performance contracting

Educational vouchers

Consolidation of undersized educational units

Spread of the "Open Classroom" concept

Development of "Open Universities"

Introduction of Delphi, PERT, PPBS, OR, MIS, and MBO into education along with other modern management practices

Use of teacher aides and other paraprofessionals

Employing team teaching, modular scheduling, "classrooms without walls," and the like

Use of newer forms of educational technology — television, CAI, CMI, programmed instruction, dial access, audio and video cassettes, and the like

Greater emphasis on well-planned interdisciplinary and self-instruction programs

Introduction of the concept of accountability into education

The foregoing, in some instances, suggests some significant changes from conventional administrative practices. Others can be implemented with relative ease. All the foregoing unquestionably, when imaginatively and vigorously applied, can achieve considerable gains. We need not only the best of the tested traditional procedures, but such promising newer ones as have been cited in this chapter. Added to the best of the older, and the promise of the newer ones, are the *nonformal* educational practices. These include such learning experiences as viewing television, traveling, working, and having discussions with peers, siblings, parents, and admired older persons. Nonformal education probably provides the highest learning ratio to cost of any of the formal procedures. Obviously, nonformal education is less costly than formal education — but nonformal education seldom can provide as complete or as rounded an education as the individual and society needs.

As Chapter 11 has shown, management is a complex process. It has innumerable facets. But it can be efficient and productive. It provides the means for achieving the kinds of results that really count. This chapter has particularly focused on the process of management. In the next chapter, the focus will shift to the managers themselves.

Chapter 12

MANAGERS OF EDUCATION

When the best manager's work is done the people shout, "We did it ourselves!" – paraphrasing Lao-tzu

In this chapter 3 major topics will be discussed: what managers are; who are the education managers; what education managers do. The importance of these topics lies in the fact that effective management can be learned just as any other skill. The effective manager acquires his skills more through training and experience than through innate aptitude.

What Managers Are

There are a number of definitions and characteristics which are commonly used to describe what managers are. Few definitions, of and in themselves, are adequate, however. Management is too complex a task for 1 simple definition to do.

The standard definition of a manager is one who is in charge of other people and their work. This definition is too narrow because the *first* responsibility of a manager is *upward* to his superordinate, to the enterprise whose instrument he is, to the system's goals and objectives. The manager's relationship to his superiors and peers is as essential to his effective performance as are his relations and responsibilities to those who report to him.

Another distinguishing characteristic usually given to denote a manager is his so-called "importance." But there are few enterprises in which everyone is not important. In most instances the absence of a custodian, a secretary, or a teacher is markedly felt by an institution – usually more significantly so over the short term than even the absence of the chief executive.

A common idea of what defines a manager is his rank and pay. But this does not necessarily distinguish a manager from others either. For example, the school district plumber may earn a higher annual salary than the elementary school principal. The superintendent of buildings and grounds may not be a "professional" either, yet his management responsibilities and salary may be substantially greater than that of many academic administrators.

In the final analysis, what distinguishes the manager from the nonmanager is his *educational* contribution. The manager is uniquely expected to give others vision and to provide the climate for them to effectively perform their jobs.

Who Education Managers Are

Managers of education include school, college, and university trustees through chief educational officers to administrators, teachers, counselors, educational technologists, librarians, and other professional knowledge workers.

Trustees manage their chief executive. He in turn manages his administrators. They in turn manage teachers, counselors, educational technologists, librarians, and other professional knowledge workers. Most of the latter knowledge workers manage students.

It cannot be overstressed that most nonadministrative educational professionals, like administrators, are managers. Teachers, for example, are in charge of students and their assignments. Teachers enjoy professional esteem. Most importantly, teachers are expected to give students vision and the opportunity to perform to the best of their capacities. Counselors, educational technologists, librarians, and some other knowledge workers have similar relationships to students.

Increasingly, superior *education managers can be distinguished by their acceptance of personal accountability for achieving measurable results.* Trustees are beginning to insist that their chief executive officer be able to demonstrate positive measurable outputs for the measurable inputs of time and dollars that are allocated to the educational enterprise. In turn, the chief executive is insisting upon the quantification of results down through the system. As a result, teachers are increasingly specifying performance objectives for their students so as to be able to demonstrate learning mastery. The counseling office is being asked to prove that their function makes a difference by documenting decreased dropout rates. Educational technologists are having to demonstrate that the professional staff are learning and using "systems" tools. Librarians are being asked to provide more sophisticated circulation figures in support of large budget requests traditional of libraries.

In sum, every educational professional is a potential educational manager, no matter what his title might happen to be. The true education manager is distinguished from the traditional administrator by 1) giving others vision and the opportunity to perform their jobs effectively, and 2) accepting personal accountability for achieving established measurable results.

What Education Managers Do

H. Igor Ansoff and R. G. Brandenburg list 3 activities which distinguish managers from nonmanagers:

> They administer
>
> They plan
>
> They lead (1:61)

George S. Odiorne suggests 4 major tasks of managers:

> They accept responsibility for what their subordinates do
>
> They make things happen
>
> They organize
>
> They are oriented towards results and responsibility (21:10-11)

Peter F. Drucker suggests 5 characteristics associated with what effective managers do:

> They know where their time goes
>
> They focus on outward contribution (needs of society)
>
> They build on their own strengths, the strengths of their superiors, colleagues, and subordinates
>
> They concentrate on a few major areas where superior performance will produce outstanding results
>
> They make decisions (7:23-24)

These descriptions by Ansoff and Brandenburg, by Odiorne, and Drucker as to what effective managers do make it readily apparent that most knowledge workers' jobs can be classified as managerial in theory if not in practice. Most of the characteristics given apply to *effective* knowledge workers most of the time. In short, a manager is distinguished from an administrator by the fact that he is a leader who moves his organization or unit towards goals and objectives that he has planned and initiated, whereas an administrator is one who strives to keep what has already been established running smoothly.

Managers are responsible for leadership contributions that materially affect the capacity of the organization to perform effectively so as to obtain desired results. By virtue of their work managers are expected to make a significant impact on the performance and results of the whole. Drucker puts it thusly:

"The manager has the task of creating a true whole that is larger than the sum of its parts, a productive entity that turns out more than the sum of the resources put into it." (8:341)

In addition to maximizing results, managers harmonize every decision and action to the requirements of both the immediate needs and the long-range future goals of the organization.

There are 4 basic operations necessary for educators to perform so as to maximize results and to harmonize immediate and long-range goals. Education managers:

Establish precise goals and measurable objectives

Evaluate progress toward predetermined goals and objectives

Organize

Motivate and communicate

Strengthen superordinates, peers and subordinates

The manager has a specific tool: information. He does not "handle" people; he motivates, guides, organizes others to do their own work be they sub-administrators, teachers, or students. The manager's effectiveness depends upon his ability to listen and to read, on his ability to speak and to write.

Managers spend a great deal of time thinking through the establishment of measurable objectives as well as systematically thinking through what to do about recurrent problems.

The most effective managers spend more hours on *upward* than on downward communication. That is, they listen more to subordinates than talking *to* them. The principal encourages teachers to discuss impediments to their success in the classroom more than he directs them. The teacher organizes his class more around student activities and discussion than on lecturing. The counselor listens more to students than offering advice. The educational technologist and the librarian seek out students and teachers to ascertain their curricular problems rather than passively waiting for them to come to them.

The manager who utilizes his time well also spends a great deal of time considering his superordinate's problems, and on thinking what he can do to contribute to his success and the success of the entire system. In short, to be a manager means accepting responsibility for the success of one's superordinate as well as accepting the responsibility for achieving success in one's own job. Each are inextricably interwoven and linked with the other. Likewise, managers accept accountability for the results of their subordinates — including students.

Managing means developing others. But in the process the manager is being developed in direct proportion to his success in developing others. Whether he develops his subordinates in desirable directions, helps them to grow, to become wiser and more ethical persons, will directly determine whether he himself will develop, will become wiser and a more ethical person.

The reader will find it helpful at this point to briefly return to Exhibit 11-1 in the previous chapter to review *The Management Process* chart. It will aid in synthesizing the commentary of the last chapter and the present one — and in the discussion on problem solving to follow. What is remarkable about Exhibit 11-1 is the fact that R. Alec MacKenzie who prepared the chart is a business man, not an educator. MacKenzie prepared The Management Process chart for business executives, rather than for academic executives. Yet, as the chart plainly shows, the processes of management are as applicable to the educational sector as to the economic sector — or in any other major sector of society for that matter.

Managers make decisions. Too often, however, managers make decisions on the wrong questions. Effective managers spend considerably more time on determining the right questions to ask than on finding the right answers which all too often are to the wrong questions. The right questions should usually pertain to recurring problems rather than responding to an immediate crisis which, more often than not, is rooted in fundamental questions that have not yet been clearly asked. Until the right questions are posed, crises administration will endure rather than preventive management.

The truly important decisions, the decisions that really matter, are *strategic* rather than tactical. Strategic decision making has 5 distinct phases, each of which must be carefully thought through: 1) defining the problem (a problem is the difference between what one has and what one wants); 2) analyzing the problem; 3) developing alternate solutions; 4) deciding upon the best solution; and 5) converting the decision into effective action. Each should be listed and written out so as to properly focus on the problem.

Effective decision making can be the manager's best means for solving the problem of time utilization. Time is necessary to define the problem, to analyze it, to develop alternate solutions, and to make the solution effective. But much less time is necessary or should be spent on finding the "right" solution. And any time spent on "selling" a solution after it has been reached is a waste and evidence of poor time utilization in the earlier problem-solving phases.

To arrive at the definition of the problem the manager begins by finding the "critical factor(s)." This is the element(s) in the situation that has to be changed before anything else can be changed, moved, acted upon. Two critical factors always inherent in every problem are: 1) how much improvement is needed over the current situation, and 2) within what period of time must the improvement be effected.

To analyze a problem it is necessary to classify it in order to know who must ultimately make the final decision, who must be consulted in making it, and who must be informed. There are 4 principles which need analysis in classifying any problem. They are: 1) the futurity of the decision (the time-span for which it commits the institution to a course of action and the speed with which the decision can be reversed; 2) the impact of the decision on other areas and functions; 3) the kinds of qualitative considerations that enter into it; and 4) the uniqueness or periodicity of the decision. These steps force the manager to see his own problem from the point of view of the entire institution and therefore are essential.

It can be seen from the foregoing that the first task in decision making is for a problem to be defined and classified — *not* to "get the facts." Definition and classification determine what facts need to be known as relevant to the problem needing solution. In solving a problem the manager asks: What information do I need to make this particular decision? He uses conceptual thinking.

It is unlikely that a manager will ever be able to get all the facts he should have. Most decisions are based on incomplete knowledge. Though it is not necessary to have all the facts to make sound decisions it is necessary to know what information is lacking in order to judge how much of a risk the decision involves, as well as the degree of precision and rigidity that the course of action can afford.

Alternative solutions are the only means of bringing our basic assumptions up to the conscious level, forcing ourselves to examine them and to test their validity. Moreover, alternative solutions are our only means to mobilize and to train the imagination, to produce creative innovations. They are at the very heart of what is meant by the "scientific method." One alternative consideration should always be to take no action on the problem at all. Sometimes any action is worse than no action at all.

With a problem defined, analyzed, and with alternative solutions considered, generally the best solution can then be determined. To aid the manager to pick the best solution among several (seldom should there be less than at least 3 alternatives) there are 4 criteria he considers:

1.   *The risk.* The manager must weigh the anticipated defined gains of each course of action against the possible defined losses, in terms of odds, prior to any action being taken.

2.   *Economy of effort.* Which of the possible courses of action will achieve the requisite results with a minimum effort of time and/or money and with the least disturbance to the organizational unit and the institution.

3.   *Timing.* If the situation has great urgency, the preferable course of action usually is a decision that is a highly visible one, one that dramatizes the decision and serves notice on the organization that something important is happening. If, on the other hand, long consistent effort is needed to effect the decision, a slow start that gathers momentum usually is preferable.

4.   *Limitation of resources.* The most important resource whose limitations must be considered are the human beings who will be required to carry out the decision. The decision-maker must ask: Do we have the means for carrying out the decision? Do we have the numbers and right kind of people?

So as to make the decision effective there are 2 cardinal rules that managers remember. First, those individuals who have to carry out the decision are brought in to participate in the decision making process at the development of alternatives stage. And second, the decision is one which helps these people to achieve their objectives, to assist them in their work, to contribute to their performing better, more effectively, and with a greater sense of achievement.

Even under the most careful analysis of alternative solutions managers do not always choose the best one. Bias can creep in. Important unknown facts or unforeseen developments can militate against the chosen decision. But alternatives not used can serve as contingency plans (or a new beginning point) if it becomes clear that the chosen alternative will not work. If a decision still must be made, the effective manager admits that an ineffective alternative was chosen rather than persisting with a decision which disregards long-range consequences so as to avoid a possible short-term embarrassment.

Exhibit 12-1, *Problem Solving Work Sheet,* provides a guide managers have found useful and effective in working through the solution to problems. Each item listed ensures that important steps and processes are not overlooked. Moreover, the filling out of the form aids the manager to focus more intensively and sharply on his problem.

Exhibit 12-1

PROBLEM SOLVING WORK SHEET

Date: No.

1.   *Definition of the Problem:*

   1)   Critical factor(s):

      a.   Minimum acceptable level of improvement over the
           current situation:

      b.   Maximum allowable time for implementing the decision:

      c.

      d.

      e.

2.   *Analysis of the problem:*

   1)   Committed length of time and speed with which the decision
        can be reversed:

   2)   Impact of the decision on other areas and functions:

   3)   Qualitative considerations:

   4)   Uniqueness or periodicity of the decision:

Exhibit 12-1—*Continued*

3.　*Alternative solutions (at least 3):*

　　1)　Take no action at all.

　　　　a.　The risk:

　　　　b.　Economy of effort:

　　　　c.　Timing:

　　　　d.　Limitation of resources:

　　2)

　　　　a.　The risk:

　　　　b.　Economy of effort:

　　　　c.　Timing:

　　　　d.　Limitation of resources:

　　3)

　　　　a.　The risk:

　　　　b.　Economy of effort:

Exhibit 12-1—Continued

c.   Timing:

d.   Limitation of resources:

4.   *Implementation:*

1)   Those to be involved in developing alternative solutions and the solution's implementation:

2)   Ways in which the solution will help the implementers to achieve their objectives, to assist them in their work, to contribute to their performing better, more effectively, and with a greater sense of achievement:

3)   Implementing steps to be taken:

This chapter has outlined what education managers do, who they are, and their major tasks. Emphasis was placed on strategic decision making since *strategic decision making is the chief task of managers.* And it has emphasized that effective knowledge workers are first strategic managers and second task specialists. Performing as managers will make for a more effective total learning environment at all layers of a school district or institution. As a consequence, it is more likely that greater numbers of Education Persons will enter society as effective citizens.

The next chapter, Chapter 13, will provide the would-be education manager with a proven management systems instrument which will enable him to become more effective. To reiterate, management can be learned as a skill just as math or foreign languages can be learned. Indeed, if educators are to effectively meet the challenges of the 21st century, management *must* be learned and practiced.

Chapter 13

MANAGEMENT-BY-OBJECTIVES

If you treat an individual as he is, he will stay as he is, but if you treat him as if he were what he ought to be and could be, he will become what he ought to be and could be – Johann von Goethe

Management-by-objectives (MBO) is managing by demonstrable, measurable results toward predetermined goals, and objectives. It provides a viable alternative to administering by abdication, crisis, fear, charisma, or "common sense."

The system of management-by-objectives goes beyond applying a set of rules, engaging in a series of procedures, or even a set method of managing. It is a particular way of *thinking* about management. It is a system of management which can be described as a process whereby the superordinate and subordinate managers of an organization *jointly* identify its common goals, define each individual's major area of responsibility in terms of results expected of him, and use these measures as guides for operating the unit and assessing the contribution of each of its members. It, therefore, can, and will, be seen that the system of management-by-objectives is operationally immersed with the leading principles of Theory Y, Contingency Theory, and the Situational Theory of management.

The primary effects of employing management-by-objectives in education are to be seen in such tangible results as improved learning, more relevant curricula, lower drop-out rates, and more efficient use of available dollars. The system of management-by-objectives improves the efficiency and effectiveness of a school, college or university. Its visible effects are seen in such areas as improved morale, improved delegation of decision-making, identifying more promotable people, and an improved institutional image.

The conceptual framework of the system of management-by-objectives includes the following:

1. The basic structure of an educational system is the organizational form often called a *hierarcy*. This hierarchial system is best seen in organizational charts which show the relationship of subordinates to superordinates. MBO is a system for making the structure work, and to bring about more vitality and personal involvement of the people in the hierarchy. Yet,

the system also takes full cognizance of the collegial and lateral relationships between professionals in an academic setting.

2. MBO provides for the maintenance, orderly growth, and innovative breakthroughs of the educational system by means of statements of what is expected of everyone involved, and measurement of what is actually achieved. It is a system of assigning responsibility by accountability for achieving measurable results. It measures results against standards. It evaluates the achievements of its managers rather than their personalities.

3. As a system, MBO is especially applicable to professional and managerial employees, of which education almost entirely consists vis-à-vis, eg, industrial workers. There are few, if any, positions in education (including the classified or support staff) in which MBO cannot be applied with a resultant improvement in performance.

4. MBO helps overcome many chronic problems of managing administrators, teachers, counselors, educational technologists, librarians, and other professional knowledge workers by:

1)   providing a means of measuring their true contributions.

2)   defining common goals of the educational system and the measurable contributions of the individuals to these goals.

3)   enhancing coordinated effort and teamwork without eliminating personal risk taking towards reaching common goals.

4)   providing solutions to the key problems of defining the major areas of responsibility for each person in the system, including joint or shared responsibilities.

5)   processes which are geared to achieve the results desired, both for the system as a whole and for the individual contributors.

6)   eliminating the need for individuals to change their personalities, for appraising them on the basis of their personality traits.

7)   providing a means of determining each knowledge worker's span of control (who and how many he supervises).

8)   providing a means for objectively providing merit pay should the system choose to pay for clearly demonstrated results.

9)   aiding in identifying promotable individuals based upon superior performance.

Setting Goals

As has already been emphasized earlier, for a district, school, college, or university to function without clear yearly goals, 5-year goals, and 15-year goals is to be more irresponsible than to sail an ocean liner without the trim tab of its rudder. Put plainly, without defining the objectives for the whole organization, for all its subordinate units, and for the individuals in them the all too typical, inexcusable outcome as follows can be expected:

No one knows whether they are on the right track or not.

Results cannot be objectively assessed because there are no clear prior expectations with which to measure them against.

No one knows when things are drifting because no one is clear as to what goals would comprise "nondrifting" or when purposive action is occuring.

No one performs with maximum effectiveness since no one knows what goals the organization is seeking (and why), nor does one know how well one is doing in absence of succinctly spelled-out goals.

The 1st task, then, under a system of management by objectives, is to establish 1-year, 5-year, and 15-year goals which are *annually* refined and updated (as discussed in Part I).

By establishing long-range goals, we can measure an organization's performance. In establishing these goals, as self-evident as it may seem, they must be stated as *educational* goals.

Educational survival is the primary demand placed upon management, and all other measures of institutional performance must follow and fit this goal. If a system is not relevant to its clientele, and/or does not produce desired results, society will provide other alternatives, eg, performance contracting, education vouchers, "free" schools, and external diplomas and degrees.

Educational survival is the primary demand placed upon knowledge workers. The closing of parochial schools and private colleges witness this fact. The early closing of public schools is further stark testimony to the fact that formal education, as we know it, is faced with a survival problem. Particularly, our schools failure to teach basic reading and computational skills threaten the very survival of formal education. Our country cannot afford the estimated 25 percent of our population who are functionally illiterate. Indeed, with the possible exception of the nation's comprehensive 2-year public colleges all other segments of education are generally out of public favor for well-known reasons. Unless we face up to the serious fact that formal education is fighting for its very survival, we are not likely to set the necessary supportive goals and take the necessary radical steps to assure education's survival. We simply must do a much better job of teaching, of providing more useful and applied research related to man's social and ecological environment, and provide more relevant and intensive community service programs — especially as applicable to the economically disadvantaged.

To meet the demands of the times nothing short of the establishment of measurable, overall organizational goals, accompanied by the establishment of measures of performance for each unit therein, will do. Out of the measures of total organization performance must come the measures of performance from its units, eg, the instructional division, the counseling center, the library, the business office.

One schematic way of looking at measurements of an educational organization's performance is to simulate the organization chart via goals as illustrated in Figure 13-1.

Figure 13-1

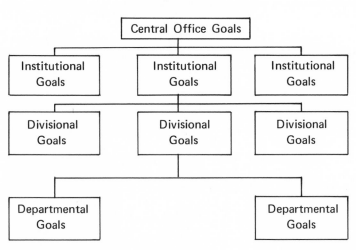

It can be readily seen from the above hierarchial structuring that *the measure of a manager's performance is the magnitude of his contribution to the achievement of central office goals.* To achieve this objective, the *MBO Agreement* of the manager must have a "goodness of fit" with central office goals, ie, the MBO Agreement must complement, reinforce, not add to or take away from the total organizational goals as reflected by central office goals. In short, the organization chart of higher level managers should be a close proximation of their major areas of responsibility. Finally, as Figure 13-1 shows, the manager is measured by the performance of his subordinates rather than his own personality.

By way of illustration, take the group reporting to a high school principal of a school having 2,000 students. He has a staff of 125. He and the superintendent of schools have agreed that his duties consist of: "Directing and administering the operation of the instructional, counseling and guidance, food services, and plant maintenance programs." The principal's organizational structure (showing immediate subordinates only) is diagrammed in Figure 13-2.

Figure 13-2

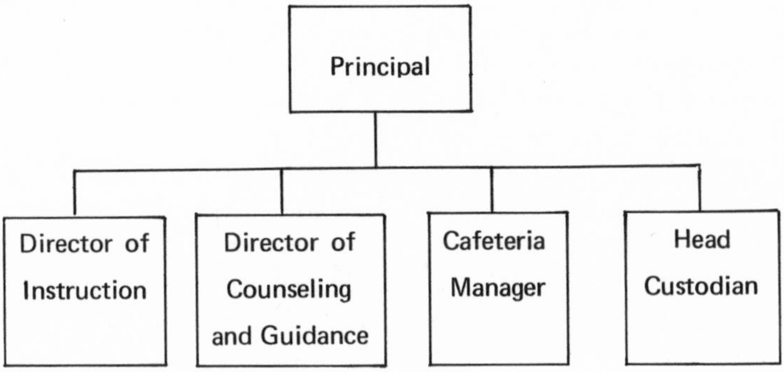

The list of responsibilities for the principal's position would include all the major divisions he directs and those things he does personally, such as recommending policy to the superintendent. If this high school principal were using management-by-objectives for his own position his first step would be to define his major areas of responsibility, and the *measures* for each:

MAJOR AREAS	MEASURES OF SATISFACTORY PERFORMANCE
Instructional Program	Students standardized mean achievement test percentile results will not fall below 5 percentile points of the standardized mean intelligence test percentile results.
Counseling and Guidance Program	Not less than 95 percent of the present Junior Class who remain in the district will return to school in September and graduate in June.
Food Service Program	Not less than 10 compliments received by the superintendent on the quality or service of the food during the school year.
Plant Maintenance	Not less than 10 compliments received by the superintendent on the quality of plant cleanliness and maintenance during the school year.

The actual measure of performance used would, of course, include the objectives imposed by any given situation, including the superintendent's perceived needs, as well as the suggestions of the principal's subordinates. Each subordinate, in turn, under MBO, defines the specific responsibilities of his own position and discusses them with his superordinate until mutual agreement is reached and *committed in writing.*

The higher-level manager does not include in his objectives all the detailed objectives and measures of all of his subordinates. If he did so, the pyramiding effect would soon make such a system unworkable. Each subordinate must define the common objectives for his divsion, department or unit consistent with the goals of the organization. The statement of common organization goals of the immediate subordinate units thus become measures of the *superordinate's responsibility.* Subordinates, in turn, have committed themselves for total results and assisting their superordinate to succeed. The superordinate has succeeded if his subordinates achieve the objectives for their area of responsibility, which combined with the accomplishment of objectives from other areas, results in total organizational goals being achieved.

Once yearly, 5-year, and 15-year goals have been set they must be implemented. Exhibit 13-3 is illustrative of how a school system, college or university might depict in a total way the duties and responsibilities of each component part. Preparing such a chart helps to more clearly identify these duties and responsibilities so as to minimize unnecessary overlapping. It avoids confusion and overcomes weaknesses. In short, such a chart helps to ensure that roles are complementary so as to maximize the possibilities for achieving organizational objectives.

Obviously Exhibit 13-3 can and should be refined in accordance with the uniqueness of each individual situation. With such a master chart of delineated responsibilities (beside an organizational goals chart as in Exhibit 2-1, in Chpt. 2), aids the organization to continually focus on what it is about. It also serves as a reminder of the interdependency and complementariness of roles, each necessary for organizational success. Figure 13-4 depicts these linking relationships.

Setting Individual Goals

The key premise in the system of management-by-objectives is that the objectives established between the subordinate and his superordinate will achieve better results than what random methods alone can produce. And the guiding principle of setting objectives demands high achievement in every area of responsibility, and in every position, where performance and results directly and vitally affect the organization. Further, as has been repeatedly pointed out, the process must begin with a system first establishing its short, intermediate, and long-range goals. Then and only then can individual objectives be meaningfully established.

An effective goals and objectives system provides every manager with a means of planning and measuring his own performance and that of his subordinates. It gives him some means for knowing when he is deviating from system goals and objectives in sufficient time to do something about his errors before it is too late. It provides for ample feedback and the opportunity to obtain genuine satisfaction for achieving agreed upon individual predetermined objectives. Finally, an effective individualized objectives system should eliminate anxiety about possible failures due to ignorance of what is expected.

In the actual setting of statements of objectives good statements concentrate on *what* and *when* (hard criteria) rather than on "why" and "how" (soft criteria). Thus, good objectives:

1.   Start off with an action verb.

2.   Identify a single key result for each of the objectives.

Exhibit 13-3

STANDARDS TO MEASURE PERFORMANCE OF	END RESULTS SOUGHT	INTERMEDIATE VARIABLES	SOME KEY CASUAL VARIABLES
Board of Trustees	The organization will survive and produce a maximum number of Educated Persons.	The organization has objectives, policies, plans, controls; is well-managed in depth; has ample facilities and equipment.	Board members are experienced, proven individuals; show strong interest in the organization, and attention to their role.
Superintendent of Schools or President	*Learning*, qualitative growth, increase cohort survival rate, meaningful research and community services consistent with Board defined "Educated Persons."	Strong executives; capable faculty, sound operating procedures; clear goals for the entire organization focused on producing Educated Persons.	Chief executive has strong proprietory interest; creates a desire to excell; provides a supportive environment to key administrators; promotion opportunities encouraged within and without the organization.
Principals or Deans	*Cost per student* per learning achievement per subject produced, as needed (in time) as measured by standards, (eg, standardized achievement tests, pre-test/post-test, behavioral objectives), estimated, PERT, or learning curve.	Productivity, quality, standards and performance, months of achievement per $100 (yield) is high; faculty and student absentee rate low; cohort survival rate of students and faculty is high.	Skilled executives, possessing technical excellence, necessary controls and encouragements, ample training; staff motivation towards excellence; organizational environment conducive toward achieving results; favorable attitudes, opportunities and incentives for growth.
Faculty	*Program budget* achieves pre-determined program within budgeted limits as agreed upon as elements toward producing Educated Persons.	Programs, objectives, lesson plans, procedures produced, installed or reviewed so as to contribute to the overall organization's short-term, intermediate and long-range goals.	Skilled individuals possessing technical excellence, ample training; capable of producing a learning environment conducive to achieving favorable affective and cognitive learning results.

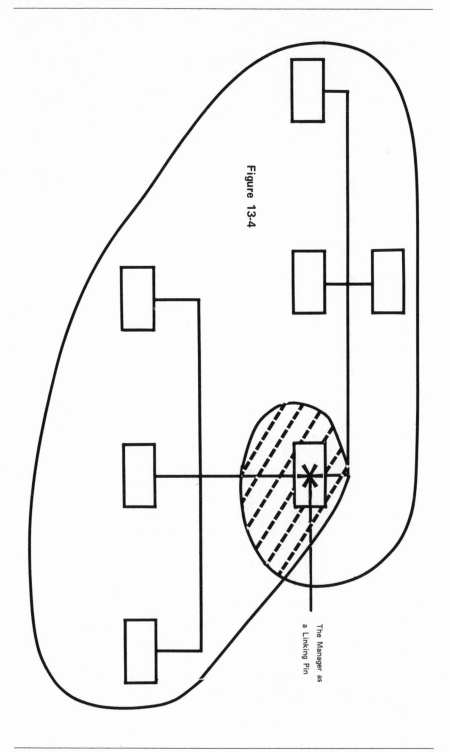

Figure 13-4

The Manager as
a Linking Pin

3. Give the day, month, and year of estimated completion for each objective (usually using PERT to establish time of completion).

4. Identify costs — ie, dollars, time, materials, and equipment needed to complete each objective.

5. State *verifiable* criteria which signal when the objective has been reached.

6. State only those objectives controllable by the person setting the objectives, or, if not totally controllable, at least those parts which are isolatable.

The initial attempt at setting objectives between a superordinate and his subordinate often results in generalized statements of objectives in which accountability is totally lacking. Typical of these evasians are such proposed objectives as:

I will perform all my duties in a superior manner by devoting more time and energy to my work.

I will meet all established deadlines so as not to delay the work of others.

I will get to know the students better so as to better meet their needs.

I will show professional growth and development by taking a class at night school.

Though such sentiments are laudable they are hopelessly vague. They are "soft criteria" — they focus on the "why" and the "how" instead of the "what" and the "when". Implicit in them is the avoidance of measurable results sought and the acceptance of personal accountability. For the superordinate to accept such objectives (or worse yet, not to demand any objectives at all) is tangible evidence of aimless leadership. By contrast, the measurable results-centered leader insists upon such "hard criteria" statements of objectives from subordinates as these:

I will provide the board of trustees with next year's budget completely in PPBS format

By January, I will have documented for the superintendent and the board the need for establishing a special education class for the mentally retarded in my school. By May, I will be authorized to establish such a class.

By June, I will have eliminated Latin from the curriculum and replaced it with not less than 3 classes of Ethnic Studies.

By August, I will have installed an automated library check-out system.

By September, recruiting efforts will have resulted in not less than 10 percent of the faculty and administration being Black, Chicano, Native American, or Oriental.

During the next fiscal year a management consulting team will be budgeted for to advise on improving the operations of the business services division. During the subsequent fiscal year the agreed to recommendations will be implemented.

The final examination in my algerbra classes will result in at least 80 percent of my students correctly solving at least 80 percent of the problems.

Not less than 95 percent of the nursing students will pass all parts of the State Boards given in August.

Such commitments, though admittedly more risky than others for a manager to commit himself to, are more tangible. They are attached to the risk that the individual may fail — with attendant consequences for promotion or even maintaining one's present position. But we should, after all, be paid for results, not good intentions.

In the objectives setting process in the system of management-by-objectives there are 4 major individual objectives: routine objectives, problem solving objectives; creative objectives; personal development objectives. Corollary to each are *emergency objectives* and *management by exception* (MBE).

Setting Routine Objectives

Every job includes some routine duties which must be carried out. Though commonplace and repetitive they need to be spelled out specifically for a variety of reasons:

1.   The superordinate must be made aware of routine duties since the failure to do them, or not to do them well, could have serious consequences for the organization.

2.   Effectively managing routine responsibilities often serves as a preventive action against what could become a serious problem later in absence of such clearly spelled out routine coverage or effectiveness.

3.   Routine achievement objectives can form the basis for a more orderly clustering of duties and distribution of assignments to allow for a fairer balance among subordinates and to maximize the effectiveness of the results.

4.   Identifying all of the important routine objectives of sub-ordinates enables the superordinate to insist and ensure that in the absence, resignation, or dismissal of the subordinate that at least 1 other inidividual can temporarily serve as a backup person for each routine task.

By way of example, here are some typical routine responsibilities of a registrar:

To prepare the college catalogue.

To prepare monthly enrollment reports for state and federal agencies.

To register students each semester and summer school

To send out grade cards to instructors twice a semester.

To record grades on permanent record cards of students.

To send out transcripts which have been requested each Friday.

Such routine responsibilities make up the typical *job description.* The job description states the minimum responsibilities which must be done well in order to hold that job. The system of management-by-objectives enlarges the job description in 3 significant aspects:

1.   All such duties are reviewed annually with changes made in writing. Mutual agreement on these duties results.

2.   Measures are established which specify when these routine responsibilities are done well.

3.   The estimated percentage of time devoted to each task is recorded which serves as an appraisal of significance of each. Such an appraisal may also result in certain rearrangements or redistribution of duties so that sufficient time is allowed for the more significant objectives.

The measurement of performance of routine duties has 2 aspects:

1.   There is prior written agreement between the superordinate and the subordinate upon what these routine duties are.

2.   There is prior written statements of *exceptions,* if any, agreed upon which both the superordinate and subordinate agree are reasonable to expect.

For example, the dean of business services and the college president agree that the measure of exception for getting the monthly payroll checks out at the scheduled time is zero. Failure to achieve this routine objective will be considered an exception that calls for an explanation by the dean. An unsatisfactory explanation will be considered a failure on the part of the dean.

Another example might be that the dean of business services and the president agree that any maintenance or repair request by a member of the faculty which would cost less than $15.00 will be completed within 5 working days of the written request, with an upper limit exception of 20 percent (one extra day). Thus if the dean habitually sees to it that faculty requests are taken care of within a 5 working day span of time, and occasionally a sixth day, he has satisfactorily performed. But if his failure to satisfactorily respond within the 20 percent exception allowance, and the causes for delay were attributable to conditions under his control, the dean must assume personal accountability for the failure.

Some further typical responsibilities of a routine nature which can be measured by the exception principle might include the following:

To notify the chairman of the board of trustess of any serious student disruptions within 4 hours of the occurence, without exception.

To notify the superintendent of a major new curriculum proposal from the Council for the Future within 5 working days of its recommendation, with an exception allowance of 2 additional days.

To notify the counseling office of the name of every student whose classroom work falls more than 20 percent below *or above* the previous quarter within 10 school days of the quarter's ending, with an exception allowance of an additional 5 days.

To notify the principal and health office of an average daily attendance (ADA) rate falling below 90 percent or above 95 percent of the enrollees within 1 day of each exception to the standard.

To notify the vice-president of instructional services within 10 days of each enrollment period the name of each instructor in each department with the smallest and largest total class enrollment, with an exception allowance of an additional 5 days.

To notify the director of curriculum within 10 days after a semester ends when less than 30 percent of the full-time students and/or faculty have failed to check out any library materials the previous semester or in which more than 50 percent have, with an exception allowance of an additional 5 days.

Common to these statements is a specification of an ideal condition that would exist if the routines were performed according to a *standard*. The measure of compliance covers what variances from the standard are permissable, and the point at which they become exceptions. In short, for MBO to effectively work, 2 premises must be observed:

1.   Reduce everything quantifiable to numbers.

2.   Where numerical measurement is impossible (eg, elements of community relations and employee relations) prepare written descriptions of the ideal conditions and of permissable variations.

There always will be emergencies and "fire fighting" in any job. They represent one form of exception (others being changing yearly routine, problem solving, creative, and personal development goals and objectives for good and acceptable reasons) just as moving outside the opposite side of the range generally represents a highly favorable condition. Though confronting emergencies will always be with the manager, to devote a high percentage of the time to such unforeseen conditions, often is evidence of a lack of thorough planning, and such planning should be sought for the future.

Some means for effective planning, and for reducing the time necessary to devote to the unexpected, include the following:

The job description itself should make allowances for the unexpected, probably not less than 5 nor more than 10 percent of the total job time requirements.

Where joint responsibilities exist, as it must in many instances, specific statements as to what measures of exception should be attributed to which subordinate, will diminish confusion and exceptions.

It must be made plain to subordinates that most activities presently seen as emergencies or unforeseeable could be planned for if a deliberate effort were made to do so; that such activities will rarely serve as an excuse to escape accountability for failure to achieve agreed upon objectives.

Only those events which could not under any circustances be predicted or estimated in advance, should be permitted to be identified as acceptable emergency or unpredictable objectives.

Finally, evidence exists that a listing beyond a *maximum* of 15 routine objectives (items in a job description) is superfluous for most any job.

Setting Problem Solving Objectives

In any situation there are bound to be problems — some minor, some more serious. The minor ones almost always should be able to be taken care of as a matter of course, without undue attention, in the efficient and effective performance of routine objectives. Essentially then, the focusing on problem solving objectives is the focusing on those problems that are recurring and of sufficient seriousness as to have an adverse effect on the efficient and effective performance of the organization. Problems are often most useful in setting objectives when they are stated as questions. Examples might be:

How can a means be found, without immediate funds, to effectively use, supplement, or supplant primary grade reading texts which are not reflective of the life-styles of the students in the school nor of the true "vegetable soup" nature of American society?

How can the poor lunchroom behavior of this junior high school be improved?

How can public demands for substantially more vocational education in this senior high school, which was designed and built 25 years earlier as a "college preparatory" institution, be met?

How can this public, 2-year college faculty, most of whom were originally high school teachers, be convinced that being a college instructor does not mean emulating the liberal arts faculty of a university?

How can a more effective means of participatory democracy in this university's governance be developed while at the same time obtaining agreements as to who is accountable for what?

What can be done so as to reduce library transaction costs below $1.00 per item?

What can the counseling office do to help decrease the alarming increase in venereal disease on campus?

These kinds of problems generally cannot be solved through the effective and efficient performance of routine duties. Moreover, it is not likely that problems such as these can be solved in only a matter of a few days. Frequently, some or all problem solving objectives make up an institution's yearly goals. As with routine objectives, problem solving objectives are set against an acceptable end result. This means reducing everything, where quantifiable, to numbers, otherwise a verbal description of the ideal condition, and of permissable variations is given. Two classroom examples of problem solving objectives against measures are shown below:

Third grade standardized arithmetic achievement test scores in this school have consistently fallen short of grade level. Therefore, the superintendent will be notified quarterly by the principal of *each* class which performs below grade level *and* of each class that achieves more than 3 months above grade level.

The senior high school English department chairman was notified by his counterpart in the nearest university that less than 20 percent of the high school's June graduates in attendance there were successful in "testing out" of the grammar portion of the *Freshman English Placement Examination.* The senior high school department chairman brought the problem to the attention of the English department and it was agreed that more emphasis on grammar would result. It was further agreed that standardized testing would occur quarterly and that the department chairman would be notified of *each* class section which failed to achieve an averaged minimum class score of 75 percent and of each class section that achieved above 85 percent on the tests.

The foregoing points up the fact that before problem solving objectives are established, facts should be arrayed in such a way as to give greater precision as to what the problem really is. It must be determined if a problem is indigenous to the entire population of the organization, or only part of it. This arraying process should reveal those accountable and for what part of the problem. By way of further illustration, if the average reading achievement test score of 5 classrooms of 5th graders at midterm was 4.9 instead of the expected 5.5 (based on students of average intelligence in heterogeneous classrooms) it might be thought, without arraying the problem, that all 5 5th grade teachers should devote special attention to reading instruction for the remainder of the school year. However, the arrayed Figure 13-5 in this example reveals that this premise is false.

Figure 13-5

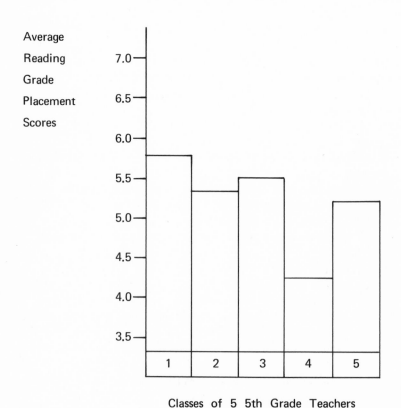

Classes of 5 5th Grade Teachers

A casual inspection quickly reveals that by sorting out and arraying the reading test score results of all 5 5th grades that Teacher 4 is the one whose students are not satisfactorily achieving. Obviously, the first step is to recheck to see if all 5 classes indeed are heterogeneous with respect to academic ability. Assuming that there are no significant differences in academic ability of the students, or any other significant differences in students from one class to another, it can only be assumed that the problem lies with the individual classroom teacher. Perhaps not enough time is being devoted to reading. Perhaps the teacher is unskilled in teaching reading skills. Perhaps the teacher is being "managed" by the students instead of managing them. Perhaps there are serious psychological or personality problems interferring with the teaching/learning process. Whatever the problem, it must be satisfactorily resolved. The school principal becomes accountable for the resolution of the problem to his superintendent and the teacher is accountable to the principal for finding a satisfactory solution to the problem. By arraying the reading problem, the principal is freed to concentrate his energy on helping 20 percent of the teachers rather than all 100 percent.

There is more here, however, than sorting out and arraying, of effort and concentration of energy, which solves 1 significant problem in 1 elementary school. There is a principle that is more important than the details of this particular elementary school's 5th grade reading test scores:

There is a normal and natural maldistribution among possible causes or focal points of trouble and the dispersion of effects. (21:120)

To be even more specific, for every problem or for every result, Pareto's "Law of 20/80" can be assumed to be at work. This is the "rule of the vital few" among the causes of specific results. To illustrate, on the average:

20 percent of the parents account for 80 percent of the complaints.

20 percent of the students account for 80 percent of the questions missed on a test.

20 percent of the staff account for 80 percent of the grievances filed.

20 percent of the faculty account for 80 percent of the innovations.

20 percent of the students account for 80 percent of the discipline problems.

20 percent of the vending machines account for 80 percent of the "down time"

All the above examples, of which there are countless more, illustrate this normal tendency for maldistribution between causes and effects.

The practical implications of the Law of 20/80 lies in the fact that the opportunity for mitigating or eliminating a problem lies in concentrating effort on the vital 20 percent of the factors concerned. This often requires a sorting and an arrayment of the problem as illustrated in Figure 13-5. This effort of sorting and arrayment is the only objective means to get at the vital few that are causing most of the problem.

As might be adduced from the foregoing, experience has shown that it is unrealistic for an individual manager to establish more than 2 problem solving objectives a year. As with routine objectives, agreement is agreed to in writing between subordinate and superordinate as to what the 2 yearly problem solving objectives are to be and the measures to be used to determine if they have been solved or reduced to a satisfactorily tolerable level.

As with all elements of the system of management-by-objectives, MBE applies. Thus if a more critical, unforeseen problem emerges which needs the manager's attention, he can request of his superordinate ⟵⟶ subordinate a modification of their beginning year agreement. As with the original agreement, the modified agreement is committed to writing. Generally, however, a critical, unforeseen problem is an "emergency" situation rather than a matter which demands the "dumping" of what should have been a carefully thought-through recurring problem demanding a priority solution. Moreover, time for emergencies are to be allowed for by the manager and his manager in their MBO Agreement so that it seldom becomes necessary to substitute one problem for another.

Setting Creative Objectives

The 3rd area making up an MBO Agreement is one which has the greatest potential for the improvement of organizational results, the establishment of creative or innovative objectives.

Performing routines well and solving problems are largely maintenance objectives. They do not move an organization ahead. Progress is only achieved through the creation of better ways of doing existing tasks or by achieving important breakthroughs by inventing new systems methods, or articles.

During the annual objectives setting process between superordinate and sub-ordinate several factors must be borne in mind:

1.   The rate of failure may be expected to be higher where creative or innovative projects are undertaken than in any other objectives area.

2.   More opportunities exist for making important breakthroughs or generous strides in some positions than in others.

3.   Since success in achieving major breakthroughs is what vitalizes an organization, all staff should be made to realize that achieving creative objectives carries with it heavy weight when it comes to perquisites, pay increases and promotions.

Creative objectives setting in a technical, managerial or staff position can be divided into 2 major categories:

Extrinsic creativity – the introduction of new ideas from outside the organization.

Instrinsic creativity – the discovery of new ways, combinations, methods, or systems of doing the present job.

Extrinsic creativity usually manifests itself by the alert and the curious who continually ask themselves whenever they come across a new invention or technique, "Would this likely make a desirable *difference* in my organizational unit (classroom, counseling center, library, et al)?

Intrinsic creativity usually manifests itself in the non-technological area by using present conditions and results as a basis for systematically improving upon the existing situation. This is generally best achieved by the superordinate and subordinate collecting, classifying, analyzing, and interpreting past facts and results before the annual objectives setting meeting. This forces both to think deeply about the results obtained in the past with a view to improvement of the organization in the future.

Some examples of creative objectives might include:

Introducing programmed reading into the primary grades.

Establishing an "open classroom."

Obtaining acceptance of the "45-15 Year-Round School Plan."

Introducing the 4-day school week.

Changing the traditional 12-year program leading to a high school diploma to 10 years.

Reorganizing the 2-year college from a divisional structure into 4 interdisciplinary colleges within the college.

Reorganizing the university into a bicameral, representative system of government with students as "congressmen," faculty as "senators," the president as "chief executive," and the board of trustees as the "supreme court."

Reorganizing subjects taught by the lecture method to performance-based teaching (behavioral objectives).

Providing a library-centered teaching workshop for faculty conducted by the library staff.

Establishing an open circuit radio station operated and maintained by the educational technology department.

Introducing a drug education program offered by the counseling and guidance personnel prior to drug usage being a campus problem.

In inducing creative objectives setting, the superordinate's major role is to ask specific questions that require reflective answers and to channel the subordinate's thinking toward constructive analysis of how he can improve the area for which he is responsible, consistent with yearly, 5-year, and 15-year goals. The main question he asks is what the subordinate should also be continually asking himself, viz, "What can be done in your (my) area of responsibility that likely will lead to a desirable difference?" This requires that the superordinate lead the subordinate to the point where he sufficiently examines the facts of his situation; sees if the rearrangement of facts into new combinations can lead to a more desirable condition; considers the relations between possible causes and effects as possible solutions.

Too, it is the responsibility of the superordinate to make it clear to the subordinate what major criteria he will use for evaluating the creative objectives established.

As with problem solving objectives, experience has shown that it is unrealistic to expect of a manager more than the achievement of 2 creative
objectives in a year (or even longer, depending upon the nature of the
objectives). Solving problems and achieving creative objectives normally
takes considerable time to achieve. If solving 2 significant problems and
achieving 2 creative objectives by each member of the staff each year is
achieved — or even an 80 percent success rate — it is likely that a dynamic
organization exists. Surely it can be expected to be a much better situation
than is typical of many of our educational institutions today where so much
emphasis instead is placed on "housekeeping" chores (ie, routine tasks) and
"firefighting" emergencies.

As with all other MBO objectives, MBE also is operative. Changes in creative
objectives can be made to capitalize on unexpected opportunities or to
modify the existing commitment as a result of a revised written agreement
between the subordinate and his manager. Such changes or modifications
should be rare but MBE provides the flexibility to capitalize on occasional,
unexpected opportunities or to modify overly ambitious creative objectives.

Setting Personal Development Objectives

The final element included in an MBO Agreement is the setting of personal
development objectives between superordinate and subordinate. Achievement
of personal development objectives should be those which make it possible
for an individual to perform his job better whether he is promoted or remains in his present position. This kind of development may result from
guided experience on the job, through formal classes in management skills,
technical and professional subjects, and so on.

As with problem solving and creative objectives, experience has generally
shown that the setting of more than 2 personal development objectives
during the yearly objectives setting period tends to overextend the manager,
when added to the other objectives, so that his overall quality of performance is threatened. As with most things, a reasonable balance, which is
well-rounded, usually proves most advantageous to the organization and to
the individual in the long run.

The array of self-development objectives presents an almost limitless selection to choose from, for example:

The completion of courses toward an advanced degree.

Attendance at two professional seminars or workshops during the year.

Membership and active participation in a professional group

Subscription to and the diligent reading of two job-related journals during the year.

Enrollment in a management training course

Carefully planned visits to professional counterparts in other institutions

Active participation in 1 or 2 community service organizations

Embark on a personal health-building program (with medical advice)

Prepare 2 papers for professional publication

Finish preparing one-third to one-half a book during the year

Prepare and present a scholarly paper at a professional meeting

Read 2 professional management books

Read 2 job-related technical or professional books during the year

Read 4 best seller books — 2 fiction and 2 nonfiction

Read 4 classics — 2 fiction and 2 nonfiction

Take a carefully planned vacation which is culturally enriching and/or one which will give direct insights into present job

These examples make it evident that some managers could spend most of their time just on self-development at the expense of performing some function of direct and immediate value to the organization. This is another reason why there should not be more than 2 self-development objectives listed on the MBO Agreement. Yet, this caution in no way is to be interpreted as denigrating the value and the necessity of personal development. An individual needs to personally grow so that an organization can grow. To ensure that personal development activities serve the purpose of the organization, the following rules should be observed:

1.   There should be a specific reason in mind — the why — for the undertakings which are stated in writing.

2.   The effect of the desired change in behavior on the job performance, either present or potential, should be weighed (How will this make the
individual a more valuable employee?).

3.   The commitment should state what tasks will be done and when
and how.

Again, as with the other 3 elements making up the yearly MBO Agreement,
MBE is operative. If, for good and acceptable reasons, an individual wishes
to substitute some other personal development objective than the ones
agreed to at the yearly objectives setting session, the system allows for it.
But, like the others, changes should not be allowed to serve as an excuse
for the inability to achieve earlier commitments which should have been
carefully thought through in the 1st place.

To reiterate, management-by-exception functions in 2 ways: 1) for changing
yearly routine, problem solving, creative, and personal development objectives of the MBO Agreement for good and acceptable reasons to the superordinate, and 2) as a "thermostat" to alert management to unusual conditions, especially insofar as routine objectives are concerned. It is the responsibility of the subordinate to notify his superordinate in accordance with
the conditions of their agreement should the expected range of acceptable
results be bridged — either below or above expectations. Just as a thermostat
turns on the air conditioning to cool the temperature down when it becomes
too hot, a thermostat, likewise, is used as a warming device. Thus, MBE is
used to identify desirable conditions as well as undesirable ones. It is used as
a "firefighting" device in emergency situations and as "fireworks" in celebra-
tion.

Such measures as the business manager notifying the superintendent within 1
day of tax receipts which fall below 2 percent of projections or above 2 percent of projections, and other illustrations in this chapter, are illustrative of
MBE at work. Such measures should be incorporated as an integral part of
the MBO Agreement at the yearly objectives setting period (not later than
September under most academic calendars — usually better in May). In short,
all 4 elements of the "contract for results" should be set against measurable
standards. Exhibit 13-6 shows an MBO Agreement form which has been effectively used in an academic setting.

This chapter concludes with findings which have been found to be the most
common *errors* commited by managers in setting objectives:

1.   The manager has not clarified common objectives for the whole
unit.

Exhibit 13-6

Period: July 1 – June 30, 19 ____

MBO AGREEMENT

Agreement Date: May ____, 19 ____

Routine Objectives	Why?	Measures of Satisfactory Performance	Allowable Range of variances (if any) Before Becoming an Exception	Estimated Percentage of Job Time Required
1.				%
2.				
3.				
4.				
5.				
6.				
7.				
8.				
9.				
10.				

Comments:

Exhibit 13-6 [*continued*]

Problem Solving Objectives

1.

2.

Comments:

Creative Objectives

1.

2.

Comments:

Personal Development Objectives

1.

2.

Comments:

Emergencies and Exceptions allowed for 100%

Additional Comments:

Agreement Signatures

2.   Objectives are set too low to challenge the subordinate or to have significant results for the department or the organization.

3.   Prior results have not been adequately analyzed as a basis for setting objectives.

4.   The unit's common objectives do not clearly fit those of the larger unit.

5.   Patently inappropriate, or impossible, or too many objectives are agreed to.

6.   Yearly objectives are rigidly adhered to that subsequently prove unfeasible, irrelevant, or impossible rather than admit to error.

7.   Responsibilities are not clustered in the most appropriate positions.

8.   Two or more individuals are allowed to believe themselves responsible for doing exactly the same things.

9.   Methods of working are stressed rather than clarifying individual areas of responsibility.

10.   It is more important to please the superordinate than to achieve the objective.

11.   There are no guides to action, only *ad hoc* judgments of results.

12.   Every proposed objective by the subordinate is accepted uncritically without a plan for its successful achievement.

13.   The needs of the superordinate (or his superordinate) are not openly and clearly made known to his subordinates.

14.   Very real obstacles are ignored that are likely to prove a hindrance in achieving agreed to objectives.

15.   The superordinate denigrates the objectives proposed by his subordinates, and imposes only those he deems suitable.

16.   The superordinate fails to think through and act upon what he must do to help his subordinates to succeed.

17.   The superordinate fails to determine with his subordinates standards of measurement and exceptions.

18.   The superordinate fails to conduct quarterly reviews of progress.

19.   New ideas from outside the organization are not encouraged (the NIH syndrome).

20.   Yearly objectives are rigidly adhered to even when a new and exceptional opportunity presents itself.

21.   Yearly objectives can be changed with ease even in absence of compelling reasons to do so.

22.   Successful behavior is not reinforced when objectives are achieved, or unsuccessful behavior corrected when they are not achieved.

23.   Subordinates are not allowed a *major* voice in setting their yearly objectives.

24.   Individuals are not allowed to set their own pace in achieving yearly objectives.

25.   The superordinate does not allow for a high degree of interaction and participation in all decisions which have a direct effect on the subordinate's area of responsibility.

Chapter 14

MANAGEMENT APPRAISAL

The best kind of pride is that which compels a man to do his very best work, even if no one is watching — Anon

The sole purpose of management appraisal should be to improve the effectiveness of the system, unit, and individual so as to achieve predetermined results.

Typically, however, management appraisal ignores evaluation of the school, college, or university system per se. Neither does appraisal of a unit within an organization often occur. Every 3 to 10 years an accrediting body of 3 members or so makes an on-site evaluation visit for 2 or 3 days to secondary and postsecondary schools. Presecondary schools seldom even have this infrequent outside evaluation. Notwithstanding this condition, there is little formal self-evaluation at any level or outside evaluations beyond these infrequent accrediting visits to secondary and postsecondary schools.

The extent of appraisal by school management usually is limited to individual yearly evaluations, typically a painful process requiring checking a list of input and process traits "below average," "average," and "above average" of subordinates rather than their output results. The forms used, more often than not, assess personality and character traits which emphasize "cooperation," "understanding," and "clerical skills" rather than achievement.

The remainder of this chapter will suggest ways for improving system appraisal, unit appraisal, and individual appraisal.

System Appraisal

It is not good enough for secondary and postsecondary schools, colleges, and universities to intensively engage in self-evaluation activity for 3 to 6 months once every 3 to 10 years in preparation for a largely subjective 3 member or so accreditation visit. Moreover, such preparations and such evaluations, like the annual evaluation, too often tend to focus on input and process rather than output. The visitors tend to seek answers to nonrelevant questions which truly do not measure the quality of an institution. Typically, what is evaluated by accrediting teams are such inputs into the

the system as degrees, graduate hours, and salaries of staff and the number of volumes in the library as if these institutional characteristics somehow have been demonstrated to correlate with output (eg, how much have students actually learned and the percent of students who actually are using the library). Far better would be concrete evidence of what entering students knew and what they now know as a result of the educational experience. Such output information is not difficult to obtain. Standardized tests of achievement of entering students against their present ranking can reveal this information. Such tests are now almost as readily available at the postsecondary level as at the elementary and secondary school levels. Student attitude scale results also provide important measures of institutional climate which can serve as an institutional mirror. Significant community projects and services which have made a positive difference is another element frequently not given enough attention. At the university level significant research findings are important as a measure of the system's success.

At the elementary school level the extent of evaluation of the system tends to be limited to the administration of achievement tests at the close of the school year when it is too late to do anything about the outcome. Moreover, without a correlation of academic ability to achievement obtained, the achievement tests are almost worthless. Only when we know that achievement and ability results reasonably coincide can the validity stamp of approval be proclaimed.

As previous chapters have emphasized, for an organization to have direction and to improve it must have short, intermediate, and long-range goals. This is where the primary appraisal need of an educational system lies — evaluation of its results against its goals.

Yearly goals of school, college and university systems, as well as individual components within each, need to be reviewed *quarterly* by key management personnel as a *group*. Generally, at least 1 full day exclusively focused on yearly goals is required each 3 months. This evaluation review of progress serves to clarify any misunderstanding, to shore up weaknesses, and to further strengthen successful approaches toward achieving system and institutional goals. Through the process of quarterly reviews, off course directions are set right in time to achieve goals. To simply review results against yearly goals at the end of the year, with no quarterly reviews in between, seldom results in any port being reached, let alone the agreed one. Instead, the system and its individual institutions flounder like a ship without a rudder, moving aimlessly on the seas of input and activity, never delivering their cargo of outputs and results to the port of goals. Exhibit 14-1 illustrates a means whereby the right goods can be delivered to the right place at the right time.

Exhibit 14-1

SYSTEM AND UNIT YEARLY GROUP OBJECTIVES AND RESULTS

Year's Objective	Completion Date	Person(s) Responsible	1 Q Results	2 Q Results	3 Q Results	4 Q Results	Year's Results
Routines							
1.							
2.							
3.							
4.							
5.							
Problem Solving							
1.							
2.							
Creative							
1.							
2.							

Unit Appraisal

Just as key managers of educational systems, schools, colleges and universities need to quarterly appraise their progress toward yearly goals, component units need to likewise make this quarterly effort — shortly after the system and institutional revisions have been completed. The "linking pin" manager needs to sit down with key managers of subordinate units to ensure that their activities toward goals and objectives are consistent with the linking pin manager's *superordinate's* interpretation of goals and objectives to be achieved. Thus, the chief administrative officer in charge of instruction will confer for at least half-a-day with division chairmen and the librarian; the chief administrative officer in charge of student personnel will confer for at least half-a-day with the counseling and guidance staff; the chief administrative officer in charge of business services will confer for at least half-a-day with his staff. Principals of elementary and secondary schools, who do not have second level administrators in charge of component parts as above, will meet directly in a like manner with academic and nonacademic staff.

Quarterly reviews serve as a vitalizing force, as a purposeful means for increasing morale. Individuals sense that the MBO oriented institution they are associated with knows where it is headed, that it is "well administered." Quarterly appraisals by component units bring professionals together in small enough groups so that a collegial relationship is fostered. All feel they are participating and thus can provide meaningful input toward achieving unit objectives, which together with the achievement of objectives by other units, achieves institutional and system goals.

Individual Appraisal

Just as educational systems, individual schools, colleges, universities, and component units of these make quarterly appraisals against yearly set goals, so must there be individual quarterly appraisals under the system of management-by-objectives. The individual quarterly reviews of progress should begin shortly after the quarterly unit review has been completed.

The individual quarterly review is just that. This appraisal takes place on a dyadic (one–to–one) basis between subordinate and his immediate superordinate in a private review of progress session. Each should allow at least 1 hour for this conference. No one in management should be excluded from the process. This means that the process begins with the chief executive officer and his board of trustees in executive session. When this session has been completed, and the chief executive is clear on his direction, he then meets in individual sessions with all those administrators (and his secretary) who report directly to him. After their quarterly review session with him, these key administrative officers meet individually with all those reporting directly to them — and so on down the line until every single employee in the system (nonacademic as well as academic!) has had a quarterly review of progress toward agreed upon objectives with their superordinate.

The process of individual quarterly reviews is seldom a "painful" experience. It is *not* used primarily as an evaluation of the individual. Rather, it is primarily used as a facilitating method toward achieving agreed upon system and institutional goals and unit and individual objectives. It is objective in nature, for the quarterly review of progress toward achieving agreed upon objectives limits itself strictly to the signed MBO Agreement discussed at length in the previous chapter. Exhibit 14-2 shows a form successfully used just for this purpose.

Before superordinate and subordinate sit down together for the quarterly review of progress session, the subordinate is asked to complete the *Quarterly Review of MBO Agreement* except for "Suggestions Agreed to for Overcoming Obstacles" and to return 1 copy to the superordinate upon completion. This saves the time of each. It forces the subordinate to think about his progress and any obstacles he has encountered which resist achievement of agreed upon objectives. Likewise, it provides the superordinate with advance information so that the conference time is not wasted on going over ground that has not been carefully thought through. A conference that is well planned makes for better use of precious time and usually assures a better result. The superordinate, thus, sets a mutually agreeable review time *after* he has had the opportunity to study his subordinate's quarterly report.

Though the one-to-one formal quarterly conference serves as a review of results to date session, this is not its main purpose. Its main purpose is to solve problems blocking the achievement of agreed upon objectives.

Reviewing results to date has a salutory effect on an organization. Few individuals like to be placed in a position where they have to admit that little or no results have occured which have been within the power of the individual to achieve. Thus, just knowing that a review of progress is to occur quarterly helps to reduce procrastination which as often as not becomes "permanent" under most of education's "common sense" system of administration.

Solving problems which are blocking desired results is usually where MBO, and its component part of quarterly reviews, most effectively manifests itself. In this situation, the superordinate has an important, or more important, a role than the subordinate. His responsibility is to serve as "teacher," "coach," and "blocking back" all wrapped up in 1 person. The superordinate must *really* study the quarterly review and listen to what his subordinate is saying. In his teacher role, he must be Socratic in method and carefully think through just the right, analytical questions to ask so as to hopefully provide the subordinate with fresh insights towards overcoming his obstacles. As coach, the superordinate must advise and direct his subordinate as to what must be done to overcome any problems the subordinate is facing which is militating against realization of objectives. As blocking back, the superordinate must always ask 2 questions of each subordinate: 1) "What can *I* do to help you to succeed?" and 2) "What must I *stop* doing to help you to succeed?"

Each role of the superordinate — teacher, coach, and blocking back — in the quarterly review session is important, but accountability squarely falls upon the superordinate's shoulders in his role as "blocking back." This may require obtaining additional financial or human resources — or both. It may require modifying an objective downward. It may require abandoning the objective all together. In this respect, any changes to the original "game plan" calls for MBE. Often this requires agreement up the hierarchy as well.

The other side of the blocking back role of the superordinate may be to stop (!) doing certain things he now is doing which interferes with the subordinate achieving his individual objectives. This point can perhaps be best explained by way of illustrative statements by subordinates:

A teacher says: "The assistant principal received 'Cindy's' file from her previous school 4 weeks ago which stated she had been in an adjustment class with serious learning problems. I only found out today by accident from another teacher that he knew this from the first day she enrolled. This is now the second time that this kind of withholding of vital information from me by the assistant principal has occured. How can I be expected to achieve my agreed upon yearly objective of a minimum class average reading growth of 10 months if he doesn't stop putting 'problem' children in my class without my knowing it?"

An assistant principal says: "My duties call for me to be in charge of discipline in this school. Yet, on more than 1 occasion the principal, after receiving an irate telephone call from a parent, and without saying anything to me, has countermanded my order for a student to remain after school. Teachers and students are confused as to who *really* is in charge of discipline here. As a consequence I cannot see how I will be able to meet my objective of reducing the number of faculty complaints on discipline by at least 10 percent over the previous year."

The principal says: "I have accepted responsibility for achieving this year's system-wide goal of increasing the percentage of graduates in June by 10 percent with a professional staff of 45. But the superintendent insists on assigning specific individuals to specific jobs in my high school even though I better know the strengths and weaknesses of each."

The superintendent says: "The board of trustees has insisted that average math achievement scores improve this year over last by at least 3 months, but at budget adoption time they slashed my request for 1 remedial and 2 regular math teachers necessary to accomplish this goal."

In sum, interferring behavior by superordinates can be as much a cause for militating against the achievement of goals and objectives as their failure not to provide supportive help of teaching, coaching and requisite material and human resources. This, then, requires that during the quarterly review conference the superordinate ask the pointed question, "What must I *stop* doing to help you to succeed?" Conversely, the subordinate has the responsibility to candidly answer this question.

Annual Appraisal

At year's end, under the system of management-by-objectives, an appraisal occurs of results obtained during the past year against the standards set. Because quarterly reviews have all along occured, the resultant outcome at the end of the 4th quarter should not be expected to produce outcomes too far removed from expectations predicted at the close of the 3rd quarter.

At the end of the 4th quarter, key staff analyze goal results against standards set for the organization as a whole (using a form such as shown in Exhibit 14-1). They try to account for factors contributing both to under and over expectations. As a result, they begin to revise 5-year and 15-year goals. They begin to detail next year's yearly goals against the current year's results. This process obviously cannot and does not begin until results from subordinate units are first obtained.

In a similar way, each component unit analyzes its results against the agreed upon standards set 12 months or so earlier. Critical and objective self-examination of results against written unit goals can serve as a spur to better achievement vis-à-vis the current state of affairs in education of no stated measurable goals or vague goals which are at best only verbally stated in a randomized way. It is true that many boards of trustees and institutions have a written philosophy and/or a statement of purposes and objectives. But few make clear yearly written commitments towards implementing these worthy ideals. MBO can serve as this vehicle. Though it is not always necessary to postpone evaluating unit results until individual appraisals are conducted it is generally poor practice not to do so. It might be possible to ascertain that certain goals were or were not reached – or even surpassed – without first conducting individual appraisals. But it is very unlikely that the *why* of the results can be learned without first having conducted individual appraisals. Therefore, under most circumstances, unit appraisals should not occur until after the yearly individual appraisals of those in the unit have first been completed. Then the evaluation of unit yearly results can take place with greater confidence on all counts. The results, and their perceived causes, are then forwarded upwards through the hierarchy.

The individual appraisals should bring few surprises. There have been quarterly reviews of progress made towards achieving individual objectives (using a form such as shown in Exhibit 14-2). There have been opportunities to exercise MBE when clearly called for. Time has been allowed for emergencies. The appraisal does not attempt to measure such nebulous factors as personality and character. Rather, the annual performance appraisal interview focuses on results against agreed upon objectives, stated measurably and committed in writing. This is results management. Little subjectivity enters into the evaluation. The subordinate has known for a year what he was to be held accountable for. There, then, can be few surprises. Of course, the annual appraisal of results obtained not only serves as an individual evaluation tool but of still greater importance serves as a means of aiding the subordinate to become more effective the subsequent year. The annual evaluation also provides an objective means for assessing the potential of individuals for more responsible leadership roles and for merit increases. In extreme cases it can serve as an objective device for justifying dismissal. Exhibit 14-3 is illustrative of an individual appraisal form used with success by 1 MBO oriented educational institution.

System Benefits

The primary benefit to be derived from the MBO system of appraisal is the much greater likelihood of realization of goals and objectives. Knowing what is expected and knowing that is what the system, its subgroups, and its

Exhibit 14-2

QUARTERLY REVIEW OF MBO AGREEMENT   19___ — 19___

July 1 — September 30*

Routine Objectives	Measures of Progress Toward Achieving Objectives	Obstacles Encountered Toward Achieving Objectives	Suggestions Agreed to for Overcoming Obstacles
Routine 1. 2. 3.			
Problem Solving Objectives 1. 2.			
Creative Objectives 1. 2.			
Personal Development Objectives 1. 2.			

*A similar form is prepared and compared for the quarterly periods of October 1 - December 31; January 1 - March 31; and April 1 - June 30.

Exhibit 14-3

19 __ – 19 __   ANNUAL REVIEW OF MBO AGREEMENT Review
                                                                    Date:

Routine Objective Set	Results	Comments
1.		
2.		
3.		
4.		
5.		
6.		
7.		
8.		
9.		
10.		

Problem Solving Objective Set

1.

2.

Creative Objectives Set

1.

2.

Personal Development Objectives Set

1.

2.

Additional Comments: **Agreement Signatures**

_____

_____

individuals will be held accountable for results in focusing on outputs rather than reacting to tangential events. Research confirms the fact that just knowing what outputs are expected will lead to improved results by systems, units, and individuals.

The importance of using the MBO appraisal system is perhaps best illustrated in the direct superordinate/subordinate relationship. Studies have revealed that when the superordinate prepares a list of what he believes his subordinate's major routine responsibilities are, and the subordinate does likewise, when the two compare their lists they will find a 25 percent disagreement. Moreover, when each independently describe what they perceive to be the subordinate's major problems, their thinking diverges by 50 percent. And, insofar as desirable creative objectives are concerned, there is a 90 percent disagreement! Figure 14-4 illustrates this divergence.

It can be well imagined in the typical school, college or university that by the time objectives filter down from the chief executive, through several layers of the organizational chart, to those who must do the implementing, there is little resemblance between the perception of the initiator and the implementer of regular objectives, problem solving objectives, or of creative objectives. Without a system of management-by-objectives, with its written objectives, quarterly reviews, and yearly appraisal of results towards achieving these objectives, the system can only gratuitously be described as pulling in multiple directions. With losses occuring in the perception of assumed objectives by superordinate and subordinate at the rate of 25 to 90 percent at each link means that by the time several links have been passed there is little resemblance between what the initiator and the implementer perceive as to what the objectives really are. This loss of perception rate remains nearly the same even when verbally expressed rather than simply an assumed understanding. To perceive the full impact of this loss of objectives congruence all one need do is to recall the old parlor game of whispering a message from 1 person to the next. When it is time to report to the group what the original message was the laughter that emerges is stark evidence of the distortion of the end message to the original. Goals and objectives are too important to leave to assumption or verbal chance. They must be written down, reviewed, and appraised.

Incentives and Rewards

Educators, for good reasons, have long resisted incentives and rewards for performance. They have largely done so because they, unfortunately, have not trusted their superordinates to make a fair and objective appraisal. Moreover, many have claimed that there is no objective way to evaluate an educator's performance. Educators have feared that their personality

Figure 14-4

JOB PERCEPTIONS WITHOUT MBO

Subordinate's
perception of
his major
routine duties

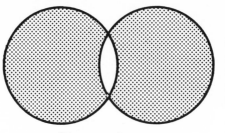

Superordinate's
perception of
subordinate's
major routine
duties

25 percent divergence

Subordinate's
perception of
his 2 major
problems

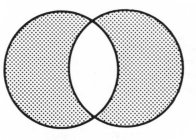

Superordinate's
perception of
subordinate's 2
major problems

50 percent divergence

Subordinate's
perception of
his 2 most
desirable creative
objectives

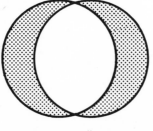

Superordinate's
perception of
subordinate's 2
most desirable
creative objectives

90 percent divergence

217

and character traits would be the subject of such merit appraisal rather than a difficult to define superior performance. Until now there has not been a system which has proven fair, objective, and practical to use. MBO overcomes most of these past difficulties. Certainly, though most of the difficulties can be overcome by MBO, Valhalla will not emerge in the education profession. Resistance to change eternally will remain with us. The incompetent likes it as it is. Competent individuals will remain skeptical for good past reasons, too. But, nevertheless, the time has come to take a fresh look at merit pay because exceptional performers are deserving of greater material rewards and because of the new tools we now have available to us which make it possible to evaluate on a criterion-referenced basis. Payment for results need not encompass an entire educational organization. Incentive pay can end between the board of trustees and its chief executive. It can include only administrators. It can include 1 or more divisions and departments – and not others – so long as a like opportunity is given to all to participate in a results plan.

Higher education faculty have long been paid according to results rather than alone for degrees and length of time in service to an institution (2-year college faculty excepted). Unfortunately, though, even in higher education there have been problems of objectivity and priorities. But MBO provides an adaptation to make the current evaluation system of higher education more fair and objective and even to aid in establishing priorities (eg, teaching vis-à-vis research). The MBO appraisal system, likewise, can be used effectively for all positions and at all levels of the education ladder.

In short, MBO provides the means to pay bonuses, "sweeten" other perquisites, and increase salaries based upon objective analyses of results by those educational systems not now satisfied with economic rewards based alone on academic training and experience.

Chapter 15

MANAGEMENT INSTALLATION

Greater than the tread of mighty armies is an idea whose time has come.
– Victor Hugo

Installing a system of management-by-objectives with its theories, techniques, and tools begins with the establishment of 15-year goals, 5-year goals, and 1-year goals. Not until an organization knows where it is headed can there be optimal management. It has been suggested that 1 effective means for establishing organizational goals is through a Council for the Future since such a council can cut across organizational lines – curriculum, counseling and guidance, teaching strategies, finances, etc.

Ideally, replacing "administration" with "management" begins at the highest possible level of the organization. Thus, the best beginning is with the board of trustees establishing policy goals and objectives, with the aid of such a medium as a Council for the Future, which they then hold their chief executive officer accountable for as described in Chapter 13. An example of a board policy directed toward the achievement of measurable outputs is shown below.

Sample Board Policy

LOCAL BOARD
John Tyler Community College
Proposed Resolution
Concerning Accountability for the Effectiveness of Educational Programs

December 1, 1969

Whereas equal opportunity for all persons is a cherished American ideal;

Whereas personal opportunity in the contemporary world is largely dependent upon competencies gained through the process of formal education;

Whereas John Tyler Community College is a public institution existing for causing students to learn in accordance with their own goals and the needs of our society and economy;

Whereas   accountability for student learning is an accepted responsibility of the entire college community;

Whereas   the Local Board of John Tyler Community College is desirous of continuing the development of an instructional program that accommodates differential learning rates of students and produces measurable evidence of student learning;

Now, Therefore, Be It Resolved that the

1. college president shall periodically inform the Local Board of:

   1) the success of students in attaining course objectives, including their attrition and failure rates;

   2) the success of students in occupations assumed upon leaving the college, including the employer's perception of the value of the college's programs;

   3) the success of students who transfer to other institutions;

   4) the extent to which the programs of the college are attaining the stated aims of the college.

2. college community is encouraged to:

   1) continue the development of an instructional program that accommodates differential learning rates of students and produces measurable evidence of student learning;

   2) foster an "open and frank atmosphere" focused on enhancing the "teaching-learning climate" for which the college has been commended by the accrediting agency;

   3) emphasize research-based planning for the continuing refinement of the instructional program to the end that college resources contribute maximally to opening the doorways of opportunities for students.

Reprinted from *Accountability and the Community College* with permission of the American Association of Junior Colleges, 1971.

Policy statements, as the above, make clear to an entire organization what its goals and objectives should be. From policy statements to MBO Agreement, to cumulative reviews and to annual appraisal there logically follows the management of education for results.

The setting of measures of organization performance before individual measures are set *defines the parameters* within which subordinates can then legitimately propose their own implementing objectives. Once these parameters are known individual objectives and program budgets should be solicited. To every extent possible the proposed individual objectives should be used if they are, or can be made, adaptable to organization goals and objectives. Thus, the establishment of measures of organization performance *precedes* objectives and the annual objectives setting meeting between manager and submanagers. These measures of organization performance delineate the areas of decision by both parties in the objectives-setting process.

Though many of the measures of organization performance will be summations of the individual objectives of managers, those which are not should be clearly identified as such.

Outlining the actual organization structure follows the setting of organizational goals and objectives. The reason for this is similarly logical. The organizational structure must be organized to optimize the achievement of organizational goals and objectives. Goals and objectives are to shape organizations, not organizations to shape goals and objectives. Possible changes in organization can lead to changes in individual areas of responsibility and authority and should be clarified before subordinate managers are asked to work out their recommended performance objectives, and their measures for the coming budget period.

Theoretically, ideally, and logically the installation of MBO, along with its supporting management techniques and tools, should be done throughout the entire organization in one fell swoop. But practically, this is seldom possible due largely to the NIH syndrome — the natural resistance to change — and because of lack of managerial experience by the staff itself. Moreover, it is better to tread lightly and slowly so as to attain ultimate genuine acceptance of the new procedures than to announce 1 day installation of modern management approaches for the next day. Lack of knowledge can be overcome through reading, consultant aid, role playing simulations, and practice.

Though not nearly as good results can be attained by only a portion of the staff operating under MBO as compared to all, nonetheless, the installation of MBO by steps is a worthy intermediate creative goal in itself, and in the long term more likely to attain desired results. Too fast an installation only leads to the inexperienced leading the inexperienced. For this reason, it is recommended that MBO installation be confined between only the board of trustees and its chief executive, and between the chief executive and his immediate subordinates, during Year One. As a result of a year's MBO experience all participants will gain in knowledge and skill in "teaching," "coaching," and "blocking".

All administrators can, and should, be brought into the MBO system during the 2nd year it is operative. During the 1st year every administrator, not included in the MBO system the 1st year, should have been given several books to read such as this one in preparation for the changeover from "administration" to "management". It also would be highly desirable to bring in at least 1 management consultant for several days at several different times to facilitate the ultimate organizational changeover. Between reading and consultant aid, and top management having acquired a year's MBO experience, the transition should move along quite smoothly.

In the 3rd year, each individual reporting to an administrator should be brought in to the system of management-by-objectives. This might include such individuals as division and/or department chairmen, program directors, support staff (classified as well as academic), etc. Similar to preceding groups, a smoother transition to the acceptance of the system of MBO will occur with reading and with 1 or more workshops on the subject during the preceding year.

Any employee not included during the 3rd year, since the inauguration of the MBO system, should be brought into the system during the 4th year. Among these, most likely, will be such paramount groups as teachers and counselors as well as certain other academic support staff and classified staff. Like other groups, reading and workshops on the subject will facilitate acceptance and a smoother transition.

Students should be brought into the system of management-by-objectives during the 5th year. The degree to which students should be included in the MBO system will depend largely upon their age and maturity. It is particularly noteworthy that a great many teachers already are using the most salient features of MBO through the use of measurable performance objectives. Students are given learning *tasks,* to be performed under certain *conditions,* and evaluated by preset *criteria.* It is only a short step from here to include a more formal "contract" for each student which is reviewed quarterly with respect to routine, problem solving, creative, and personal development objectives. Classroom teachers, as group, have thus been *managing* through the use of performance objectives and criterion-referenced evaluation instruments far longer than most administrators. The heart of MBO is the employment of performance objectives and criteria-referenced measures long familiar to classroom teachers. Incidentally, pointing out this fact to teachers will do much toward overcoming the NIH syndrome. MBO is only applying the principles of performance objectives (tasks, conditions, criteria) in and beyond the classroom in a more complete and sophisticated way. Students operating under the intelligent application of the system of MBO will have their learning considerably enhanced vis-à-vis the traditional method of instruction (lecture / text / chalkboard) where they really are not sure what is expected of them. Under MBO, a systematic means is provided for students to participate in objectives setting. They can solve problems of their own interest and opportunities for creative achievement are enhanced. Education is given greater meaning and purpose, and responsibility is taught through commitment. In a very real sense MBO provides the bridge to join the best elements of Skinnerian psychology (behaviorism) and Piaget psychology (heuristicism) as represented by "programmed" learning on the one hand and "open" learning on the other.

As should be reiterated with respect to the preceding, only a small group is first involved in management installation. The effects of mistakes are minimized in this way as increased expertise is gained through experience, reading, and management training workshops. As skill is gained by higher management, it is reflected in an orderly way, by example, down through the hierarchy. If MBO implementation proceeds cautiously, it will generally be found that because of its logic and its clear and open purposes, MBO will not only readily overcome the natural resistance to change, but actually will be warmly embraced. Individuals like to know where they stand, precisely what they are to be held accountable for.

As Figure 15-1 shows, the system of management-by-objectives is a cycle. Its uniqueness over present day practice in most places is threefold: setting *measurable* objectives; *joint* establishment of subordinate objectives; *quarterly* reviews of progress toward achieving objectives.

Since many faculty have for a long time, though unknowingly perhaps, been successfully employing leading aspects of the system of MBO with their students through the use of performance objectives, criterion-referenced measurements, and increasingly using written student contracts as well, it is self-evident that even where there is no overall organizational direction, or superordinates employing the system, subadministrative units, nevertheless, can still improve their performance through MBO. True, the effectiveness of MBO will be substantially diminished if it does not begin at the very top of the organizational structure, but there still remains sufficient degrees of

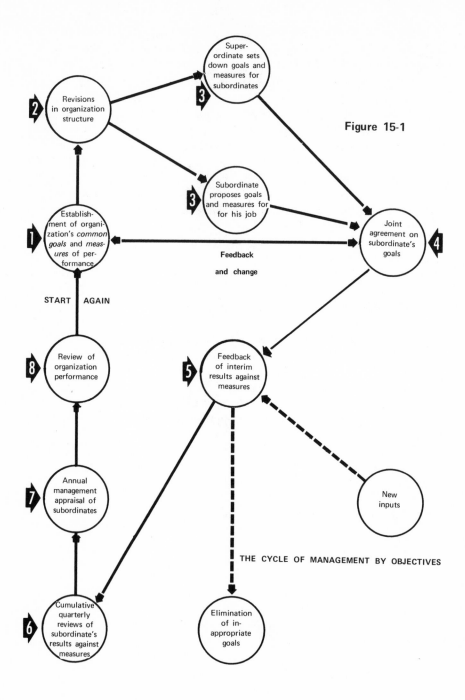

Figure 15-1

THE CYCLE OF MANAGEMENT BY OBJECTIVES

freedom to substantially improve upon extant randomized administration at any level. Individual building principals and deans can significantly improve their unit's performance by following MBO principles. Individual divisions and departments can likewise substantially improve their performance by installing modern management systems. Islands of innovation are better than none at all even though education sorely needs continents of innovation insofar as modern management is concerned. It should be cautioned in the preceding, however, that the primary condition that must first be met in installing a system of management-by-objectives is the support, endorsement, or permission of the principal manager in the organizational unit where the system is to be used when the system is initiated from below. Here, Law 7 applies: "Communicate contemplated controversial actions beforehand to superordinate . . ."

In sum, though management installation should begin at the very top, it can begin at any level to the benefit of the organization as many teachers have already demonstrated during the past half-a-dozen years or so. The principles, techniques, and tools discussed in this book are as applicable to subunits as to the organization as a whole. The ultimate objective, however, should be to install MBO and its techniques and tools throughout the entire organization. Only in this way can the organization achieve goals stretching beyond a year or so — if even that.

The very logic of modern management systems will facilitate its own installation in educational organizations in all but the 20 percent who fall under Pareto's Law of 20/80. There it will take a little longer. But where there is the will to make a change for the better, it can even happen among the resisting 20 percent. MBO is an idea applicable to education whose time has come.

Chapter 16

MANAGEMENT POTENTIAL

There is only one straight road to success, and that is merit. The man who is successful is the one who is useful. Capacity never lacks opportunity. It cannot remain undiscovered, because it is sought by too many who are anxious to use it – Bourke Cockran

There is a story of an individual named "Peter" who was called into his superordinate's office where he was told, "In this envelope is a problem I want you to work on. Return your recommendations to me by 5:00 P.M. today."

Peter returned to his office, sat down, and curiously and swiftly tore open the envelope. He withdrew a blank piece of paper. At first he thought a mistake had been made. Then he thought, No, my resourcefulness is being tested for a more responsible position. Still later, he thought he was being made a fool of. But later still he became concerned that if he did nothing, it might even be cause for dismissal so unimaginative would he be considered. The cycle of frustration kept revolving through his mind and stomach throughout the day giving him a headache and gas pains. Finally, Peter wrote down on the blank sheet of paper ways he believed that the unit and the organization could be improved. At 5:00 P.M. he handed the now filled out sheet of paper back to his superordinate.

The superordinate took the sheet of paper from Peter without even so much as a glance at it. He then handed his subordinate another envelope and said, "Now, I'd like you to work on this problem at home tonight and let me have your recommendations first thing in the morning."

When Peter got to his car at the parking lot, and sat down inside, he hurriedly ripped open the second envelope. In it was a second blank piece of paper!

Though "The Peter Test" might be one effective way of measuring certain important characteristics of higher management potential, the system of management-by-objectives provides a better way. That way is the study of past performance. Studied reaction of an individual to unfamiliar and/or disorienting test problems is no substitute for what an individual has proven he could or could not do previously on a job.

The Peter Test simulated a complex and frustrating problem. But as valuable as simulations are they are no substitute for the real thing. Thus, the first consideration in assessing the potential of an individual for promotion to a higher management position must be how the individual has performed in previous jobs, and particularly his present one. "Simulations," such as The Peter Test, can be effectively employed, analyzed, and discussed in management courses and workshops. But simulations are of questionable value in initial employment, and almost completely so for advancement, vis-à-vis other alternative evaluation procedures available.

Assessing Potential

Present staff can best be evaluated for management potential by past *performance*. Potential new employees can best be evaluated by visiting their present place of employment (or training institution) to observe first-hand their performance and/or to talk in person to *several* individuals having first-hand knowledge of the potential employee's present performance.

Making on-site visits is among the most underused but most valuable means for assessing potential. The typical excuse for not making such visits is the cost and the time involved. But compared to the potential good or damage that professional and high level classified staff can contribute to an organization, the cost is small indeed and the time well invested. Recent court decisions mandating due process for nontenured as well as for tenured staff in nonrenewal of contract decisions requires that there be at least as careful an evaluation of potential employees as for those already employed.

Next best to making on-site visits to where potential employees are now in training or where they currently are working is to make *several* judicious telephone calls to references provided — or to others that might have first-hand knowledge of an individual's present or past performance. Under no circumstances should the potential of a possible new employee be assessed by professional placement file papers alone. It unfortunately, but understandably, is true that the authors of most professional recommendations cite only the strengths, often exaggerated, of the individual they are writing about — but leave out the critical factors that can make the critical difference in the effective performance of the requirements of the open position. A more complete picture of the individual will be revealed, and to a surprising degree, by personal or telephone contact. The voice is anonymous whereas there is a real hesitancy to commit something to writing which might be construed as negative and which might get back to the individual so evaluated. Information sought should not focus on personality characteristics which are subjective but rather on objective *results* that the individual under consideration has achieved or failed to achieve. Results, in the final analysis, is the summation of the individual's total personality, knowledge, and skills as related to his present job.

There are other factors of assessment of management potential besides desirable past results achieved. The open position itself must first be clearly described since several individuals may have equal management potential but for *different* kinds of upper level positions. This requires that an individual's professional training and experience be assessed against the job as well as against past results achieved. For example, if there were a dean of students position open and there were 2 individuals who each had performed exceedingly well in current positions, but one had been trained in psychology and the other in business administration, it seems evident that the individual trained in psychology most likely should be the one selected to fill the vacancy. In short, the needs of an open position should be well defined with applicants assessed against the needs of the position rather than trying to fit a position around the talents of an individual.

Other Assessment Considerations

There are still other assessment considerations which cannot be "swept under the rug," but rather must be squarely faced. Such factors as *age, race,* and *sex* must be taken into account when it comes to assessing the best person to fill a particular position. All 3 factors are subject to federal discrimination clauses and must be given due consideration. *All things being equal,* there will be many instances in which a job would be *best* filled by an older person, an individual from an ethnic or racial minority group, or a woman. Managers must be especially sensitive and careful not to be chauvinistic in this regard. Each position to be filled should, as a matter of standard procedure, be assessed by formally asking, "Would this position be best filled by an older person? An individual from an ethnic or racial minority? A woman?" Unless these formal steps are followed there is a distinct possibility that the best person will not be promoted or sought out for initial employment, for, like fish, we are sometimes oblivious to the environment that surrounds us and make little effort to look outside ourselves.

A further consideration in assessing management potential, aside from considering past results and our sometimes own blind chauvinism, is the *health* of the candidates under consideration. If the position opening is one which demands considerable energy and/or time and/or tension and frustration, it would be a grave mistake to place an individual in a position where an existing health problem could be seriously exacerbated. Finalists should be required to undergo a thorough physical examination at the system's expense.

Finally, a genuine, thorough analysis of the job finalists' past performance must be made not only in light of what he has accomplished in the past, but what he likely can accomplish in the future at a higher level of responsibility. There must be clear signs that indicate he can produce effective results at the higher level.

The Peter Principle

Laurence J. Peter and Raymond Hull have written, "In a hierarchy every employee tends to rise to his level of incompetence." (22:26) This statement has come to be known as "The Peter Principle." Though this principle was promulgated somewhat with "tongue in cheek" it nevertheless is true that the Peter Principle represents "more truth than fiction". There *is* a real danger of promoting an individual beyond his level of competence. It is far better to keep an individual in a job where he effectively performs and is happy than to promote him to a higher level of responsibility and decision making where the organization suffers and where the individual feels miserable. It, therefore, is not enough that an individual only perform routine objectives well and achieve his personal development objectives. Rather, he must have shown exceptional performance, particularly in achieving *problem solving objectives* and significant *creative objectives,* to be considered seriously for the next step up the hierarchy. All of us know only too well of individuals who performed well enough in lower positions but who now occupy positions too difficult for their competencies. We know of teachers who are teaching subjects they were competent to teach at lower levels, but not at the present level. We know of incompetent principals and superintendents, deans and presidents, and certain members of boards of trustees who performed well enough at less demanding levels in the educational hierarchy. Still, each of these incompetents might yet be doing a competent job at a lower level or in another area of the educational structure if they had remained there. But for money and pride many incompetents would gladly return to their level of competency where though there might be less money and prestige there might be the gain of a longer, happier, and more satisfying life.

Under the system of MBO most every education manager can be made more effective for the simple reason that he knows what is expected of him, his performance is reviewed quarterly, he is "taught" and "coached," and his superordinate serves as a "running back" to aid him in being successful. In short, though there is much truth in the Peter Principle, it still is true that more managers are made than born. The competency of managers depends more on training than inherent native managerial ability — a potential yet to be subject wholly to predictive tests.

At the same time that MBO enhances managerial effectiveness, it also serves as an objective evaluation guide. In instances where it has been clearly revealed, even with all the aids of modern scientific management, that an individual has not effectively performed, it can be reasonably certain that the Peter Principle is operating.

Just as upper management has the responsibility to promote on the basis of perceived ability of individuals to handle more responsible positions, management likewise has the responsibility to *demote* when an individual cannot handle existing responsibilities. If an individual, on his own, will not request a transfer back to his level of competency (perhaps at first with subtle and kind suggestions) it is upper management's responsibility to offer an individual an opportunity to perform at a level not so demanding. The offer of a demotion (or in some cases a lateral move from a line to a staff position) is far kinder and fairer to the individual than to simply dismiss him. Likely, he cannot help his unsatisfactory performance. A sensitive organization will try to place the individual in a position where he has the potential to satisfactorily perform rather than to defensively dismiss him by placing all the unsatisfactory performance blame on the individual alone. The organization, after all, mistakenly placed him in a position which he could not handle in the first place. Thus, the organization, in part, is responsible for the unsatisfactory performance. Moreover, if the individual accepts the offer of a demotion or a lateral move to an area where he may be able to satisfactorily perform, the organization can gain from his strength in his reassignment. If an individual so situated does not accept the offer of reassignment, he and the organization can part via a resignation knowing that the organization was as sensitive to individual needs as to organizational needs. This "intermediate" procedure generally has a salutory effect on organization morale vis-à-vis the traditional straight dismissal procedure.

While it is the duty of the superordinate to consider the alternatives of a demotion or a lateral move of a subordinate to a less demanding position before considering a dismissal action, it is also his responsibility to foreclose any consideration of leaving the incompetent individual in his present position. It is the superordinate's duty to remove anyone from his current position who consistently fails to achieve high results. To allow such an individual to remain in his present position corrupts others. It is grossly unfair to the whole organization or unit. It also is grossly unfair to the incompetent's subordinates (or students) who are constantly frustrated by his inadequacies. Moreover, it is senseless cruelty to the individual himself. Most individuals so situated know that they are inadequate where they are whether they admit it to themselves or not. To help them to "escape" their "torture" is to often to do them a favor. But let this escape, in most instances, first be the offer of a lateral move or a demotion, rather than taking a dismissal action.

In sum, management potential can chiefly be determined by past performance which complements the demands of the position opening at a higher level. Acquiring management skills is more dependent upon learning and experience than upon innate ability. There is danger, without careful analysis of past performance to future needs, that an individual will be promoted to his level of incompetency. Should a promotional error be made, demotion or a lateral move to a projected level of competency should be offered and given as careful a consideration as the original promotion itself. But when all else fails, managers must dismiss those that cannot produce the desired results — results against measures of performance, *not* on personality characteristics.

Management Potential Scale

On the remaining pages, the reader is provided with a *Management Potential Scale* which can serve as a guide in assessing management competency in the present position. The results are also suggestive of how one *might* do up the next rung of the organizational ladder. Finally, the statements provide hints as to how one can become a more competent and effective educational manager.

MANAGEMENT POTENTIAL SCALE

Score each characteristic in a range from 0 through 10.

In my present job, I am

1.   . . . available. If my subordinates (or students) have a problem they cannot solve, I am there to help. But I am also forceful in making my subordinates do their level best to bring in solutions, not problems.. . . . . _____

2.   . . . inclusive. I am quick to let my subordinates in on information or people who might be useful to them or who are stimulating or who are of long-term professional interest.. . . . . _____

3.   . . . humorous. I can be light-hearted as well as serious. I laugh even harder when a joke is on me.. . . . . _____

4.   . . . fair. I show concern for my subordinates and how they are doing. I give credit when and where credit is due, but I also hold subordinates to their commitments.. . . . . _____

5.   . . . decisive. I do not procrastinate. . . . .   _____

6.   . . . humble. I admit my mistakes openly. I learn from them and expect subordinates to the same. . . . .   _____

7.   . . . objective. I can distinguish between what is apparently important and what is truly important. . . . . .   _____

8.   . . . firm. I won't let superordinates or important outsiders unduly waste my time or my subordinates' time. . . . .   _____

9.   . . . effective. I teach my subordinates to bring their mistakes to me and show them how to correct them. I teach them not to interrupt me with possible good news on which no action is needed.   _____

10.   . . . patient. I can keep from interfering with subordinates' problems until they solve them or seek my help. . . . .   _____

Total* . . . .   _____

_____

*This is your rating as a manager on a scale of 0 through 100. If it is below 60 better seek a lateral move or a demotion; if above 80, you show strong potential for promotion.

As might be suspected, self-evaluation is not nearly as accurate a predictor as ratings obtained from subordinates. Therefore, the validity of the Management Potential Scale will substantially increase if subordinates can be induced to anonymously complete and return the 10 item scale to their superordinate. The *averaged* results will not only aid the superordinate to see himself as his subordinates see him, but will serve as an aid to improve self-perception.

Of near equal importance to having subordinates do the evaluation is to have one's superordinate do the rating. In this way the manager can see himself in a kind of 2-way mirror. Without a positive consensus by both one's subordinates and one's superordinate, it is not likely that one will rise in an organization.

A final use of the scale is to evaluate subordinates for management potential.

In sum, the Management Potential Scale can be used as a self-rating device, a device to rate one's superordinate, and a device to rate one's subordinates (with slight word revisions according to how used). It is most valid as a predictor of promotable potential when used by subordinates to evaluate their superordinate.

Managers who accept the call for accountability by setting and implementing goals and objectives, who use system theories, techniques, and tools, and who employ modern management principles and practices, are capable of successfully managing education for results.

BIBLIOGRAPHY

1. Ansoff, H. Igor, Brandenburg, R. G. "The General Manager of the Future," *California Management Review,* Spring, 1969.

2. Blaschke, Charles. "Performance Contracting Costs, Management Reform, and John Q. Citizen," *Phi Delta Kappan,* December, 1971.

3. Borton, Terry. "Reform Without Politics in Louisville," *Saturday Review,* February 5, 1972.

4. Coombs, Philip H. *The World Educational Crisis: A Systems Analysis.* New York: Oxford University Press, 1968.

5. Dempsey, David. "The Right to Read," *Saturday Review,* April 17, 1971.

6. Diebold, John. *Business Decisions and Technological Change.* New York: Praeger Publishers, 1970.

7. Drucker, Peter F. *Effective Executive, The.* New York: Harper & Row, 1966.

8. _____ . *Practice of Management, The.* New York: Harper & Row, 1954.

9. _____ . *Technology, Management & Society.* New York: Harper & Row, 1970.

10. Freire, Paulo. *Pedagogy of the Oppressed.* New York: Herder and Herder, 1970.

11. Hartman, Edward. "The Cost of Computer Assisted Instruction," *Educational Technology Magazine,* December, 1971.

12. Havelock, R., Benne, K. "An Exploratory Study of Knowledge Utilization." In G. Watson (Ed.), *Concepts for Social Change.* Washington, D.C.: National Training Laboratory, N.E.A., 1967.

13. Holderman, James B. "Executive Director's Report No. 86," State of Illinois, Board of Higher Education, May 5, 1970.

14. Hostrop, Richard W. *Teaching and the Community College Library.* Hamden, Conn.: The Shoe String Press, Inc., 1968.

15. Hubbard, Charles, Jahoda, Gerald, Torter, Robert. "A Systems Approach to Library Problem-Solving." *Educational Technology Magazine,* February, 1972.

16. Lawrence, Paul R., Lorsch, Jay W. *Organization and Environment.* Homewood, Illinois: Richard D. Irwin, Inc., 1969.

17. Livingston, Samuel A. "Will a Simulation Game Improve Student Learning of Related Factual Material?" *Educational Technology Magazine,* December, 1971.

18. Mackenzie, R. Alec. "The Management Process in 3-D," *Harvard Business Review,* November-December, 1969.

19. McGregor, Douglas M. *The Human Side of the Enterprise.* New York: McGraw-Hill, 1960.

20. Marland, Jr., Sidney P. "Accountability in Education," *Teachers College Record,* February, 1972.

21. Odiorne, George S. *Management by Objectives.* New York: Pitman Publishing Corporation, 1965.

22. Peter, Laurence J. Dr., Hull, Raymond. *The Peter Principle.* New York: William Morrow & Co., Inc., 1969.

23. Thompson, Robert B. *A Systems Approach to Instruction.* Hamden, Conn.: The Shoe String Press, Inc., 1971.

24. Toffler, Alvin. *Future Shock.* New York: Random House, 1970.

25. Townsend, Robert. *Up the Organization.* New York: Alfred A. Knopf, 1970.

26. Van Dusseldorp, Ralph. "Some Principles for the Development of Management Information Systems," *Management Information Systems in Higher Education: The State of the Art.* Durham, North Carolina: Duke University Press, 1969.

27. Zani, William M. "Blueprint for MIS," *Harvard Business Review,* November-December, 1970.

GLOSSARY:

Common Terms
Used in
Management Technology

ACCOUNTABILITY

The acceptance of personal responsibility for the achievement of pre-determined measurable objectives.

ACTIVITY

The work effort involving time and resources required to complete a task or job to a given level of performance. It is represented on the network by an arrow and connects two network events.

ACTIVITY NETWORK

A network that uses activities rather than events as the basic building block.

ALGORITHM

A procedure for solving a problem or processing information in which the various steps, and their sequence, are specified beforehand.

BLACK BOX

A convenient term to describe a system component whose function is known, but whose mechanism is unspecified.

CONTINGENCY THEORY

A theory that emphasizes that the appropriate pattern of an organization is *contingent* upon the nature of the work to be done and upon the particular needs of the people involved. But one central need of all people is the need to achieve a sense of competency.

COST ACCOUNTING

That method of accounting used to establish all the elements of cost incurred to carry on an activity or operation.

COST-BENEFIT ANALYSIS

The process of examining and comparing alternative courses of action with respect to two main considerations: the cost in terms of needed resources, and the benefits (in general, the gains, utility, value, or effectiveness) in terms of the objectives to be attained. The results of the analysis can serve as one of the factors assisting the decision maker in a choice of alternatives.

CRITICAL PATH

That sequence of events and activities that has the greatest negative or least positive slack, or the longest path through the network.

CRITICAL PATH METHOD (CPM)

An activity-oriented network representation of the relationship and duration of tasks of an entire project. The longest path, in terms of time, through the project is known as the critical path. Each task on this path must be completed within the time allotted in order for the project to be completed on time. Tasks not on this path can have extra time for completion. Costs and resource availability can be associated with each task to give management a basis for a choice of schedules, and to monitor the project. Most projects use a combination of CPM-PERT.

CYBERNETICS

The field of technology involved in the comparative study of the control and intracommunication of information-handling machines and the nervous systems of animals and man in order to understand and improve communication.

DATA

A general term used to denote any or all facts, numbers, or letters and symbols that refer to or describe an object, idea, condition, situation, or other factor. It connotes basic elements of information which can be processed or produced by a computer. Sometimes data are considered to be expressible only in numerical form, but information is not so limited.

DATA PROCESSING

A series of operations used for handling information. Data processor may be defined as any group of people and/or machines organized and acting together to perform the processing of information.

DELPHI TECHNIQUE

A method for assessing group opinion by individuals through responses to a series of successive questionnaires, rather than through a series of face-to-face group meetings.

EFFICIENCY

The achievement of goals and objectives using the optimum ratio between time, dollars, personnel, and quality standards.

EVENT

A specific, definable accomplishment in a program network, which is recognizable at a particular instant in time. Events do not consume time or resources. They are usually represented on the network by circles.

EVENT SLACK

The difference between the Earliest Expected Date (T_e) and the Latest Allowable Date (T_i) for a given event. If the T_e for an event is later than the T_i, the event is said to have negative slack. When the T_i is later than the T_e, the event is said to have positive slack.

EXPECTED ELAPSED TIME

The time which an activity is predicted to require based on the formula:

$$t_e = \frac{a + 4m + b}{6}$$

Expected Elapsed Time is usually represented by the symbol t_e and has a 50-50 chance of being equaled or exceeded in practice.

FEEDBACK

Procedures, built into a system, which provide information on how well the actual performance of the system matches the planned performance.

FLOW CHART

A pictorial description of a plan showing the interrelationships of all required events. It is also called a network, arrow diagram, etc.

GAMING

A simulation of competitive processes in which strategies are chosen mathematically. A game is specified by the number of players, the established rules for play, and a set of end conditions with which payoffs are associated.

HEURISTIC PROGRAMMING

The use of computer programs to carry out complex information processing by attempting to simulate the process by which humans solve problems. Stored in the computer are a number of separate programs for performing small identifiable tasks. Which tasks will be performed, and in what sequence, is not determined beforehand but rather under the control of the simulation program while the problem solving is in process.

INFORMATION RETRIEVAL

A method of cataloging vast amounts of related data so they can be called up any time they are needed, with speed and accuracy. The recovery of desired information or data from a collection of documents or other graphic records.

INFORMATION THEORY

A mathematical theory describing the efficiency of the transmission of information through a communications channel.

INNOVATION

A new or novel tool or technique used as a *means* to achieve goals and/or objectives.

LINEAR PROGRAMMING

A mathematical technique for optimizing the overall allocation of resources to various activities where restrictions are such that not all activities can be performed optimally. A requirement is that the relationship between the activities and the restrictions and objectives be linear in a mathematical sense. The objective is to maximize or minimize some function. The decision problem is solved by finding the levels of the various activities that maximize (or minimize) the objective function while satisfying all restrictions.

MANAGEMENT

Its function is to decide on the most effective expenditure of manpower facilities, materials, and funds needed to achieve goals and objectives. It is the acceptance of personal accountability determined by measurable results. Management is concerned with *planning, administration,* and *leadership.*

MANAGEMENT-BY-EXCEPTION (MBE)

A procedure which alerts those "who need to know" when monitored expectancies are not reached or are exceeded by a predetermined margin.

MANAGEMENT-BY-OBJECTIVES (MBO)

A systemic way of *thinking* about management which emphasizes the achievement of predetermined system, unit, and individual goals and objectives by demonstrable, measurable results.

MANAGEMENT INFORMATION SYSTEM (MIS)

An organized method of providing management with information needed for decisions, when it is needed, and in a form which aids understanding and stimulates action.

MILESTONES
   Key program events, the accomplishment of which are essential to the
   completion of a program. A milestone is usually represented on the
   network by a rectangle or square.

MODEL, MATHEMATICAL
   The general characterization of a process, object, or concept in terms
   of mathematics which enables the relatively simple manipulation of
   variables to be accomplished in order to determine how the process,
   object, or concept would behave in different situations.

MONTE CARLO METHODS
   The use of sampling methods to solve mathematical problems involving
   a random variable. An example is observing the pattern of winning
   numbers on a roulette wheel, developing a mathematical model that
   describes the bias of the wheel, and then testing the model by
   attempting to predict the winning numbers during actual play.

MOST LIKELY TIME
   The most realistic estimate of the time an activity might consume in
   the opinion of the estimator. It is usually represented by the symbol
   (m). This time would be expected to occur more often than any other
   time if the activity could be repeated many times under the same
   circumstances.

NETWORK
   A flow diagram consisting of activities and events which must be
   accomplished to reach the program objective. The flow diagram shows
   the planned sequences of accomplishment, interdependencies, and interrelationships of the activities and events.

OPERATIONS RESEARCH (OR)
   The use of analytic methods adopted from mathematics for solving
   operational problems. The objective is to provide management with a
   more logical basis for making sound predictions and decisions. Among
   the common scientific techniques used in operations research are the
   following: linear programming probability theory, information theory,
   game theory, and Monte Carlo method.

OPTIMISTIC TIME
   The time in which an activity can be accomplished or completed if
   everything goes extremely well. It is represented by the symbol (o).
   An activity may have one chance in a hundred of being completed
   within this period.

OPTIMIZATION

A strategy to maximize objectives. If there is one objective, or multiple independent objectives, which do not vary with time, then optimization may be possible. When objectives are dependent, or vary with time, maximizing one objective usually results in suboptimization in which there is less than maximum attainment of the other objectives.

PARETO'S LAW

There is a normal and natural maldistribution among possible causes or focal points of trouble and the dispersion of effects, ie, 20 percent of a given group is responsible for 80 percent of the results.

PERT

An acronym for program evaluation and review technique. An event-oriented network representation of the time and duration of tasks of an entire project. An event is a point in time marking the start or completion of a task. PERT uses three time estimates for each task — optimistic, pessimistic, and most probable. The probability of meeting scheduled dates can then be calculated to assist management in evaluating project status. Most projects use a combination of PERT-CPM.

PETER PRINCIPLE, THE

In a hierarchy every employee tends to rise to his level of incompetence.

PPBS

An abbreviation for the planning-programming-budgeting-system. A decision system for allocating resources to various objectives based on cost-effectiveness analysis.

PAYOFF

In a game, the amount gained by one player and lost by another in a given move.

PESSIMISTIC TIME

An estimate of the longest time an activity would require under the most adverse conditions. It is usually represented by the symbol (P). An activity may have one chance in a hundred of being completed within this period.

PROBABILITY

A statistical statement of the likelihood of occurrence of a particular event in the network. It is represented by the symbol P_r.

PROBABILITY THEORY

A mathematical tool useful to the decision maker who is forced to make decisions in the face of uncertainty as to what will happen after the decision is made.

PROCESSING DATA

(1) The preparation of source media which contain data or basic elements of information and the handling of such data according to precise rules of procedure to accomplish such operations as classifying, sorting, calculating, summarizing, and recording. (2) The production of records and reports.

PROGRAM BUDGETING

The preparation of a budget which reflects explicit consideration of present and future costs of various programs designed to realize objectives. It is essentially a task of determining priorities for the various objectives, because of limitations on resources, in order to achieve a coherent program of action for the organization as a whole. A programmatic classification system for budget accounts. Sometimes equated with PPBS.

QUEUING THEORY

A theory which deals with the nature of waiting lines, particularly, but not exclusively, as such waiting lines relate to people. It is an important member of a class of models which are used to minimize the total of 2 sets of costs which move in opposite directions.

RELIABILITY ANALYSIS

Based on statistical analyses of educational tests (for example), the reliability of the result is that part which is due to permanent systematic effects and therefore persists from sample to sample, as distinct from error effects which vary from one sample to another.

RESOURCE

An available means whose store is reduced in quantity through use. Resources can be financial, facilities, equipment, material, or personnel.

SAMPLING THEORY

A mathematical description of the processes by which a specified part of a whole population is deliberately selected as representative of the whole for the purpose of investigating the properties of the whole.

SCHEDULED COMPLETION DATE

A date assigned for completion of an activity or event for purposes of planning and control. It is usually represented by the symbol Ts.

Where no specific date is assigned, Se equals Ts.

SERVO THEORY

A mathematical description of the processes by which automatic control of an operating system is maintained. When the system varies from specified performance, the error is detected and, through a feedback process, timely corrective procedures are automatically instituted in the system to eliminate the error.

SIMULATION

The study of realistic systems through the use of analogous models. The application of computer methods to mathematical models permits many possible system variations to be examined in a relatively short span of time.

SITUATIONAL THEORY

A unifying theory of management which applies the best management principles known to any given situation rather than trying to fit every situation under the umbrella of a single theory.

SLACK

The difference between the Latest Allowable Date and the Earliest Expected Date (Tl–Te). It is also the difference between the Latest Completion Date and the Earliest Completion Date (Sl–Se). Slack is a characteristic of the network paths. Slack may be positive, zero, or negative.

SPAN OF CONTROL

The number, kinds of positions, and individuals a superordinate is directly responsible for supervising.

STANDARD DEVIATION

A statistical statement of variability about the expected completion date of an activity. Common PERT practice uses a standard deviation equal to one-sixth of the difference between the Optimistic and Pessimistic Time Estimates.

$$\sigma = \frac{P - o}{6}$$

STRATEGY

Choice of a specific course of action or a specific utilization of resources by a decision maker.

SYSTEM

> An organized assemblage of interrelated components designed to function as a whole to achieve a predetermined objective.

SYSTEM, INFORMATION

> The network of all communication methods within an organization. Information may be derived from many sources other than a data-processing unit, such as by telephone, by contact with other people, or by studying an operation.

SYSTEM, INFORMATION RETRIEVAL

> A system for locating and selecting, on demand, certain documents or other graphic records relevant to a given information requirement from a file of such material. Examples of information retrieval system are classification, indexing, and machine-searching systems.

SYSTEMS APPROACH

> A rational procedure for designing a system for attaining specific objectives. The methodology includes specification of objectives in measurable terms; restatement of the objectives in terms of capabilities and constraints; development of possible approaches; selection of appropriate approaches as a result of a trade-off study; integration of the approaches into an integrated system; evaluation of the effectiveness of the system in attaining objectives.

TASK

> A related group of activities that clearly defines a segment of a program. Small programs may be considered as one task, while a system program may have a hundred or more. Tasks in a program are relatively stationary, while activities are dynamic.

TECHNOLOGY

> The science of the systematic application of knowledge to practical purposes.

THEORY X

> A theory which views the average person as lacking in ambition, as disliking work, and of preferring to be treated this way, so as to be able to avoid responsibility.

THEORY Y

> A theory which assumes that people do not hate work; that people do not have to be forced or threatened; that motivation, potential for development, capacity for assuming responsibility, and readiness to direct behavior toward organizational goals are all present in people.

TIME ESTIMATE
An estimate of time required to perform an activity, based upon technical judgment, experience, and knowledge of the job. Time estimates are not commitments or schedules.

TRADE-OFF
The weighing, on the basis of selection criteria, of the use of alternative approaches to attain an objective, with the intent to select a "best" alternative. Appropriate criteria, with differing relative importance, might include performance, timing, risk, cost-benefit, or policy.

WORK BREAKDOWN STRUCTURE
A family tree subdivision of a project beginning with the end objective which is then subdivided into successively small units. The work breakdown structure establishes a framework for defining work to be accomplished, constructing a network plan, and summarizing the cost and schedule status of a project for progressively higher management levels.

INDEX

Accountability, 3-7, 20, 47, 53
ADP (EDP), 122-25
Allen, James E., 3
Ansoff, H. Igor, 170
Appraisal (evaluation), see management
Armor, David J., 17-18, 20
Assessment, 15, 30-47, 50, 59-61, 223

Barber, Larry, 55
Behavioral objectives (see performance
    objectives)
Bruner, Jerome, 56

Cockran, Bourke, 226
Coleman Report, 17, 20
Communications, 131-46, 153, 171
Computers (see ADP)
Cost-Ed model, 12-13
Councils for the Future, 24-29, 48
Counseling, 40-44, 183
Critical path, 90, 94

Delphi Technique, 67-87, 101, 110, 114,
    121
Dixon, James, 158
Drucker, Peter, 136, 158, 170-71
Dupont, 90

Engbretson, William E., 77, 78, 81
Evaluation (see assessment)

Food services, 117-18, 183
Freeman, Roger A., 14

Gallup survey, 11-12
Gerjuoy, Herbert, 26
Goals and objectives
    board of trustees', 30-31
    counselors', 40-44
    creative, 196-99
    deans', 190
    education's, 22-23
    implementing, 48-63
    individual's, 184-88
    librarians', 37
    personal development, 199-201
    principals', 32-35

Goals and objectives *(Continued)*
    problem solving, 192-96
    routine, 188-92
    setting, 21-24, 29-45, 180-84
    superintendents' (and presidents'), 31-32
    teaching, 37-40
    teaching team, 35-37
Goethe, Johann von, 178
Governors State University, 77-85
Grant, Harold, 158

Heinich, Robert, 158
Helmer, Olaf, 68
Hesburgh, Theodore, Father, 158
Hostrop, Richard W., 67, 87, 101, 110,
    121, 132, 143, 146
Hubbard, Charles L., 118
Hugo, Victor, 219
Hunter, Guy, 17

Information
    levels of, 121-22
    management sources of, 56-57
    problems, 132-33, 139
Instruction (see teaching)

John Tyler Community College, 219-20
Johoda, Gerald, 118
Jungk, Robert, 29

Lahti, Robert, 158
Lao-tzu, 168
Lawrence, Paul R., 150
Libraries, 37-38, 113-15, 118-19
Lorsch, Jay W., 150
Louisville Public Schools, 30-46, 50-61

MacKenzie, R. Alec, 162-63, 172
Management
    appraisal, 206-18
        annual, 212-13
        incentives and rewards, 216-18
        individual, 209-12
        system, 206-08, 213-16
        unit, 209
    at work, 157-58
    at work in education, 152-53